W. K. Kellogg Foundation Grant

By Joseph Wechsberg

LOOKING FOR A BLUEBIRD

HOMECOMING

SWEET AND SOUR

THE CONTINENTAL TOUCH

BLUE TROUT AND BLACK TRUFFLES

THE SELF-BETRAYED

AVALANCHE!

RED PLUSH AND BLACK VELVET

RED PLUSH
AND
BLACK VELVET

RED PLUSH
AND
BLACK VELVET

The Story of Melba and Her Times

By Joseph Wechsberg

WITH PHOTOGRAPHS

LITTLE, BROWN AND COMPANY
BOSTON   TORONTO

TO ALL MY PRIMA DONNAS
with apologies and affection

Acknowledgment

I AM INDEBTED and grateful, first and foremost, to Nellie Melba who set down the facts of her life in her autobiography *Melodies and Memories* (London, 1925), and to her biographers Agnes G. Murphy (*Melba*, London, 1909) and Percy Colson (*Melba*, London, 1932); to Melba's trusted friends Thomas Hazelton-Cochrane, Elena Danieli and Stella Murray; and to others, who prefer to remain anonymous; to Hector Berlioz (*Evenings with the Orchestra*), Colonel J. H. Mapleson (*The Mapleson Memoirs*), Clara Leiser (*Jean de Reszke*), George Bernard Shaw (*Music in London*, 1890-1894), Henry C. Lahee (*Famous Singers of Today and Yesterday*), Vincent Sheean (*Oscar Hammerstein I*); to Melba fans, friends and colleagues — Irving Kolodin, Francis Robinson, Harold Rosenthal, Desmond Shawe-Taylor — and to everybody connected with the wonderful and exciting world of grand opera.

J.W.

Contents

Contents

Illustrations

RED PLUSH
AND
BLACK VELVET

❦ 1 ❦

Even Angels Have Off Days

THE PRIMA DONNA is still with us — and long may she live!
Without that fascinating creature a night at the opera
would be as dull as a bottle of flat champagne.

The prima donna radiates excitement, spreads magnetism,
creates argument. Her friends admire her passionately. Her
foes hate her violently. She is the spark plug of grand opera,
the delight of her public, the nightmare of her colleagues,
the cross of her managers. Her emotional flights off stage are
often better known than her artistic achievements on stage.
Her tantrums belong in opera as spices belong in food.

To her enemies the prima donna is imperious, demanding,
mean, arrogant and jealous. To her admirers she is divine,
lovable, generous, harmonious and broad-minded — her mere
appearance raises her audience's blood pressure.

Both her friends and her foes agree that the prima donna
is unique. She herself has no doubts: she alone is perfect;
her rivals are terrible.

But the poor prima donna pays a terrible price for her
glory. A single cracked high tone may ruin the fragile edifice

of her fame. She is as insecure as a French cabinet minister. Her work routine is more competitive than that of a lion tamer. She never sings *for* anybody, always *against* someone: against the orchestra ("They are too loud"), against the conductor ("He knows so little of singing"), against her rivals ("They're just waiting to take my place"), against the critics ("Worse than women!"), against her colleagues ("Why don't they like me?") and against her public ("When they have no more use for me, they'll toss me out").

To be able to sing a sustained high C under such pressure with bright lights in her eyes and in front of four thousand people demands steady nerves, physical strength, and absolute self-confidence. If the prima donna is not convinced of her own superiority, how can she convey it to other people? All evening her audience is waiting for that one high C — the big climax — with sadistic excitement. Suppose she doesn't make it? Are they going to witness the dramatic downfall of the great prima donna?

Now the diva takes a deep breath before attacking the critical note. (No one is supposed to see her breathe, of course.) Everybody sits, a little tense, in pleasant anticipation of disaster, as in the circus when the music stops, the drums start rolling, and the daring middle-aged man on the trapeze swings out into space.

For one horrible moment, that may last an eternity, the celebrated prima donna is alone — utterly and unspeakably alone. No one can help her in this agonizing second of trial. No matter how beautifully she has sung all evening long, all the preceding nights and weeks and years — if she doesn't sing that high C with perfect ease and stunning bravura, she's had it.

Unfortunately the normal human voice does not produce high C's. The prima donna's famous top tones are the result of years of physical effort, hard work, nervous concentration, correct breathing. She needs perfect health, peace of mind — and luck. Without luck, no singer ever became a prima donna.

The orchestra has stopped playing. The conductor keeps his baton in mid-air while he looks up at her. The stagehands in the wings interrupt their card game, the hairdressers and white-coated wardrobe women have come out of their rooms, the electricians on the lighting bridge have stopped being bored. Even the firemen who hate music and the nondescript old party (there is one in every opera house) who sits by the stage door and never listens to anyone show a faint trace of interest. Thousands of people in the stalls, the boxes, the galleries, among the standees, suddenly hold their breath although they don't know it.

Now the stillness around the prima donna has become almost three-dimensional. An invisible wall of sheer horror stands between her and her audience.

And then the high C rings out, gloriously and brilliantly, with an incandescence and inner life of its own. It spreads an invisible shower of sparks over the vast auditorium and shatters the wall like glass, casts a magnetic spell and gives everybody one moment of perfect happiness.

Of course she made it. What else did you expect? She is still the great prima donna.

The perfect prima donna should be endowed with good looks and a beautiful voice, musical taste and correct breath control, a sense of style and the ability to act, perfect vocal technique and at least relative pitch. She should look as exciting in a five-thousand-dollar gown as in a long white nightshirt. She must have that mysterious thing called personality. Above all, she must spread a magic — the mystic ability of casting a spell. Without that magnetic force she will never become a genuine prima donna. Beauty alone can be boring. The greatest prima donnas were not very beautiful women. But they were fascinating.

Nellie Melba was *the* perfect prima donna. If there ever was any doubt of this while she was alive, there is none today. The implacable judgment of history has confirmed her.

Melba had everything — commanding presence and beautiful voice, talent and technique, wealth and power. The moment she came on stage, even before she sang a tone, she could cast a spell. There would be that subtle quickening of her audience's pulse. She was worshiped even by people who had never heard her. She lived at a time that adored its prima donnas, and she was the symbol of that time: the best-known woman in the world, the most applauded and the most highly paid.

At the zenith of her career, Melba could dictate her terms, pick her associates, choose from an abundance of offers from the world's great opera houses. London's Covent Garden, New York's Metropolitan, Milan's La Scala, the Paris Opéra, Vienna's Court Opéra, Berlin and St. Petersburg were begging for her. In New York she got three thousand dollars for an appearance. In Sydney she once received eleven thousand, seven hundred and fifty dollars for a concert — and the dollar was worth a considerable amount more than today. She once said, "If I had only the money that has been spent in flowers for me and nothing else, I should be a rich woman." Even without the flower money she was a millionairess. She would travel like a queen with her own pink silk sheets, silk cushions and eider downs. On the train her drawing room would be transformed with her own paintings and silver candlesticks to look like the salon in her home.

"The word Melba has come to mean crowded audiences, doubled prices, long packed lines of motorcars and carriages, rows upon rows of waiting footmen, flowers, emotions, a golden superfluity of money, and that touch of solemnity with which we crown our enthusiasm," Filson Young wrote in 1908.

Melba lived the life of the fairy-tale prima donna, before radio, the prying television camera and modern press-agentry began to deglamorize great divas. She always remained remote and enigmatical — a goddess. There was a cloud of mystery about the great passion of her life; she loved Philippe, the Duc d'Orléans, Pretender to the throne of France, an elegant cavalier in the classic tradition. Her romance was worthy of a great prima donna and created much of Melba's legend. She had everything: beautiful jewels and expensive automobiles, elegant houses and dresses from Worth and Reville-Terry. She was a leading figure in the Court of King Edward VII and Queen Alexandra. Among her friends were the rulers of great countries. And why not? She was a queen in her own right — "the

Queen of Song." At Covent Garden she was the ruling prima donna during that wonderful, lavish age around the turn of the century, which will always be remembered as the Edwardian era — a time of big men and exciting women who loved beautiful things and enjoyed life to the hilt.

It was a perfect time for the perfect prima donna. "Melba" was a "household word," as they would say today. (A great prima donna is known by last name only.) No one remained indifferent at the mere mention of Melba's name; this alone proves her genuine prima donna status. Celebrated chefs called their culinary creations after her, parents their little girls, manufacturers their soaps and perfumes. She often received photographs of babies that had been named after her. Nellie Melba was what the Italians call *"prima donna assoluta"* "absolute first lady" of the operatic stage, outdistancing her rivals by light-years. She became a legend in her own lifetime.

The first prima donna was perhaps Vittoria Archilei, who enchanted Florence during the early seventeenth century. She soon lost her crown to Adriana Basile, whose endowments were a beautiful voice, a perfect figure, blond hair and dark eyes. But the title "prima donna" comes from Naples, where it was first used in the early eighteenth century. The *prima donna* had the main soprano part, and the *primo uomo,* often a castrate, sang the male part.

The *castrati* were the great singing stars of the seventeenth and eighteenth centuries. In 1601 the first *soprano castrato,* a young priest, made his debut in the Papal Chapel in Rome. The Church had banished women from the stage for "moral" reasons, but didn't object to the (officially forbidden) operation that castrated young boys, since it provided suitable material for the choirs of the *musica sacra*. The unpleasant, often bloated appearance of the *castrati* didn't bother their *aficionados*, since their artificial soprano or alto voices had a larger range than women's voices and a great deal more power, owing to the larger male chest. If we can believe contemporary reports, some of the *castrati* sang with as much brilliance, sweetness and charm as women. Their technique was formidable, and they sang their virtuoso "coloratura" (the expression was first used by the Venetian composer Pietro Andrea Ziani) with astonishing perfection.

Famous *castrati* were pursued by their fans as are movie stars today. The celebrated Caffarelli, a contemporary of Louis XV, was able to buy a duchy from his enormous fees. The great Farinelli received fifty thousand francs a year from melancholy King Philip V of Spain, who forgot his sorrows when he listened to this youth. Farinelli had to sing four arias a day.

Eventually nature prevailed and people preferred to hear their soprano arias sung by women. Ever since, every era has had the prima donna it deserves.

There were seldom more than two real prima donnas at the same time — and never, at the most, more than three. Survival is short in the operatic jungle, and the inexorable law of supply and demand limits the exalted ranks. Adriana Basile, who married Muzio Baroni from Naples, became prima donna at the court of Vincenzo Bonzaga in Mantua — a great connoisseur of women, music and art who kept Tor-

quato Tasso, Rubens and Claudio Monteverdi, the early
genius of opera, at his court. "La Baroni" earned two hundred escudos a month, Monteverdi only fifty. The income of
prima donnas has always surpassed that of even great composers, but their fame has been more perishable. Baroni's
daughter Leonora became more famous even than her
mother; she was admired by Cardinal Mazarin, who brought
her to Paris, and by Milton, who praised her charms in a
Latin poem.

The great prima donnas of the Baroque were Giulia de
Caro, a *femme fatale* with an exciting voice; the celebrated
Giorgina, mistress of the Venetian Viceroy Medinacoeli;
Marthe Le Rochois, who was Lully's great Armide in Paris;
and the notorious Maupin, whose vices fascinated her public
and who left a trail of scandal wherever she went. The
golden era of *bel canto* had Faustina Hasse-Bordoni, Angelica Catalani and Giuditta Pasta. The early Romantics adored
Henriette Sontag and Maria Malibran, Giulia Grisi and
Michelle Pauline Viardot. Later, people who fell for the
crazy antics of Phineas T. Barnum loved Jenny Lind, opera's
"*casta diva*," who was managed by Barnum in his inimitable
fashion, made ten thousand dollars at a concert, and retired
from the operatic stage at the age of twenty-eight, though
she continued for many years as concert singer. The Victorians
had Adelina Patti, and the Edwardians, Nellie Melba — the
last of the truly great prima donnas.

Our own age of noise and neurosis has produced a different species. We've had Maria Jeritza and Lotte Lehmann,
Toti dal Monte and Kirsten Flagstad. And today we have

Maria Callas, whom the Italian newspapers call "the Tigress,"
and Renata Tebaldi, whom they call "the Dove." Needless to
say, the Tigress gets most of the space and the biggest headlines. In the relatively short space of three years, Madame
Callas broke with the Lyric Opera in Chicago after some well-
publicized tantrums, had the Italian baritone Enzo Sordello
discharged by the reluctant Metropolitan because he had
dared hold out a high note while hers cracked, was dropped
successively by the Vienna State Opera, the San Francisco
Opera and the Met, considered it incompatible with her
dignity "as a woman and artist" to sing at La Scala, and
walked out after the first act of *Norma* on opening night at
the Rome Opera, in the presence of Italy's president, while
the packed house booed her. . . . Not bad by conventional
prima donna standards, but nothing extraordinary.

The eruptions of opera's first ladies are better publicized
in this era of the televised press conference, but basically
nothing has changed. The great Angelica Catalani, who
could afford to turn down Napoleon's offer of one hundred
thousand francs a year — an enormous sum of money — if
she would stay in Paris, because she disliked Napoleon, was
once reprimanded in Munich by the Court Chamberlain
when she mistakenly sat down in the church pew reserved for
a princess. The enraged diva called off her concert and swore
that her feet would never again touch the ground of this
blasted city, and they didn't. The ground between her coach
and the entrance of the Hotel Zum Schwarzen Adler was
covered with rugs and, as the great Catalani got out, she
threw her scarf on the ground with a grand, inimitable
gesture.

When George Frederick Handel was director of London's Royal Academy of Music he hired not one prima donna but two, paying Faustina Hasse-Bordoni twenty-five hundred pounds a year and Francesca Cuzzoni a little less. These two divas often kicked each other on the stage of the King's Theatre in Haymarket while the audience screamed and whistled in delight. London was split in two camps, with Lady Pembroke leading the partisans of Madame Cuzzoni, and Lady Burlington running the party of Bordoni. Handel didn't improve matters when he wrote his opera *Alessandro*, in which both prima donnas had an equal share of *bel canto* arias. In Bononcini's *Astianatte*, produced in 1727, the two divas got into a terrible fight which turned into a free-for-all among their partisans in the public. Handel became so upset by these "devilish females" that he once pushed Madame Cuzzoni toward the open window of his office and threatened to throw her out. Rudolf Bing of the Metropolitan, at certain times, had to cope simultaneously with Maria Callas, Zdenka Milanov and Renata Tebaldi. Fortunately he is a man of calmer temperament, or there might have been wholesale defenestration on West Fortieth Street.

One prima donna is a blessing in grand opera, but two at the same time are murder. Mozart found that out during rehearsals of *Don Giovanni* and *Zauberflöte*, and Wagner in his *Walküre* and *Tannhäuser*. Verdi and Puccini knew this and generally limited themselves to one prima donna per opera. Richard Strauss, a man of courage, wrote operas for three prima donnas — such as *Rosenkavalier* and *Ariadne auf Naxos*, which caused some of the gaudiest operatic fireworks in more recent history. The participants are still around, and

each will gladly tell you her own version of the event, doubtless the truth but perhaps not the whole truth.

It is safer to write about divas of the past than about contemporary prima donnas. History's sober judgment has ap-
praised them. The passage of time and passion has distilled
some legends into facts and some doubts into truth. One
isn't constantly walking the tightrope between malicious
gossip and clumsy publicity.

The first prima donna who appeared in New York — in the
first Italian opera heard in America — was Maria Malibran.
After singing in 1825 in Rossini's *Il Barbiere di Siviglia* she
became the idol of New York's music lovers and the toast
of Knickerbocker society. She was only eighteen years old.
"Her beauty of person and charm of manner made her the
supreme prima donna, a woman who from her first appearance has become accustomed to see the world at her feet,"
the American music critic Richard Grant White wrote later,
after Malibran's death. "She had an enduring, always varying charm. By her smile not only all men but even all women
seem to have been carried captivated. . . . Her figure was
so exquisitely beautiful in all points that it was somewhat
extravagantly said she might be studied for an improvement
upon the Venus de' Medici."

White is not the only cold-blooded critic who got bowled
over by a prima donna. Later the famous Viennese critic
Eduard Hanslick, who was feared for his caustic pen, wrote
about Patti: "The irresistible charm which so surrounded her
first appearance, and her pure joy in singing and acting,
have not been lost with her youth." And Philip Hale, the

Vermont-born Bostonian critic, once rhapsodized, "Melba's voice has a fullness, a richness, and a sumptuousness that are incomparably beautiful. The hearer revels in its tonal, sensuous beauty. Thirteen years have gone by since she first gave delight to this city, but charmed and applauding Time has constantly enriched her."

Madame Malibran was a prima donna who was "as good as an angel." She was often compared to the great Catarina Gabrielli, who had bewitched Europe's opera lovers some seventy years earlier with her sweet voice and sensational affairs and was "far below Malibran morally." In New York Malibran sang on Sundays in the choir of Grace Church, then at the corner of Broadway and Rector Street. But even angels have off days. At Covent Garden Madame Malibran once refused to sing with John Templeton, a Scottish tenor with a beauitful voice and tepid personality. The manager asked Madame Malibran why.

"Last evening Mr. Templeton was going to kiss me," she said, with appropriate hauteur.

The horrified manager sent for the tenor and in the presence of the prima donna told him of the accusation.

The stolid Scotsman gave a shrug. "Modum Molly Brawn," he said, "I wadna kuss ye on ony account." Madame "Molly Brawn" began to laugh and all was well. She could afford to be generous. She was admired by Rossini, Bellini, Chopin, Liszt, Alfred de Musset and Lamartine. She was so completely immersed in her art on the stage that people said she was in a trance, and doctors claimed she suffered from "hysterical spasm." Once she was numb with her cramps and had to be carried to the theater, where she immediately became quite normal and gave a great performance, only to succumb again at the end of the evening. At least that's the version we read today.

Madame Malibran may have been as good as an angel, but she knew that a prima donna must always remain the center of the universe. The moment she stops being controversial and people no longer talk about her, she is in trouble. And she must be the whole show. When the "golden-voiced" Angelica Catalani was the great star of Covent Garden during the early nineteenth century, the manager once complained to her husband that her high fees made it impossible to engage other good artists.

"Does it matter?" said the worthy husband. "My wife and a few puppets are quite sufficient for any theater." That's the spirit!

Patti had a clause in her later contracts which absolved her from appearance at any rehearsal whatsoever. She took full advantage of it, so that "occasionally she had to be pointed out from the wings to minor artists who had not sung with her before and were now obliged to accost the unfamiliar diva and engage her in a duet."

When Emma Nevada, the daughter of a physician from Nevada City, California, sang the Mad Scene from *Lucia di Lammermoor*, people were unable to determine which were her notes and which the notes of the accompanying flute. "Now and then a pathetic vibration would move the human voice and make it rise triumphantly above the instrument." Occasionally Madame Nevada forgot the words, but it didn't matter: "the flutist improvised a few sparkling variations" to enable her to regain her breath.

You might think people would have hissed. On the contrary. The prima donna can do no wrong, so far as her admirers are concerned. W. J. Henderson, the eminent critic of the *New York Times* and later of the *Sun,* wrote after a performance by Geraldine Farrar: "All the little gerryflappers were out last night, striving to fill the Metropolitan with their hysterical squeaks of rapturous approval of everything done by the prima donna. . . ." A gerryflapper was a "flapper," a girl about teen age, and had a half-baked mind and "a goddess called Farrar." In a performance of *Faust* the goddess, playing the part of the simple peasant girl Marguérite, wore shoes with genuine diamond buckles, which impressed her audience no end. The goddess had fights with Caruso that made all the front pages; she was denounced from the pulpit for showing too much epidermis in *Zaza,* and had a clause inserted in her Met contract that she was to have her own dressing room (No. 14, which she described as "a miserable airless little box used for odd articles"). The goddess eventually met her equal, when she told Toscanini during a rehearsal, "Maestro, I am a star," and the maestro (though he admired her) answered coolly, "Madama, I know only the stars in heaven."

But old-timers at the Metropolitan speak reverently about Madame Farrar, perhaps because she had her own dressing room, a feat accomplished after her only by Kirsten Flagstad. "Dressing room assignments and appointments probably have caused as lively prima donna fireworks as any other single thing in the opera house," writes Francis Robinson, the urbane assistant manager of the Met, a man who knows. The dressing room assigned for any given evening to the first soprano is No. 10, "a cheerless chamber with a bilious pink dressing table, a couple of inelegant chairs and a day bed." The temporary tenant generally brightens it up for the evening with satin covers, family portraits, holy pictures, mascots and flowers. On Saturdays, when another singer occupies No. 10 for the matinee, the redecorating arrangements in time for the evening performance sometimes create serious diplomatic problems that have to be straightened out by the general manager himself. Not everybody has the cold courage of Giulio Gatti-Casazza, whose technique it was to listen in silence to a prima donna's complaint and then walk away while she was still sputtering.

At Covent Garden a German prima donna, convinced that her dressing room appointments were inferior to those of a rival, arrived early one evening and with her fair little hands changed the furniture of the two rooms. Covent Garden's dressing room problems severely tested the patience of Sir Thomas Beecham when he was in charge there. In his memoirs he remembers the day when an angry figure came storming into his office and asked what the deuce he meant by painting her room green. It was Nellie Melba "and very upset she seemed to be." Sir Thomas had never come into working contact with "this imposing personality." Considering attack the best method of defense, Sir Thomas simply pretended not to remember who she was and asked her what the deuce she meant by entering his office unannounced, adding that he knew nothing of private ownership of rooms in the building.

"This produced a fresh explosion of wrath, which, as I remained grimly silent, gradually subdued and was eventually succeeded by resignation and the complaint that she would not have minded so much if the green would have been of a cheerfully light instead of a depressingly dismal hue."

Having scored a victory and remembering that Melba was to sing on the opening night under his direction, Sir Thomas decided to be "magnanimous as well as diplomatic" and offered to repaint "her" room any color she liked. "This little present delighted her more than the most costly present could have done, and we soon became excellent friends."

Unlike Sir Thomas, most conductors were terrified of the "formidable Nellie" and didn't dare interrupt her during rehearsal. The age of the conductor had not yet dawned. When the famous maestro Cleofonte Campanini stopped Melba in the middle of a rehearsal at the Manhattan Opera House and asked her to do the same passage all over again in a different tempo, "Melba stared at him in unaffected amazement — that had not happened to her in years." But she accepted the authority of a conductor whom she respected: she started all over again, and sang the phrase in Campanini's tempo.

Solo curtain calls are another source of prima donna wrath and managerial ulcers. John McCormack, the Irish tenor, after his first appearance with Melba, was about to step out with her in front of the curtain when he was told, "At Covent Garden nobody takes bows with Melba." Melba's old friends claim this was just a malicious rumor and point out that later on she did take bows with other artists. Perhaps the ravages of time and the exigencies of breath control had somewhat mellowed the prima donna's strict principles.

At least Melba would not step out of character and take

bows in the middle of a performance, which is still a wide-spread bad habit. Once Melba watched with Puccini in a box at Milan's La Scala during a performance of *Tosca;* when after Tosca's great aria *"Vissi d'arte"* the diva collapsed on the stage in despair at the feet of satanic Baron Scarpia, there was an ovation; the diva got up and stepped forward, hands to her heart, her face wreathed in smiles, to repeat the aria all over again. Melba asked Puccini indignantly why he allowed this practice. The whole act was spoiled for her.

Puccini shrugged in his tired way. "If people don't shout *Bis* in an Italian opera, there is no real success," he said.

A few nights later, during a La Scala performance of *Lucia di Lammermoor,* Melba was in the middle of an impassioned love duet with Edgardo, when the music suddenly ceased, Edgardo turned swiftly away from his beloved, and the orchestra began to play the national anthem. Melba found herself suspended in space, standing with outstretched arms, as in a film that has suddenly stopped running. Edgardo informed her in a whisper that the Queen of Italy had just entered the royal box and this was the "customary" method of doing homage to her. When the anthem was over, Edgardo raised his arms in customary tenor style and started to continue his love scene exactly where he had left off as though nothing had happened.

"I felt like a complete fool," Melba said later. "How can I stop in the middle of a tense scene and be expected to continue? One's operatic emotions may be fairly elastic but they are not as elastic as all that."

Toscanini stopped the silly practice at La Scala, but at the Vienna State Opera Herbert von Karajan, considered by his admirers to be the heir to Toscanini's throne, has not yet stopped the singers' bad habit of bowing with a silly grin on their faces in the middle of stark tragedy.

At a recent performance of *Carmen*, the tenor who played Don José sang *"Carmen, je t'aime"* at the end of the "Air des Fleurs," and broke down passionately in Carmen's lap. Applause and cheers, whereupon Don José got out of Carmen's lap, leaving the poor girl in emotional suspense, and bowed to the audience. Then as if he had just remembered Carmen he went right back into her lap again. No wonder her first words were, *"Non, tu ne m'aime pas."* No real lover ever acted that way.

But things could be worse. The eighteenth-century English actress Mrs. Farrell, who noticed that the audience didn't like her way of dying as the heroine of *The Mourning Bride*, "rose from the dead to express her regrets to the audience."

At the Metropolitan, "The audience is respectfully, but urgently, requested not to interrupt the music with applause," but the intrepid fans get around the taboo of solo curtains by applauding their star's first entrance, often at the worst possible moment. What is known in the Met annals as "The Great Curtain Call Clash" occurred one night when Maria Jeritza, then the ruling prima donna, and Beniamino Gigli, then the ruling tenor, were skillfully and effectively stealing each others' curtain calls. At last the diva lost patience and, behind the curtain, kicked Gigli in the shinbone. The chivalrous tenor retorted by slapping the prima donna's face. Madame Jeritza went before the curtain and confided to her thirty-eight hundred friends: "Mr.

Gigli has not been nice to me," which was the understatement of the evening. A few years later, during a *Tosca* performance, Ljuba Welitsch asked Lawrence Tibbett to act "realistically." Always glad to oblige a lady, the baritone threw the diva on the stage with such vehemence that she was hardly able to collect her breath in time for her great aria *"Vissi d'arte."* But Madame Welitsch got even with Tibbett. After stabbing him to death, she kicked his prostrate body in the stomach, "exactly as Tosca would have done." She must have known. Floria Tosca, the heroine of the opera, is a prima donna herself.

Grand opera, often declared dead and buried, is very much alive and getting more popular than ever. Handicapped by absurd librettos, and hamstrung by implausible acting — harassed by financial crises and production problems — an opera house rarely manages to break even and to get all the singers it needs. But still grand opera gladdens the hearts of its addicts and continues to win new ones. Pompous esthetes call opera fraud; cold fish call it a bore. Even Dr. Samuel Johnson, who was neither, called it "an exotic and irrational entertainment." But some exotic and irrational entertainment is extremely exciting, and I think the good doctor just didn't know what he was talking about. Anybody who remains totally unaffected by the divine beauty of Mozart's *Le Nozze di Figaro*, Wagner's *Parsifal*, or Verdi's *Falstaff* misses a lot in life, as does the man who doesn't enjoy the first touch of spring in the air, the colors of a Renoir, the sight of a lovely woman, the aftertaste of an old claret, or the afterthought of a good book.

Grand opera thrives on exaggerated emotions. The prima donna spends her professional life in a heavily supercharged atmosphere of musical melodrama. In most operas people either love or kill one another with great gusto and violence; often they do both, love inevitably leading to death. Normal human relations are rarely tolerated because they are thought to be dull. The suffering in Wagner's *Musikdrama* is always on a heroic scale with endless climaxes.

No wonder the prima donna often doesn't know where make-believe ends and real life begins! On stage she is rarely permitted to enjoy a happy ending or at least the comforts of a peaceful, bourgeois death. During her thirty-eight years on the operatic stage Melba was many times stabbed to death in *Rigoletto* and *Pagliacci,* strangled in her bed in *Otello,* buried alive in *Aïda,* driven mad in *Hamlet* and *Lucia,* dying of acute tuberculosis in *La Bohème* and *La Traviata,* perishing of shame in *Faust,* of a broken heart (a popular operatic disease unknown to medical science) in *Lohengrin* and *Tannhäuser,* of excessive love (another strange operatic epidemic) in *Roméo et Juliette.* She once tried to study the title part in *Madama Butterfly* but gave it up. Perhaps the prospect of hara-kiri was too much for her.

And there are other problems. The prima donna is always threatened by horticultural hazards. Fashions come and go, but flowers remain popular as tokens of admiration. This is a definite sign of progress; the Romans used to throw bracelets and ornaments at their favorite actresses. At least one perished under the weight of popular enthusiasm. Yet the prima donna must remain smiling and composed under concentrated fire of small bouquets. H. Sutherland Edwards, the

eminent music critic of London's *St. James's Gazette*, suggested that the public shouldn't hurl its missiles at the *head*
of a diva it desires to honor, but at some distant point from
the spot where she is standing. Unfortunately opera fans are
often so excited at the end of the performance that their aim
is bad and their pitch unreliable. The prima donna must
look radiant while flower rockets hit her face. But at least
she has the satisfaction of seeing the heavily corseted tenor
bend down to pick up the flowers and present them to her.

All prima donnas love flowers, especially flowers for which
they don't have to pay. During the first weeks after Melba's
first appearance at the Paris Opéra a large bouquet of magnificent yellow roses would be delivered at her dressing
room every time she sang. She never found out who had
sent them, and for many years remained pleasantly mystified
about the mysterious donor. She was just as happy with a
small bunch of violets which an Australian soldier gave her
during the war as with the orchids which she received from
her millionaire admirers.

Once on a cold, snowy night Melba was leaving the stage
door of the Opera House in Philadelphia and found an old
lady waiting for her with one rose in her hand. "Madame,"
said the old lady, "I've just heard you sing, and I've waited
here for you. Will you let me touch your hand?" Melba im-
pulsively kissed her on both cheeks and gave her all the
flowers she had in her arms; and the old lady began to cry
and said, "God bless your beautiful heart, my dear."

The Edwardian prima donna lived before the invention
of modern press-agentry. Advertising was done by her man-

ager in a routine way. Public relations were amateurish,
stunts were frowned upon. Once in a while "suggested
rumors" were spread by a rival clique and had to be "con-
tradicted." Melba had a conspicuous weakness for "conversations" with a couple of carefully selected, highly distinguished music critics. Conversations — not interviews. No
one would have dared ask Madame Melba any questions,
especially impertinent questions of a private nature. Some
mysteries might be answered in her autobiography, but there
again it was the art of omission that counted. Her autobiography was interesting for the things it left unsaid rather than
for what was in it. The Edwardian prima donna was too
subtle for direct attack.

Melba knew that unbiased judgment is often impossible
when the critic and the diva are close friends, and she never
became very friendly with the leading critics. The best of
them respected her sensible attitude but some considered it
an autocratic arrogance. She was too smart to ever try to influence the critics. Her only appearance in the editorial offices of several London newspapers was one night late in
1899, after a Covent Garden performance, in which another
singer, whom she liked, had blundered badly. Melba pointed
out that the lapse might retard the singer's career for years,
and asked the critics not to mention it. The critics did not
oblige.

Despite her reticence Melba was good copy. "Her name
was on everybody's lips, her doings were discussed with as-
siduity, and 'Melba' stories were so popular that almost no
newspaper could do without one," writes Agnes G. Murphy,
Melba's panegyrical biographer. And her friend, the novelist

Marion Crawford, said, "The position of a successful lyric prima donna is exceptional. No other artist enjoys such popularity."

Publicity, adverse as well as favorable, always was as important as money for a prima donna. Marcella Sembrich once got plenty of it simply by refusing to finish a performance at the Metropolitan. It was a "Gala," in 1902, in honor of Prince Henry of Prussia; the program featured the first act of *Lohengrin,* the second of *Carmen,* the third of *Aïda,* the second of *Tannhäuser,* and the first act of *La Traviata.* It was like one of those twelve-course, seven-different-wines dinners; in those days people must have had an enormous capacity for food as well as for opera. By the time Sembrich was to go on in the first act of *La Traviata,* His Royal Highness had had enough, and departed; then Madame Sembrich put her little foot down and refused to sing. Grace Moore also once managed to stay on America's front pages for three days, during a train ride from Hollywood to New York, by making comments at various stopping places on the difficulty of milking a cow and simultaneously singing a high C. It so happened that she'd had to do both in her new film *The King Steps Out.*

The only thing livelier than a prima donna is a pair of prima donnas. Happily, there are always more than one about. Angelica Catalani had Giuditta Pasta as a rival; Pasta (Bellini's first Norma) had Giulia Grisi; Grisi had Thérèse Tietjens; Tietjens had Henriette Sontag; Sontag had Maria Malibran, who abdicated to Jenny Lind, who preceded

Adelina Patti, whose mantle fell to Nellie Melba. Melba had quite a few rivals during her long career: Luisa Tetrazzini, Emma Calvé, Emma Eames, Selma Kurz. Eames had Mary Garden, Garden had Geraldine Farrar — and so it goes, down to our younger days when Amelita Galli-Curci sang against Toti dal Monte, and Maria Jeritza against Lotte Lehmann.

Today life at the opera would indeed be dull if Maria Callas didn't have Renata Tebaldi or Leonie Rysanek; and there are Birgit Nilsson, Ann Sutherland, Elisabeth Schwarzkopf, Leontyne Price and a few more. . . . But none of them is a prima donna *assoluta* in the great tradition of Nellie Melba.

It is rare to see two prima donnas giving a demonstration of sisterly love, even obviously for the benefit of public and press. However, it does happen. Madame Malibran, that angel, and Madame Sontag were publicly feuding for years, but Madame Malibran showed her angel's soul by weeping and saying "Why does Sontag sing so divinely?" (Few similar admissions have been recorded among active divas.) Once at a concert in the London home of the Countess Merlin both divas were present, which must have taken some clever politicking. The Countess suggested that the two rivals together sing the great duet from *Tancredi*. After the end of the beautifully sung duet, "the two divas looked in each other's eyes, silently clasped hands and kissed, a sight to see."

In 1892 Nellie Melba and Emma Calvé were commanded to Windsor Castle for a performance of *Carmen* before Queen Victoria, after which, to everyone's astonishment, the two prima donnas embraced each other affectionately on the stage. They would never have done so in private life. A contemporary observer compared them to the two women in a *Punch* cartoon, one writing a letter and the other looking up from her book to say, "Give Ethel my fond love, dear. Heavens! How I detest that woman!"

A few years later Madame Melba and Mary Garden, then the lovely, reigning diva of the Opéra Comique in Paris, appeared on the same program at a command performance in Windsor Castle, after a state dinner for the King of Greece. During supper with the other artists, Melba turned to Lord Farquhar, the Court Chamberlain, and said in a loud voice, "What a dreadful concert this would have been if I hadn't come."

> Twenty pairs of eyes were fixed on me [Miss Garden remembers in *Mary Garden's Story*]. I sat only two chairs away from Melba, and Lord Farquhar, who was very embarrassed, began to pay me a compliment to cover up Melba's remark, but I raised my hand.
> "I love Melba's rudeness. It amuses me."

The two divas went back to London on the train. "Before we reached London, Melba and I were fast friends," says Miss Garden. Melba asked Garden how to act Tosca and what sort of wig she should wear. Garden told Melba all about Tosca but thought it was perfectly useless, "because Melba could never sing Tosca" — and Melba never did.

> Melba grew to like me because I wasn't a coloratura singer. Later she came to visit me at my villa in Monte Carlo. . . . She could be quite funny, and wherever she went she always had people laughing. In the evening she would sing just small English songs, but she turned them all into little things of heavenly beauty.

A high point of prima donna rivalry was reached during the "mad twenties" in Vienna — a city frankly dedicated to the pursuit of operatic happiness. Not only opera lovers but the inhabitants-at-large, most of whom never went inside the Staatsoper, were sharply divided into two camps, going out either for Maria Jeritza or Lotte Lehmann. Some splinter groups rooted for Selma Kurz, the great coloratura whom Melba is said to have kept from getting entrenched at Covent Garden and who later carried on fierce feuds with other divas in Vienna, and for Maria Olczewska, the famous mezzo. Mezzo-sopranos and contraltos are the Cinderellas of grand opera. They have to study as hard as everybody else, must be able to sing a perfect high C as well as sonorous low tones, and then they have to melt into the background as duennas, nurses, spinsters, gypsies or mothers, while the prima donna warbles, trills and gets most of the applause and the highest fees. Without the kindness of Bizet, Verdi and Saint-Saëns, and an occasional assist from Wagner, the sorority of mezzo-sopranos would long ago have become extinct from frustration.

Madame Jeritza and Madame Lehmann competed in the same parts — as Sieglinde, Tosca, Turandot, Elsa (*Lohengrin*) and Elisabeth (*Tannhäuser*) — and sometimes they sang different parts on the same evening. The management of the Staatsoper showed a fine spirit of courage and a commendable sense of drama by making the two divas sing against each other on such memorable nights. Despite occasional flashes of bravery beyond the call of duty, Mr. Bing has never dared to schedule a performance of *Turandot* with Madame Callas as Turandot and Madame Tebaldi as Liu, possibly because at one point Turandot orders her soldiers to torture Liu — a delicious operatic prospect for which some *aficionados* would cheerfully pay a hundred dollars per ring-side seat.

In those wonderful years of my operatic youth, however, Madame Jeritza and Madame Lehmann appeared frequently together, in *Carmen, Rosenkavalier, Ariadne auf Naxos, Frau ohne Schatten, Walküre* and other operas. On such nights the Staatsoper was filled with a capacity crowd and with as much tension as Yankee Stadium before a world's heavyweight championship fight. Some of the beautifully gowned ladies in the audience could hardly conceal a bloodthirsty look in their eyes. Some men regretted they were not at Milan's La Scala, where vigorous booing is permissible even in orchestra stalls and where ripe tomatoes, raw eggs and tight shoes have been thrown by people in full evening dress across the orchestra pit at disappointing singers. Such gusty demonstrations of inverted enthusiasm were unheard-of in Vienna. But on big nights plain-clothes men, conspicuous to everybody, would appear in the galleries to prevent violent outbreaks of enthusiasm or displeasure.

I spent the best years of my opera life as a member of the celebrated claque in the Staatsoper's fourth gallery, a highly exclusive group of deeply dedicated opera lovers whose musical refinement was not always matched by their financial solvency. By way of using the former to achieve the latter, the claque members would receive free tickets from the claque chief, in return for which they would clap their hands at the right moment for the right person in the right

manner, a feat far more difficult to achieve than most operagoers would imagine.

The institution of the claque is much older than opera itself. Opera dates only from the sixteenth century, but the
claque was already known to the ancient Romans. Nero, an
early status-seeker, had a "body of hired applauders." Owing
to their exalted pedigree, the *claqueurs* were called *les Ro-
mains* in eighteenth-century Paris but among each other they
referred to themselves as *chevaliers de lustre*, aware of their
magic to give brilliance and glamor to a lusterless performance. Until the end of the eighteenth century the names
of the singers were not printed on the playbill. Ticket dealers were often beaten up by irate operagoers who had hoped
to hear the prima donna and instead had to listen to a
second-rate replacement. An obscure ticket-dealer became
famous for his exclamation, "How was I to know that they
would let loose Ponthieu?" But the Ponthieus of this world
deserve our gratitude, for one of them can save a performance that is almost wrecked when the prima donna cancels.
Still, there is no justice left in the operatic world: everybody
hates the substitute.

In 1837 in Paris it was seriously proposed to introduce the
claque officially in the opera houses of France, England and
Italy, to educate innocent audiences and teach ignorant amateurs the subtleties of applause, but unfortunately nothing
came of it. The best *claqueurs* are true educators; an element
of racketeering was brought in much later by unscrupulous
second-raters. In Paris many composers, authors and artists
realized that you cannot depend solely on the doubtful audible support of friends and relatives when the going gets

tough, which often happens toward the end of the second
act or after a difficult aria. A certain amount of encouragement is supplied by various "cliques" — groups of personal
friends and ferocious fans — but without carefully steered
applause the public-at-large might conclude that as a whole
the evening has been rather a failure. "Observation for more
than two decades has convinced me that the public is much
better off in the hands of a claque than in the hands of a
clique," writes Irving Kolodin. Alexandre Dumas the Older
often consulted the *chef de claque* about applause.

The experienced *claqueur* knows exactly when carefully
built-up applause will have the greatest effect. He knows the
score, has an understanding of the art of singing, is endowed
with a sixth sense for the mood of the audience, and has perfect timing. Some composers have suffered so long from the
tantrums of divas and the antics of tenors that they get even
with them, posthumously, by putting a fiendish quaver rest
at the end of a great aria — after which the music goes on
right away. Unless the applause begins exactly at the fraction of a second, there is disaster in the opera house. To applaud too early might ruin the singer's high tone and carefully calculated effect. To start applause too late incurs the
risk of the conductor's running away with the music. Conductors don't like ovations given to others. Such inept applause may fizzle out ingloriously — another of life's missed
opportunities.

The hardest thing is to applaud "into the music." It must
be done with such momentum that it literally stops the show.
We often did this after *"Nessun dorma"* in *Turandot,* when
the tenor had finished his aria with a brilliant high C. Puc-

cini has provided no pause for an ovation there. Verdi, an old hand at dramatic effects, always left a chance for a cascade of applause after a great aria, except when he wasn't so sure there *would* be an ovation. That is perhaps why the music goes on so quickly after the terribly difficult "Nile" aria in *Aïda*, which is rarely sung well enough to deserve applause. Wagner took a dim view of applause which, he felt, did not belong in his exalted scheme of *Musikdrama*. One of the few occasions when we would dare interrupt the holy sounds of Wagnerian music with brutal applause was at Hans Sachs's appearance on the festival meadow in the third act of *Meistersinger*, when we would join in the Wagner-sanctioned ovation of the stage folks in Nuremberg for their beloved cobbler-poet. This custom is still preserved in Vienna, provided the singer deserves it.

Under its celebrated chief, the great Joseph Schostal, the claque at the Vienna Opera was a precision instrument of musical timing and psychological skill, which provided friendly guidance for lukewarm ticket-holders, injected a healthy sense of competition among the artists, saved many evenings from dullness, and generally helped to raise the standard of the performances.

Schostal was a man of high principles in a *métier* not famous for lofty morals. He had uncompromising ideas about the art of subtly engineered applause. "Applause must be earned," he used to say. Even though he accepted money from the artists he made it clear that he was under no moral obligation to deliver applause unless the artist deserved it. The volume would range from a mild shower after Cherubino's *"Non so più"* in *Figaro,* appropriate to the style of Mozart's music, to a dramatic tumult after Tosca's *"Vissi d'arte."* Schostal was of the opinion, unusual for a *chef de claque,* that applause is effective only when it is genuine.

"Genuine applause," he would say, "may turn a mediocre performance into an exciting evening. The claque makes opera grand."

We members of the claque would carry out the tactical operations, but the great strategic decisions were made by Schostal himself. He might decide during the aria of one of our clients that the singer wasn't good enough that night. The artist was singing quite well but failed to radiate that peculiar excitement that fascinates the audience. Schostal would slowly shake his large bald head — he would be standing at the extreme left side of the gallery under one of the emergency lights and could well be seen — and the members of the claque, scattered all over the gallery, would know the order had been rescinded. Or it might happen that a singer who hadn't paid Schostal a single schilling suddenly electrified the audience with an unexpected display of vocal fireworks. Schostal would not hesitate to bestow upon him a deserved tribute, free of charge; he might even give the artist the supreme accolade, by booming a perfectly timed "Bravo!" into the auditorium that would be followed by a paroxysm of enthusiasm, while we congratulated ourselves on yet another superb achievement. No wonder our claque made headlines in the local papers more often than the artists. After a conspicuous claque performance Julius Korngold, the music critic of *Neue Freie Presse,* would end his review with the sentence, "The claque was in its usual top form." Malicious

rumors said that in return Schostal gave "audible support" to
Korngold's son Erich Wolfgang, the composer of *Die tote
Stadt*. The fact was that Schostal loved *Die tote Stadt*, with
its great parts for Maria Jeritza, Richard Tauber and Richard Mayr. Schostal even went to hear *Parsifal*, "as a private
citizen," since there is no applause after *Parsifal*. Most members of the claque also went to hear *Parsifal*, at their own
expense too.

The genuine *claqueur* is, in fact, a congenital opera enthusiast. He cares more about opera than about a prima
donna. He is always aware of the claque's tradition, history,
and code of ethics. In his *Evenings with the Orchestra* Hector Berlioz writes about the manners and mannerisms of the
claque of the Paris Opéra a century ago, about their grand
strategy and devious tactics. Berlioz had much respect for
the well-trained claqueur. He defined the professional as
one who is "educated, shrewd, cautious, inspired."

> The claque [Berlioz writes] has become a necessity of our
> time. In whatever shape or disguise, with whatever excuse,
> it has won its way everywhere. It reigns and governs in the
> theater, at concerts, in the National Assembly, in clubs,
> churches, and corporations, in the press and even in the
> salons. . . . The claques at our theaters have become ex-
> perts. Their profession has risen to be an art. Besides, the
> doings of the claque are a part of the fun; it is a pleasure to
> see it maneuver. This is so true that were the *claqueurs* ex-
> cluded from certain performances there would not be a soul
> in the house.
> No, the suppression of the claque in France is happily a
> madman's dream. Heaven and earth shall pass away, but
> the claque shall stand.

Of the professional *claqueur's* essential equipment inspiration is the most important single component. I happen to know quite a few singers and musicians, some of them well known, who don't really love opera or music but consider it a means of making a living. But I have never known anyone in the claque who wasn't infatuated with opera, even after thirty years of mediocre performances, uninspired playing, dull singing. The great claques in nineteenth-century Paris and Vienna were organized like embassies, with paid attachés and unpaid staff members, but all were crazy about opera.

There are subtle gradations of applause. At the end of a certain passage there might be "gentle indications of approval," at others "warmer expressions of admiration." After the great climaxes in Italian opera there would be "wild outbursts of uncontrollable enthusiasm." It was all very inspiring, well organized and tremendously effective. Efforts were made to abolish the claque at the Paris Opéra in 1830, at La Scala in 1890, at Vienna's Court Opera (under Mahler) in 1906, at the Metropolitan in 1915, but the claque, like a phoenix, always rises out of anarchy and confusion. As long as there is grand opera, there will be a claque.

Schostal left nothing to chance. He would attend rehearsals and make notes in his score, and he would carefully weigh the pro and con before making a decision when and where to applaud. He would brief us before the performance. There was no "false applause" while he was around. He had a secret intelligence network inside the opera house and knew in advance what the evening performance was going to be like. Around noon, when the singers had finished their morning rehearsals, Schostal would hold court under the Kärntnerstrasse arcades near the stage entrance, where he would receive the tributes of his clients and get the latest dope on their vocal, marital or emotional crises. A young soprano might give him a sweet smile, hoping for a solo applause after she'd sung her few lines as Hellwige in *Walküre* or Barbarina in *Figaro*. The poor woman didn't know that it took more than a smile to get an ovation from the Vienna claque.

The size of the evening force depended on the opera given. During Verdi and Puccini performances there were twice as many of us up in the gallery as when Strauss or Wagner operas were performed. A quarter of an hour before the beginning of the performance Schostal would stand near a marble column in the downstairs lobby, handing out tickets and instructions. Each member received one ticket (Schostal wouldn't permit us to invite a girl friend) and no other favor. Insinuations in the sensationalist "boulevard press" that we were paid to applaud were as false and malicious as most of their news reports. Many of our detractors were members of the rival "clique" — an amateurish outfit operating downstairs under the command of a man named Stieglitz, who was more impressed by the financial contributions of his clients than by their vocal achievements. The clique members were not "educated, shrewd, cautious" — and certainly not inspired.

On important evenings when Maria Jeritza sang against Alfred Piccaver, or Leo Slezak against Lotte Lehmann,

Schostal would summon the suicide squads of the claque, called *Hohlposcher*, courageous *condottieri* able to produce that special, dark, sepulchral sound which had the supreme professional finish. These accomplished masters of enthusiasm were the respected Commando troops of the claque. When the *Hohlposcher* clapped their hands, you thought a tank regiment was rumbling by at high speed over an old, cobblestoned street. On special occasions, when Schostal decided that floral tributes were due to a diva, the *Hohlposcher* would race down the hundred-and-fifty-odd stairs into the parquet, and toward the orchestra pit, to throw across small bunches of flowers which they had hidden under their coats. Such manifestations of enthusiasm were forbidden by the police, but the *Hohlposcher* managed to disappear before they could be arrested. The fact that the prima donna herself had paid for the bouquets didn't diminish our admiration for these brave men.

I remember a memorable *Rosenkavalier* performance in the middle twenties with Madame Lehmann as the Marschallin, Madame Jeritza as Octavian, Madame Elizabeth Schumann as Sophie, and Richard Mayr as Ochs. For reasons that cannot be divulged — much of the claque's intimate history is still classified information — the claque in those days supported Madame Lehmann, while the Stieglitz clique worked for Madame Jeritza. Both groups, incidentally, worked free for Richard Mayr, who never paid a nickel to anyone and was, in Schostal's words, everybody's honorary client. The boulevard press had hinted there might be trouble that night, and the police had sent large detachments of plain-clothes men into the house. In the lobby, Schostal was surrounded by the entire membership of the claque, standing provocatively beside a sign: "All Disturbing Manifestations of Ap- and Disap-proval Are Strictly Prohibited."

It was a tense situation. *Rosenkavalier* is an impossible opera from the claque's viewpoint; there are no arias, and applause is permitted only at the end of each act. We know that the clique downstairs would try to outclap and outshout us. Feelings between the claque and the clique that night were as friendly as, let us say bluntly, those between Madame Jeritza and Madame Lehmann. Everything depended on the volume of the applause. All divas have invisible audiometers built in to their competitive hearing systems. They know at once whether the rival's applause is a few decibels louder or softer than their own — and God help you if theirs is softer.

"Tonight," Schostal said solemnly, "it is our mission to produce volume. Men, the honor of our institution is at stake."

I will not go into details about the performance, which was spruced up by the wonderful spirit of rivalry on the stage. As the curtain went up, the Marschallin sat stiffly at one end of her couch while her young lover Octavian was crouched at the other end, a good two yards removed from the lady. Despite the orgiastic music of the Prelude, it was very hard to realize that the Marschallin and Octavian had supposedly just spent a passionate night.

Throughout their scenes the two divas outmaneuvered each other skillfully, under the watchful eyes of Richard Strauss, composer, conductor and referee of the opera. At the end of each act there were "wild outbursts of uncontrolled enthusiasm," in which even the plain-clothes men took part — most of them, it was noted, in favor of Madame Jeritza. And why not? Not so long ago the claque had also been in the Jeritza camp. . . .

Toward the end of the opera the *Hohlposcher* made a dramatic dash into the parquet but were stopped from throwing the flowers by the intervention of several guests of the clique who were usually active around the locker rooms of Sportklub Rapid, a soccer team well known for the rough manners of its *aficionados.* In the ensuing scuffle one of the flower bouquets hit the face of Richard Mayr, who threw it right back into the audience. The *Hohlposcher* and the Rapid fans were arrested. The rest of us ran to the stage doors, where we created such a tumult that at least two guests at the nearby Hotel Sacher phoned for their bills and wanted to leave because they could only assume that another minor revolution had broken out. The police, considerate as always, waited until both divas had departed and the last shout of *"Brava!"* had echoed out into the night sky, and then they arrested the entire membership present of both the claque and the clique.

Everybody was marched off to the police, where Viennese justice prevailed. Stieglitz and the clique members were fined for disturbing the peace. Schostal and members of his claque were dismissed with assurances of mutual esteem. It was well known that the claque was motivated by the highest artistic considerations.

Another great climax was reached one evening a year or so later when the foolhardy Staatsoper management put on

a *Walküre* performance with Madame Lehmann as Sieglinde, Madame Jeritza as Brünnhilde *and* Madame Olczewska as Fricka. Three "first ladies" for the price of one
ticket! Madame Olczewska was ably seconded by her husband Emil Schipper, the famous brass baritone, who sang
the part of Wotan that night. But the balance of power was
restored by Richard Schubert, the great *Heldententor,* who
sang Siegmund and was a Lehmann follower.

The three-cornered prima donna fight was extensively
reported by the local boulevard press. Special backstage war
correspondents (hired from among the stagehands and electricians) claimed there had been quite a brawl among the
divas in which Wotan, Siegmund and Hunding had also
participated. The correspondent of *Die Stunde* wrote, "It
was more fun than anything that ever happened in Richard
Wagner's *Walküre* and, as is well known, some mighty funny
things happen in *Walküre.*" There is still as much disagreement about the backstage fracas as there is about the great
military battles of the Second World War. War correspondents don't always agree on what they have seen. The event
was reported with more drama than objectivity. Local libel
laws were generous and the standards of journalistic ethics
not particularly strict.

It was a great time to be a *claqueur.* Some of the singers
needed our help and quite a few journalists sought our
opinions. The golden epoch of the Vienna Opera was under
the reign of Gustav Mahler, from 1902 to 1912, but the
golden epoch of the Vienna claque was during the twenty-
year-rule of Joseph Schostal.

Practically no week went by without a minor *Opern-skandal*. Once Chaliapin almost broke up a *Faust* perform-ance when he not only sang the part of Mephisto but also tried to conduct the orchestra from the stage. A humorless critic started a bitter argument when he noticed that in the third act of *Rosenkavalier* — after the Baron Ochs's question *"Was woll'n die Maikäfer da?"* — half the orchestra had sung *in unison* with the stage waiter: *"Servier'n, Euer Gnaden."* The critic implied that such musical jokes belonged in vaudeville, not in the august Vienna State Opera. The or-chestra angrily retorted that the joke had first been perpe-trated under the baton and with the consent of Richard Strauss, the composer, and had thus became "part of the score." (It still is; and at a recent *Rosenkavalier* performance, at the Salzburg Festival House, Herbert von Karajan, the conductor, almost got flustered and dropped his baton when the orchestra, playing a joke on the joke, did *not* sing the phrase, which is not in the score.)

In my day the State Opera's star tenor, Alfred Piccaver, a Lehmann partisan, might one week feud with Madame Jeritza, when he sang against her in Puccini's *La Fanciulla del West,* and the following week there might be excitement when young Jan Kiepura arrived on the Opera's high-voltage stage, almost directly from the unsophisticated Polish land-scape. Kiepura, naturally unable to appreciate the subtle nuances of Vienna's musical high-life, found himself in trouble with all local divas because he held his youthful high C's longer than they could hold theirs — an offense that no blue-blooded prima donna will tolerate.

Later in America, Kiepura, who was by that time an

accomplished infighter, carried on a running battle against
Grace Moore. During a *Manon* performance in Rochester,
Miss Moore walked out on him just as he was to sing
an aria to her. Undaunted, Kiepura turned around and
instead addressed the aria to the audience. Most people
didn't understand his French anyway, and no harm was
done.

This just goes to show that "prima donna" does not always
denote the female of the species. Celebrated conductors are
notorious for their tantrums and privileges. Think of Arthur
Nikisch, fastidious, vain and imperious; of Gustav Mahler,
who would tolerate no imperfection; of Wilhelm Furt-
wängler, who got more publicity than most divas he worked
with. Toscanini's outbursts were feared and famous. Every
time Sir Thomas Beecham opened his mouth in public his
delicious utterances were quoted by the newspapers. Herbert von Karajan had become a musical legend before he was
fifty. But Toscanini's temperament was directed against
sloppiness, not against a rival; Sir Thomas tried to educate
as well as to uplift his audiences, for which he deserved our
admiration. Karajan is more deeply involved in beautiful
music than in psychological warfare. Subtlety is practiced
by conductors, not kicks in the shinbone.

Tenors are a different story. Their peculiar fascination for
women has long puzzled Freudians and gland specialists.
The operatic *chronique scandaleuse* knows many stories of
the temperamental primo uomo. The tenor Luigi Ravelli
once got enraged in the middle of the stage because Minnie
Hauk, the American soprano, embraced him so passionately
that she choked his high B flat. The audience considered
Ravelli's tantrums a fine histrionic touch, and applauded

wildly. The tenor was appeased and went on with his performance. Pasquale Brignoli, another celebrated nineteenth-century tenor, often refused to go on with his performance unless he received his "proper share" of applause. The tenor Fancelli, who had a high opinion of himself, was once asked to write his name in the Golden Book of the Liverpool Philharmonic Society. His handwriting was limited, however, and when he attempted to write, "Fancelli, *Primo Tenore Assoluto*" (obviously the opposite of the prima donna *assoluta*), the signature came out like "Fanali Primo Tenore Ass."

Baritones and bassos also come in for their share of operatic tribal behavior, and have been analyzed by psychologists, who talk of complexes, and by laryngologists, who explain strain. Chaliapin at the zenith of his fame would instruct conductors about tempi, his fellow singers about interpretation, the chorus about where to stand. Michael Bohnen, the German bass baritone, also liked to conduct the orchestra from the stage. One night, after the beginning of a performance of *Faust* in Vienna, he failed to appear as Mephisto because he hadn't been paid in advance. Not long ago at the Rome Opera, Boris Christoff, during a *Don Carlos* rehearsal in which he sang the part of King Philip, got into an argument with Franco Corelli, the tenor who sang Don Carlos, and both drew their stage swords. It was a fine new climax that would have pleased Maestro Verdi, that great expert in operatic climaxes.

That is the stuff grand opera is made of. As Francis Robinson says, "What's the use of paying ten dollars a seat to hear somebody who is exactly like oneself?" Life at the opera house will never be boring as long as the great diva is alive and (literally) kicking. Long live the prima donna!

❧ 2 ❧

Melba's Magic: Trills and Thrills

"NELLIE MELBA had the sort of beauty that slowly grows on you," remembers Tom Hazelton-Cochrane, an Australian writer and opera lover who knew the prima donna as early as the beginning of the twentieth century, when he was her young, devoted admirer. Mr. Hazelton-Cochrane spoke thus at the age of eighty-six — still a passionate Melba fan. In his London flat was a nice collection of Melba memorabilia. He spoke as one of the few people alive in 1961 who had been close to the great prima donna.

"Nellie was not tall but she *looked* tall to her public. That is, of course, common among fascinating artists. The first thing you noticed about her were her eyes. They were reddish-brown and immensely alive. She had delicate eyelids and long, curling lashes. She had rich, dark hair and a wonderful complexion. She was proud of her wonderful teeth. Used to tease me because I had to go to the dentist all the time and she never did. She had small feet and carried herself very well; she always walked fast, with a quick step, head high. She gave you the feeling of being completely alive. Yes, she was a real diva. Dear Nellie had class!"

There was a misty expression in Hazelton-Cochrane's eyes that afternoon as we sat at his club and talked about Melba. And I thought, How many people who have been dead for almost thirty years can spread such posthumous magic?

Jacques Isnardon describes Melba with Gallic perception in his *History of the Théâtre de la Monnaie* (the theater where Melba made her debut). "The nose is straight, delicate; the neck's line *exquise,* superbly set; the eye wonders, searches; the mouth is frank and loving. The build of the head, neck and shoulders reveals the thoroughbred. Her ideal profile harmonizes with the charm of her carriage. . . . Her admirers went into raptures about her small ears, her musical laugh, her delicate eyelids, her strangely colored eyes." Obviously "dear Nellie" had not only class but also sex appeal — a refined sex appeal.

It's too bad that electrical recording was not perfected a generation earlier. We would have had a correct memory of some of the greatest voices of all times. We've read long descriptions of these voices, but unfortunately it is impossible to describe a singer's voice accurately. What did the "golden-voiced" Catalani sound like? Were the voices of Faustina Bordoni, Giulia Grisi, Maria Malibran really as perfect as we are asked to believe? One good recording conveys more than a thousands words. If later recording magicians hadn't succeeded in almost completely restoring Caruso's magnificent voice from his earlier imperfect re-

cordings we couldn't imagine what it was like. Caruso's 266
recordings prove it gloriously.

Melba's pure, even, beautifully controlled voice was ideal
for recording, but she lived thirty years too early. She was
the first famous singer who dared step in front of the terrify-
ing recording horn. It took courage because the technical
equipment was imperfect. On her early recordings Melba
is sometimes heard to hoot and to sing out of pitch, crimes
of which she was never guilty. She made her very first
recordings in the drawing room of her London town house
in Great Cumberland Place. She had stipulated that if she
didn't like them they would be destroyed. She sang *"Ah!
Fors' è lui"* from *La Traviata* and *"Cara nome"* from *Rigoletto.* She was horrified by the "scratching, screeching results."

"Never again!" she said. "If I sound like that, I'll go away
and live on a desert island." The recordings were destroyed.

Six years later — in 1910 — Madame Melba was once again
approached by the intrepid Gramophone company. She
carried out intricate negotiations with her remarkable mixture of business and sentiment. The recordings must remain "unpublished" — they were for her "dear Daddy" in
Australia. And she would get fifty thousand dollars for one
week of recording, in addition to royalties. She even had a
special Melba label on them, with her autograph — an honor
accorded only to her and Patti (not even to Caruso). In an
interview with the *Daily Express* a few months later, Melba
said she had been "inundated by letters from strangers, and
also from representatives of voice-producing machines, making flattering but not sufficiently tempting offers. One came

yesterday and asked me to name my own price. I did so. The gentleman left me more in sorrow than in anger."

And the Gramophone and Typewriter Ltd. promised their patrons "that they will leave no stone unturned, and let no financial consideration (however gigantic it may be) stand in the way of all Gramophone dealers being able to stock records of Madame Melba's voice." One result of the sale of Melba recordings was an avalanche of marriage proposals from men all over the world. Melba, an eminently practical woman, was not impressed. She concluded that the bold suitors were less infatuated with the sweet sound of her voice than with the pleasant prospect of her earning power.

In 1926, after electrical recording had first been tried, "His Master's Voice" persuaded Melba's protégé, the young Australian baritone John Brownlee, to persuade the prima donna to record some duets with him, "simply as a souvenir." Melba came to the studio and curiously viewed "the new instrument of torture, the microphone."

"How can anything good come out of this obnoxious little box?" she asked, stalking around the helpless microphone, while Brownlee and the engineers were terrified she might change her mind and leave at the last minute. But she calmed down and agreed to a test. The playback amazed her so much that she wouldn't believe it, and they did another recording.

By this time Melba was really excited.

"For the first time I can hear what my voice is really like," she said. "Why wasn't this thing invented before?"

The excitement grew, and Melba, always impulsive and

fast in her decisions, said to Brownlee, "John, we'll record
the duets and I will also do a couple of songs. 'Clair de
Lune' and 'Swing Low, Sweet Chariot.'"

"I felt quite sure," said Brownlee, "that the Gramophone
people who had been in on this from the start would explode
at this moment, but the English calm prevailed." The only
one who almost lost his nerve was Brownlee, twenty-five
and inexperienced, and bowled over by his chance to make
recordings with the Queen of Song.

Of the more than a hundred published records of Melba,
the first were made in 1904, when she was forty-five, the
last in 1926, when she was past sixty-seven. The earliest
records are too imperfect to show the full beauty of her
voice; and when she made her last records, her voice no
longer had its magic. At the early recordings the engineers
were so frightened by the effect of Melba's powerful top
tones that they asked her "to lean right back from the
recording horn when taking a high note." After making
what may have been "the most beautiful record, I stumbled
backwards over a chair, and then said 'Damn!' . . . That
'damn' came out with terrible clarity, making me feel as a
sinner must do on the Day of Judgment. . . . No, singing
for the Gramophone was no rest cure." It still isn't.

There exists a primitive recording which gives a brief
but electrifying acoustic impression of Melba. It was made
on the stage of the Metropolitan on March 11, 1901, during
Les Huguénots. "There is a high C sharp, attacked in full
voice, which seems to echo round the huge auditorium,"
wrote the English critic Desmond Shawe-Taylor. "There
are cascades of florid singing thrown off in a manner which

might almost be called reckless, yet not a semiquaver, even in the most rapid upward arpeggios, is out of place."

All the people who remember Melba tell me that her magic was in her voice. Her singing voice. "Her speaking voice was different," says Hazelton-Cochrane, "often harsh and strong, while her singing voice was wonderfully clear and unbelievably lovely."

It's easy to believe when you listen to a recording which she made in America in 1910 with Caruso, the magnificent duet "*O soave fanciulla*" from the first act of *La Bohème*. Melba's voice glows with an inner fire; it is full of emotion, mellow and pure. At the end of the duet, the two voices blend in a heavenly pianissimo. Melba was right when she told a friend, "When I sing with Caruso in *La Bohème*, I always feel as if our two voices had merged into one." She also made some wonderful solo recordings. When she sings "Salce" and "Ave Maria" from the last act of *Otello*, a shiver runs down your spine. And she sings "Home, Sweet Home," her most famous encore, with such feeling and warmth that the voice becomes completely alive again and catches your heartstrings. No wonder millions of people adored her!

"Melba was not fundamentally a coloratura singer but rather a *soprano leggiero*," writes H. Hugh Harvey, an English connoisseur who heard her many times between 1906 and 1926, lucky man. He was at Covent Garden the night of June 22, 1906, when Melba, Caruso and Mattia Battistini appeared in *Rigoletto*. "Melba," says Mr. Harvey, "was a light soprano with a resonant and beautiful timbre and an exceedingly brilliant vocalization, combined with an extensive compass which enabled her to sing certain coloratura roles with great success."

Melba's audiences (as audiences everywhere) were high-C-crazy. "History of opera proves, from Lind to Pons, and from Patti to Galli-Curci, that there is a kind of aural appetite which nothing satisfies so keenly as the highest notes and the swiftest scales," writes Irving Kolodin in *The Story of the Metropolitan Opera*.

One can identify certain elements of the prima donna's vocal equipment — intonation, attack, steadiness of sustained notes, precision in scales and arpeggios, all the technical details. But to convey the actual sound of the living voice one has to fall back on adjectives and impressionistic words. Caruso's voice has been called "golden," which conveys the color, the metal, the sheen, the timbre. Melba's voice, we are told, was "silvery," pure, sweet, fresh and girlish. The blend of Caruso's gold and Melba's silver created the most precious masterpieces of vocal jewelry.

John Pitts Sanborn, Jr., an American critic, called Melba's voice "sculptural — it has the quality of physical form. The voluptuous large body of her voice takes shape in the air." He also compared her singing to the art of the painter. "Melba can lay a note out on the air as a painter lays a color on his canvas, so that it seems to stay there."

What was the unique charm of Melba's voice that so fascinated the public and the critics? She had a lovely soprano voice. So had quite a few other prima donnas who never radiated Melba's fascination. Percy Colson, her biographer, thought her voice had a "siren's beauty." "One lost oneself in the joy of hearing it." Melba herself once told Colson, "My voice is like a glorified boy's voice." She meant a choirboy's voice, the refined English variety of chorister.

A siren's voice and a choirboy's voice. How much inner life must a woman's voice have to convey such divergent impressions!

One man who still has "the sound of her voice in the ears" compares her voice to the paintings by the great masters from Siena, which have "little passion but great pathos." All agree with Hazelton-Cochrane who says, "Once you've heard Melba you can never forget the sound of her voice." The great Wagnerian conductor Anton Seidl said, "Melba's voice has a magic, a fairylike tone."

Melba's old friends still talk about her "angelic" timbre. Colson remembers a lovely spring morning in Paris when he drove up in his coach in front of Melba's house and heard her voice through an open window.

> The quiet street was suddenly flooded with the quality of her exquisite singing. She ran up the scale of G major, improvised a cadenza, trilled as only she could trill, on G and A, and ended with a long drawn-out B natural. The coachman stopped at the sound of her voice, and when the last note died away turned to me and said, *"Mais, Monsieur, c'est un ange qui chante!"* I never saw her so pleased with a compliment as when I told her about it.

One of Melba's close friends remembers that when she was practicing in a hotel room in New York, a small boy in an adjoining room said to his mother, "Listen, Mummy — a birdie!" Jules Massenet called her "Madame Stradivarius." Joseph Joachim, the great violinist who said "Melba surpasses all other great singers of our time" compared her to his beautiful Stradivarius violin of 1715 which he kept all his life. "A Strad," he once explained to Melba, "sounds small in a small room and swells as the room increases, always retaining its beautiful quality."

The supreme accolade comes from Mary Garden, Melba's great competitor and a prima donna in her own right. "I have no hesitation in declaring that Melba had the most phenomenal effect on me of any singer I have ever heard," it says in *Mary Garden's Story*. This is a rare and amazing statement.

Melba was a born singer. "Melba sings because she must sing," said the Belgian composer François Auguste Gevaert. She did instinctively what other singers take infinite pains to do and never achieve: her technique was so astonishing that it was no longer apparent. There was some discussion where nature ended and art began with Melba, which was perhaps the highest tribute paid to her art. Her sustained notes were perfectly even, with no trace of tremolo; she had no vocal tricks, no mannerisms. A coloratura and a violinist must never give the impression of laboring under technical difficulties, otherwise the public suffers with (and for) them and winds up hating them. A great coloratura diva must give her audience the impression that she enjoys bringing off a formidable *tour de force*. Melba was that accomplished artist; she gave her listeners a happy feeling that she was having fun with her vocal gymnastics. A *tour de force* became a *tour de joie*. "Up and down the scale she went in trills and runs and roulades and ended like a fireworks display with a shower of golden notes," writes a critic. Melba's virtuosity gave her listeners the illusion that they could go home and perform the same chromatic scales and difficult arpeggios in the bathtub. She would execute the most difficult *fioriture* with wonderful flexibility, always using her voice within rather than beyond its true limits of resonant power.

Her trill alone would have made her world-famous. The Melba trill was facile, pure, brilliant — the trill of a bird. "*Elle chante comme un rossignol,*" wrote a French critic after her Paris debut. Melba enjoyed her "nightingale" trill. She once had "the most amazing sensation" when she visited the Taj Mahal on a trip through India. There was moonlight, the strong scent of flowers and a soft radiance of marble. Melba sang a trill, and heard her echoing voice "which never seemed to stop."

Coloratura runs can be as dull as an étude, but Melba made her vocal gymnastics sound musical. She didn't have absolute pitch but she never sang out of tune. "I must have an especially built throat," she would say. "When I sing a chromatic scale I feel like pressing down each note on a keyed instrument."

She never was a great dramatic actress. After she first played Manon at the Metropolitan Opera House, the *New York Times* critic wrote: "Madame Melba has the voice of a lark and, so far as her acting is evidence, the soul of one also." One of her close friends says, "When she tried to convey a mild emotion she would raise one arm. But it didn't matter. Her voice could express the subtlest nuances of all emotions, all the delicate shades from happiness and gaiety to sorrow and despair." Sir Arthur Sullivan, the composer of *The Mikado* and a great friend of Melba's, said, "By the mere emission of tone she can express the whole gamut of human feeling."

Melba was rarely "carried away" by her performance in opera. In her special repertoire there was no need for that. She kept both her voice and her emotions in control and saved both her vocal cords and her temperament. This sense of control, together with her impeccable technique, enabled her to sing in opera until she was almost seventy years old. "The years showed on her appearance but her voice retained much of its youthful charm," wrote a newspaper.

"What is the secret of her clarity of tone? One thing, certainly, is her ideal 'looseness.' Last night it was very noticeable how she slipped away from consonants, giving them the least possible value, to get the musical part of the word — the vowel," wrote *The Times* critic after Melba's farewell concert at Albert Hall, London, when she was sixty-seven years old. "She was in wonderfully good voice," said the *Daily Telegraph*. "The thousands who were there will have taken away the memory not of the ghost of a beautiful voice but of a still entirely delightful singer."

Melba would cast her spell even before she appeared on stage. "Time and again," says Hazelton-Cochrane, "I've been sitting in the auditorium of Covent Garden during the first act of *La Bohème*. There comes that wonderful moment when Mimi's voice is heard behind the door. '*Scusi, di grazia, mis' e spento il lume.*' She apologizes for intruding;

her candle has gone out. Just a few syllables, rather spoken
than sung. No sob stuff. But there was such sweetness and
innocence in those few tones that you could feel a ruffle
of excitement in the darkened auditorium. People would
smile and shake their heads in delight, and some would
whisper, 'Melba!' You didn't have to understand the words.
It was magic and you were caught by it."

"Put Melba behind a screen," writes J. A. Fuller-Maitland,
an English critic, "and the most rapturous exultation of
youth or the most poignant expression of sorrow will be
conveyed to all intelligent hearers."

Elena Danieli, an American singer who often appeared
with Melba in the 1920s, was particularly moved by Melba's
Desdemona in the fourth act of *Otello*.

"No one," she says, "has ever sung 'Ave Maria' as she did
it. There was piety and sweetness and warmth in it. She had
a wonderful way of fitting in the half-spoken phrases. At
the end she could sing the long 'A-ve' in one breath. I often
sat in the auditorium during that act. People around me had
tears in their eyes. No one who was there would ever forget
it."

W. J. Henderson, who heard Melba at the zenith of her
career — the ten years following her American debut in
1893 — wrote:

> No words can convey to a music lover who did not hear
> Melba any idea of the sounds with which she ravished all
> ears. . . . One could say, 'It's the unique voice of the world.'
> This writer never heard any other just like it. Its beauty, its
> clarion quality, its power differed from the fluty notes of
> Patti. Melba's voice has been called silvery, but what does
> that signify? There is one quality which it had and which

may be comprehended even by those who did not hear her; it had splendor. The tones glowed with a starlike brilliance. They flamed with a white flame.

It is easier to describe Melba's technical equipment. Melba's voice extended from the B flat below middle C to the F sharp above high C. To sing a beautiful high C is the cherished goal of all sopranos, but Melba could sing a high D, a high E and a high F — two and a half tones on top of the high C! Her breath control, phrasing and modulation were perfect. There was not the smallest change in the quality of the tones from bottom to top. There was never even a suspicion of throatiness. And the critics never stopped admiring the way she attacked the notes.

> The Melba attack was little short of marvelous [writes Henderson]. The term "attack" is not a good one. Melba indeed has no attack. She opened her mouth and a tone was in existence. It began without any betrayal of breathing; it simply was there.

People always love a great coloratura soprano. Catalani, Giulia Grisi, Jenny Lind, Galli-Curci and Lily Pons were popular idols. When Melba studied singing in Paris she heard Patti. "The most golden voice to which I have ever listened," she writes. "The timbre was exquisite, the diction crystalline. I took my lesson from her, for she had much to teach."

There is a peculiar fascination in a pure, beautiful, lovely "white" voice that soars to dizzy heights with utter facility, the song of a nightingale on a spring morning. As a young boy I first heard the great Viennese coloratura Selma Kurz in *Rigoletto*. I'll never forget her trill at the end of *"Caro nome,"* which seemed to last for ages while she slowly walked off stage. Later, when I had joined the claque, we used to time the trill with a stop watch. Once it lasted twenty-one seconds, which, I now realize, was a record of vocal bravura but also of doubtful taste.

I've since learned that coloratura prima donnas are better remembered for vocal trills and thrills than for mature musicianship, but perhaps that is the fault of the composers who wrote for them. When you spend a considerable part of your early life learning the bravura scales, *fioriture,* arpeggios and trills of Donizetti's Lucia, Delibes' Lakmé and Gounod's Juliette, not enough time remains for the sound development of genuine musicality. As a child Melba learned to play the violin, the piano and the organ. "She was more than a competent pianist, a good accompanist and a sight reader," writes Colson, who is not always benign. "She had an infallible sense of rhythm and phrased perfectly." Her recordings prove it. (Prima donnas can be versatile musicians. During a benefit concert at the Metropolitan, Marcella Sembrich first played de Bériot's Seventh Violin Concerto, then a Chopin Mazurka on the piano, and finally wound up singing *"A! non giunge!"* from *La Sonnambula.* Henderson wrote: "Her artistry was hardly less as an instrumentalist than as a vocalist.")

Colson remembers a party in London when Melba sang a waltz song by Herman Bemberg, with the composer accompanying her on the piano. Bemberg was absent-minded. Shortly before Melba's final cadenza he modulated into the wrong key. Melba took the phrase up in the wrong key, improvised a few bars leading into the right one and finished the song correctly. "Herman, you fool, what's the matter?" she said. "Are you drunk?" But no one had noticed the mistake.

When Melba sang for Verdi her part of Desdemona in *Otello* — musically a difficult part — the old maestro was enchanted. Desdemona was one of the best things Melba did. No unmusical singer could sing it as well. Certainly some of her composer friends may have been influenced by her powerful position in the great opera houses of the world, but old Verdi was too honest for flattery. The great German conductor Hans Richter, who conducted Melba in *La Traviata* at the Vienna Court Opera, thanked her because she sang "Verdi, not Melba-Verdi." And when Arthur Nikisch heard her sing her entrance phrases in *Faust* — "*Non, monsieur! Je ne suis ni demoiselle, ni belle*" — he rushed backstage to tell her that he knew from her rendering of those few bars what an artist she was, and invited her to sing with his Leipzig Gewandhaus Orchestra. An old-timer in Paris told me that no other diva managed to mold that opening phrase in *Faust* with that floating tone of Melba. "It would make me happy for the rest of the evening," the vintage *boulevardier* remembers wistfully. "*Ah, elle était une merveille!*"

John Brownlee, the great Australian baritone, remembers a phrase from *La Traviata*, "*Dite alla giovane si belle è pura.*" "How many times have I stood beside her as we sang this duet, spellbound by the way this phrase would pour out, the perfect diction, the beautiful blending of each note to the other, in other words, heavenly legato."

There are few singers on earth who can build a reputation

with a few parts. Melba built fame with the way she sang certain phrases.

But prima donnas had very bad habits in those days. After a moving performance as Desdemona, when the audience clamored for an encore (which was bad enough) Melba would tell the stagehands to wheel out a piano onto the middle of the stage, and Desdemona, still wearing the nightgown in which she had been strangled a while ago by her jealous husband, would sit down and sing "Home, Sweet Home," accompanying herself!

Melba said the public forced her to do it. When Maria Malibran appeared in Rossini's *Otello* in New York, her fans interrupted the performance with shouts of "Home, Sweet Home," and the prima donna had to sing it right away! The fans were afraid that once Desdemona was dead she wouldn't give them their favorite song. Thérèse Tietjens often wound up a performance with "Last Rose of Summer" as an encore. Patti preferred "Home, Sweet Home." Even after the First World War, when audiences' taste began to improve in opera houses and concert halls, Melba would sing as encores the sentimental songs of Francesco Paolo Tosti, "Addio" and "Mattinata," or the song of her Australian childhood, "Comin' thro' the Rye." The operatic arias in her concerts were the fireworks, and when she had her audiences in the palm of her hands she would caress them with the songs they loved to hear.

"She was a great showman," writes John Brownlee. "She could make the simplest song seem like a big event. When she sat down at the piano and sang 'Home, Sweet Home,' thousands of people went away happy, feeling *that* was the gem of the evening."

Melba herself said she was not happy about this. "Time and again I am compelled to sing the same old songs," she said. "When I try to put something new on the program I am regarded as positively eccentric. Do you realize that even now, wherever I go, I am being asked to sing the old tunes they have heard a thousand times? I try Debussy, Duparc, Ravel. I try anything which strikes me as beautiful and fresh, and I am greeted with the same response — tame compared with the positive uproar that I receive when I sing the old favorites."

Coloratura prima donnas often sin by adding minute embellishments and minor embroideries to the original score. Vain singers want to show off; tenors love to "sit" on sustained high notes. Melba, at the end of her career, wrote, "It has always been one of the golden rules of my artistic creed that a composer's score is sacred," but in her earlier days she doubtless sinned too, making minor changes not only in the scores of dead and defenseless composers but also in operas whose composers were her friends. They didn't object; if they did, no such objections are recorded. This was the era of the prima donna; Melba could make or break a new opera. In her famous essay "On the Science of Singing" Melba wrote, "The singer's mission is to interpret the message of the composer, and not to mutilate or embellish it with extraneous ideas." Perhaps she didn't always practice what she preached. The influence of the purists — mainly Gustav Mahler and Arturo Toscanini — was not yet felt. Sir Thomas Beecham, who calls Melba "the most perfect vocalist of the last sixty years — her scale rippled from low C to top C with never a change of quality" — found "something lacking," though he wasn't quite sure what it was.

She had stage instinct. In the second act of Rossini's *Il Barbiere di Siviglia* Rosina is having a singing lesson. Rossini either was too lazy to compose the scene or he had touching faith in the musical taste of prima donnas; at any rate, he left the choice of the song to the discretion of the singer. Melba, as Rosina, would sing anything that seemed appropriate for the mood of the evening — Tosti's "Mattinata" (composed two hundred years after Rossini) or the German song "Stille Nacht," in an eighteenth-century Spanish setting!

On her first trip to California Melba appeared as Rosina at the San Francisco Opera House, at a critical moment in Spanish-American relations — shortly before the outbreak of the war. It was not very wise to put on *Il Barbiere*, which might provoke a hostile demonstration. Melba noticed there was an air of tension among the audience. The atmosphere grew more tense during the second act, when Rosina was to have her singing lesson. What was she going to sing? As she stepped to the piano, she had a flash of intuition. She sat down and sang "The Star-Spangled Banner." The vast audience rose and sang the anthem with Melba. The tension was broken. Melba was the heroine of the evening.

Her cool judgment was evident on another night in San Francisco, when she saw flames break out in the gallery while she sang the Mad Scene from *Lucia di Lammermoor*.

There were shouts of "fire!" — a wild panic seemed about to start. Melba calmly stepped to the footlights and asked everybody to file out, quietly and in order.

The conductor, however, a maestro called Bimboni, got frightened and began to scramble up from his platform to the stage. Melba gave him an imperious look and shouted "Stay where you are, Bimboni!" And when the maestro continued his hazardous climb, she gave him "a resounding crack on the head." Bimboni fell back on his seat, with an angry expression on his face and a deflated feeling in his stomach.

The theater burned down to the ground, but there was no loss of life. Melba called it "a tribute to American discipline." Others called it "a tribute to Melba's *sang-froid.*" Everybody called it "a tribute to San Francisco journalism." Leaving the burning theater, Melba read a special edition of a local paper "containing a great deal more information than we knew ourselves." The singers went to their hotels wearing their costumes, Melba as Lucia, others as courtiers and soldiers, "feeling a little foolish."

Melba's favorite partner (and favorite coach) was Jean de Reszke. This gallant, romantic Pole, who had first been a baritone (under the name Giovanni de Reschi), became one of the greatest tenors of all time. (He sang Roméo, Faust and Don José, and also Radames, Siegfried and Tristan.) Jean loved beautiful women and beautiful horses, and spent his money on both as fast as he made it. Among his fans was old Queen Victoria, who once asked him for his autograph. On her eightieth birthday, after a command performance of *Lohengrin,* the Queen said, "Jean looked so handsome in his white attire, armor and helmet, and the electric light was turned strong upon him, so that he seemed surrounded by a halo."

After the Covent Garden *première* of Massenet's *Werther,* in which Jean sang the title part, Manager Augustus Harris decided not to give a second performance, press and public reaction having been less than lukewarm. Instead there would be a performance of *Faust,* with Jean de Reszke. The great tenor protested, saying, "I will draw, if the opera doesn't," and Harris gave in and announced a second performance of *Werther.*

The day before, de Reszke asked for a few stalls for his usual *faveurs de claque.* Harris went to the box office. Practically no seats had been sold except those taken previously by subscription, unheard-of for a de Reszke performance on a Saturday night! Harris wrote a short letter to the tenor:

> *Mon chèr Jean,*
> *Avec plaisir. Voilà quelques billets pour demain soir. Si vous avez besoin d'autres, écrivez-moi un petit mot. Je vous envoie 140 fauteuils, 150 balcons et 60 amphithéâtres.*

Half an hour after de Reszke had received his 350 free tickets and the letter, Harris had a telegram from the tenor who was "ill, unable to sing either in *Werther* or *Faust.*" The critic Herman Klein believes that "the *grandes dames* of the grand, and pit, tiers, and boxes, had no wish to see their beloved Jean in costumes so drab and uninteresting as that of the Goethe period, accustomed as they were to feasting their eyes upon his superb manly figure."

The de Reszkes were an amazing family. Jean's brother Édouard was a famous basso, and their sister Joséphine had been a celebrated soprano before she married and wisely retired from the stage.

Melba first heard the two brothers at a gala performance of *Roméo et Juliette* in Paris in 1887. Patti was Juliette. Jean at once became "a god" to Melba. "He is so perfect, so gallant," she said. "Never has there been an artist like him." When she sang with him in a *Lohengrin* performance, she became so moved by his portrayal of the noble knight that she burst into tears during their duet in the third act. It was one of the few recorded instances of Melba's being carried away. Fortunately she didn't have to sing much afterwards; she might have choked. A real prima donna must be hardboiled to remain one.

Jean de Reszke became one of her most devoted friends, playing a special role in the Melba legend. He was an accomplished actor and a fine musician, but he disliked hard work. He was often scolded by that formidable music critic, "Corno di Bassetto" — George Bernard Shaw — for not tackling the great tenor parts in *Meistersinger* and *Tristan*. The gallant Pole hated the exertion. In 1888, when he and his brother were taking the waters in Bad Ems with the London critic Herman Klein, the brothers "listened with excitement" to Klein telling them the plot of *Meistersinger*, and later went to Bayreuth "to see this wonderful novelty." (The "novelty" was already twenty years old and a great success in several European capitals.) Eventually, the brothers studied their parts in *Meistersinger* and had a terrific success, but it took Jean another six years to sing *Tristan* in German.

Jean's only unfulfilled ambition was to sing Parsifal, but one of his dearest friends, the Princess of Wales, said, "I couldn't imagine why you should go to Bayreuth and give pleasure to the Kaiser, that horrible old man." Jean de Reszke was an artist *and* a gentleman. He did not sing Parsifal in Bayreuth.

It was Jean who taught Melba to move gracefully about the stage, to walk in a relaxed way, to make simple gestures, and to stand still — which, Richard Strauss once said, is the hardest thing to do on stage.

Melba loved to sing with Jean, they traveled together all over the world, and there was the inevitable talk of romance, arduously promoted by their managers. The public loves to think that the great tenor and the famous prima donna are in love. This gives a feeling of authenticity to their ardent love scenes on stage, when their voices merge orgiastically. The women shiver with delight as they "positively" detect a certain smile, a tender glance, which (they think) are secret communications between the "lovers." Some people swore that when Melba sang with Jean, there was "a trace of passion in her silvery tones."

Jean told Melba to leave the score alone and to respect the composer. He loved Melba's voice, "the glorious medium, the exquisite coloratura, the facile flow of the vibrant line." After her only appearance as Micaela in *Carmen*, at the Opéra Comique in Paris — in 1890, at a benefit performance to raise funds for a statue of Bizet — Jean wrote into Melba's autograph book:

*La nature vous a doué d'une voix d'or, positivement la
plus belle voix de notre temps. Vous êtes musicienne, vous
êtes femme charmante . . .*

So now the silvery voice had become a golden voice.
"Darling Jean" knew how to make a compliment.

Life was never dull for Melba when "darling Jean" was
there. In 1891 she went with him and Édouard to Russia,
by special invitation of Tsar Alexander III. At the Russian
border things were not much different from the way they
are now. Melba was horrified to see Russian soldiers search
her luggage, throwing on the snowy ground an "exquisite
cloak," a creation of Jean Worth in Paris, which she had
brought along for *Lohengrin.* She tried to explain, in a mixture of English, French and Italian, that the cloak was for
the opera and must not be spoiled, and that they had been
invited by special wish of the Tsar. The Russian soldiers
"merely gazed at her with silent indifference." A Russian
friend on the train saved the cloak and the situation.

Russian operagoers turned out to be ardent Melba fans.
Young men took off their coats and threw them on the snowy
ground so that the prima donna wouldn't walk in the snow
on her way to her carriage, which was "crammed with
orchids." Even "darling Jean" was impressed by this display
of adoration. After she signed an autograph, a passionate
admirer "took the pencil, bit it to pieces with his strong
white teeth and distributed them among his friends."

Something always happened when Jean was around. During a Chicago performance of *Roméo et Juliette,* with Melba
and de Reszke, a man in the audience suddenly clambered

over the footlights and ran toward Juliette. Everybody was paralyzed, but Roméo drew his stage sword and "waved it fiercely in the man's face," until stagehands rushed out from the wings and dragged him off to the nearest psychopathic ward.

When Jean de Reszke died in Paris in 1925, virtually forgotten, Melba was among "the very few" who followed him to his grave. The last two pages of her autobiography, *Melodies and Memories,* are devoted to Jean. He hadn't sung during the past twenty years. When he was on his deathbed in a coma, his breathing suddenly became clear and, to the astonishment of his doctors, he sat up in bed and said, *"Enfin! J'ai retrouvé ma voix."* And he began to sing.

> . . . For three days, in that house of death, Jean sang [Melba writes]. The whole house echoed with his golden notes, pouring out with all their former loveliness. He was dying every minute, and yet the song still poured on, role after role in which he had once been so superb.

Melba must have had some afterthoughts, for she says, "I suppose it was uncanny and incredible, yet to me it was only beautiful." She was blessed with the wonderful ability for self-deception of all great performers, who believe anything they really want to believe. "It is how I should like, when my time comes, to die myself," she wrote.

But it didn't happen quite that way.

⚡ 3 ⚡

"Comin' thro' the Rye"

BIOGRAPHER Colson, a self-admitted enthusiastic Edwardian snob ("write me down as a snob for I love all the fleeting joys life has to offer"), who sometimes treats his subject with irony rather than objectivity, at one point observes that "Melba had the indefinable manner of a woman who moves habitually in the great world, and yet one knew instantly that she was not of it."

Melba was too smart for such pretense. Even when she was the spoiled darling of "society" in London, Paris and New York, she had no illusions about it. Her friends knew that she was really happy only among her own people in Australia. When the great prima donna "who belonged to the world and to whom the world belonged" retired, she did not live in one of the world's great capitals, close to her former friends among the smart sets of the world's cosmopolitan capitals. She built her Australian home in the shade of the same tall gum trees where she had been happy as a child, and there she died.

But Melba was no fool. She had found out early in her

career that the opera houses of the world could not survive without people who have education, taste, *and* the money to pay for the most complex and most expensive dramatic entertainment.

Success never spoiled Nellie Melba. She had many faults, but snobbishness was not one of them. Even as the world's undisputed Queen of Song, she remained "the honest bourgeoise." She never quite lost her Australian accent nor her common sense. "If you wish to understand me at all," she writes in her autobiography, "you must understand first and foremost that I am an Australian."

Helen Porter Mitchell (who later became Nellie Melba) was born on May 19, 1859, in Doonside, Richmond, a dreary suburb of Melbourne (and not, as many dictionaries of music claim, in 1861 in Burnley). She was her parents' third child. Her father, David Mitchell, the son of a small farmer in Forfarshire, Scotland, had arrived earlier in Australia with the proverbial sovereign in his pocket. His widowed mother had given him a purse with two hundred sovereigns when he set out from Scotland, but his purse was stolen from him on the boat coming over and he kept only the one coin he'd happened to carry in his waistcoat pocket.

David Mitchell worked in the gold mines or "wherever he could find a job." He saved his money, and eventually made a lot of it. He had foresight and a sense of adventure, and he was thrifty. Melbourne was still a relatively small city; Queensland became a separate colony only in the year of Melba's birth. Mitchell figured that a growing city would need bricks, and he decided to make them. He wound up making them by the millions. It was said that half the important buildings in Melbourne were made of Mitchell's bricks. He never stopped working. When he was seventy he went into the wine-making business, and at eighty he began to manufacture a special "fireproof" cement. Apparently Nellie inherited his business acumen, intelligence and energy.

He must have been a remarkable man: dependable, kind, taciturn. "My father could say more with his eyes than most men with their lips," Melba said. When she came back to Australia in 1902, as the world's ruling prima donna, a characteristic dialogue took place between father and daughter.

"Have you saved any money?" he asked her.

"Yes . . . A little."

"How much?"

"Oh — perhaps twenty thousand pounds."

She was fibbing, and her father knew it. He winked at her, and she winked at him, and then he took her by the arm and said, "You're quite right, lassie. Never tell anybody what you've got, not even me." When he died he left over seventy thousand pounds.

Nellie's mother, born Isabella Ann Dow of Scottish and Spanish ancestry, was a gentle, sensitive woman who played the piano "uncommonly well" and dabbled a little in painting. David Mitchell played the violin "with some skill" and had a beautiful bass voice. Two of Mrs. Mitchell's sisters had good voices and sang well. Melba's musical development was probably a case of heredity *cum* environment; there was always the sound of music in her home. As a child of three, Nellie would crawl under the piano and remain there quietly for a long time while her mother was playing. Nellie loved to listen to her Aunt Lizzie, whose soprano voice "remained even in the highest pianissimo passages." Later on Melba was often asked exactly when she had started to sing. She would say that she could not remember any time when she had not been singing. As a child she would always hum, and her mother would often say, "For heaven's sake, child, stop that humming." Nellie didn't stop. Humming, she later said, turned out to be good vocal exercise.

The future prima donna gave her first concert at the tender age of six at the Richmond Public Hall, singing "with great delight" and with a fine Scottish accent "Comin' thro' the Rye" and "Shells of the Ocean" — songs her grandmother taught her. (During the following sixty years audiences all over the world never got tired of hearing her sing "Comin' thro' the Rye.") She was very small then, so she sang her program standing on a chair; amateur child psychologists will find traces of the future diva right there. The following morning when she asked a girl friend how she'd liked the concert she heard the most honest criticism of her entire career.

The little girl looked at her coldly and said, "Nellie Mitchell, *I saw your drawers.*"

By that time the family had moved from Melbourne to a small country township in the bush, forty-five miles away. You had to take the rickety, dirty stagecoach, with its four horses "that were flicking the flies with their tails." Nellie loved these rides; she would sit next to the driver, and she

loved the first glimpse of the blue mountains in the rear.
Sometimes there would be a dangerous black snake on the
ground, and the driver would stop to break its back with his
long whip, or he would run over it. Nellie was taught that
you must never let a snake escape.

They would arrive three hours later in the small town of
Lilydale, have lunch, and continue over cart tracks in the
family wagonette, sitting sideways on hard, narrow seats.
The houses in these outlying bush districts must have been
depressing structures — shacks with corrugated iron roofs,
surrounded by broken bottles and empty cans. The Mitchell
home, called "Steel's Flats," was much better, though it was
not exactly a palace. To Melba it remained the memory of
her happy childhood. Even when the celebrated, spoiled
prima donna was at home in royal castles and millionaires'
mansions, at the London Savoy or the Paris Ritz, where
Monsieur Ritz looked after her and Monsieur Escoffier
cooked for her, she was often homesick for Steel's Flats and
the things it meant to her.

Nellie was a tomboy who liked the boys; her preference
never changed. She was always involved in some mischief.
She loved to go out with her father, riding, fishing, tramping
through the woods. She was deeply devoted to her father all
her life; he was probably the only man she really loved. He
was very strict with her. When they rode out together and
her hat blew off, he wouldn't stop but rode on until Nellie
galloped up, out of breath. Once she mounted the front seat
of a horse-omnibus whose driver had left, and drove it down
the streets of Melbourne, while frightened pedestrians scur-
ried in all directions. And she never played with dolls.

Nellie's school days were Spartan; she hated school. At Leigh House, the school in Bridge Road, Richmond, a cold shower at six in the morning was compulsory. This didn't go well with "the sybarite strain" in the nature of the latter-day diva. She would take an umbrella to the bathroom and stay dry under the shower. Unfortunately the head mistress discovered that there was always chaos in the bathroom after Nellie Mitchell had used it. One day she found the dripping umbrella. From then on Nellie had to take her baths under supervision. At the Presbyterian Ladies' College in East Melbourne, "a scholastic establishment of the very highest standing," Nellie shocked her teachers by her accomplishments in the art of whistling and delighted her classmates by making "that funny noise in the throat." Her whistling may have helped her in the development of her uncanny breath control. And the "funny noise in the throat" eventually became the world-famous "Melba trill" — proof, if needed, that prima donnas are born, not made.

Nellie's fondness for practical jokes which later irritated so many people was already apparent. Once she dressed up as a Catholic nun and "with downcast eyes and a gentle voice" asked her father for a donation. She so impressed the worthy Presbyterian, who didn't recognize his own daughter, that he gave a sovereign for a Catholic cause.

The "strict Presbyterian Sundays of gloom and solemnity" didn't go well with Nellie. One particularly distressing Sunday, when an old parson "of great piety and excessive dullness" came to the house to conduct a service — which was customary in these remote bush settlements — Nellie was asked to play a hymn on the cracked harmonium. She pulled out all stops and played the "No. 1 Hit Parade" tune of the day, "You Should See Me Dance the Polka!" Consternation. Nellie was yanked from the stool by her horrified father and send to bed for the remainder of the day.

David Mitchell was a man of strict principles. He once promised Nellie a gold watch if she would learn to play twelve pieces by heart on the organ. Nellie earned the watch, but dropped it the first time she wore it. She found it a few days later in the street. It was ruined. "You will never get another watch from me," her father said, and he kept his word. Melba kept the pieces of the old watch until her death, in a special drawer reserved for "happy memories."

As a young girl, Nellie liked to give concerts "because I loved the applause." Her father, by now a prosperous manufacturer, had an organ built into a wall of the drawing room for the musical accompaniment of the Sunday services. Nellie decided to celebrate the event by giving a concert for her friends and relatives. She went around to invite them. Her father didn't like the idea. David Mitchell saw little difference between a professional singer and a practicing demimondaine. Getting up there and showing off didn't appeal to his strict Presbyterian principles. He sent word around to their friends and relatives that they'd better stay away from Nellie's "concert." In the end two people came. Nellie was sad but undaunted, and sang the whole program for her audience of two.

At the holiday resort of Sorrento, Victoria, she once gave a concert at the Mechanics Institute, donating the proceeds — twenty pounds — for a new fence around the local cemetery.

She posted the bills herself. As a prima donna she also often donated the proceeds of a concert to a worthy cause, but she no longer posted her own bills.

When Nellie was twenty-two she had the first really bad shock in her life. Her mother died after a long illness, and four months later her four-year-old sister Vere died. Nellie was so depressed that her father took her on a business trip to Queensland, hoping she would "recover her spirits." Nellie did — in a way which she, and her father, sorely regretted afterwards. She fell in love with Charles Nesbitt Frederick Armstrong, the handsome young son of the late Sir Andrew Armstrong, Baronet, of Gallen Priory, King's County, Ireland.

Melba's friends, loyal to the very end, are reticent about what one of her oldest intimates calls "Nellie's folly." They think it simply was all a matter of youth and circumstances. To the lonely young man, who lived in the bush near Port Mackay, where he was manager of a sugar plantation, the pretty, vivacious, cheerful girl with her reddish-brown eyes and sweet voice must have seemed an angel that had descended straight from heaven. There were not many angels in Port Mackay — or, for that matter, in Queensland. And to Nellie Mitchell, the dashing young man with his easy Irish charm was Old World glamour personified.She had never met anyone like him; Charles fascinated her. They became engaged.

For a short while they were very happy. So was Nellie's father. Now Nellie would get married, have children, and forget all that nonsense about having a career as a singer. Charles agreed: singing was strictly for the birds.

They were married "on a hot, dusty day" in December, 1882, in Brisbane. The short weeks of bliss were soon followed by long years of unhappiness. They were not suited to each other; they had nothing in common. Melba later described the cheerless setting of their married life in her autobiography:

> We had a little house with a galvanized iron roof, desolate and lonely, with no other company than that of the birds and especially of the reptiles. Soon after we arrived it began to rain. It rained for six weeks. My piano was mildewed; my clothes were damp; the furniture fell to pieces; spiders, ticks, and other obnoxious insects penetrated into the house. Snakes had a habit of appearing underneath one's bed at the most inopportune moments. It rained and rained, a perpetual tattoo on the roof, and as the days passed by, and the weeks, I felt I should go mad unless I escaped.

It reads almost like Maugham. Any moment, one feels, Miss Sadie Thompson of *Rain* will appear. Nellie's only recreation was to sit on the veranda and watch the tropical vegetation, burdened with water. She might try to bathe, but on her way to the river she would see green snakes hanging from the branches of the trees. In the water she would be tortured by bloodsucking leeches until she screamed with horror. And there were rumors of giant crocodiles only a hundred yards upstream. Bathing became an overrated amusement.

The monotony was terrible; the evenings, in the house, full of mildew and hatred. The only interlude was a boat trip in a small sailing boat, which capsized. Nellie almost drowned, but she later said she considered it a welcome break in her dull life.

She waited until her child, a boy named George, was born. Two months later she left her husband and the house in the bush, and returned to her father's home in Melbourne. She never went back to that house, or to her husband.

Nellie Armstrong now made up her mind to become a professional musician. For a while she was not sure whether to be a pianist or a singer. At parties she would often play the piano and afterwards sing a few songs, and usually she had more success as a pianist. If she had chosen the piano, she would probably have become a celebrated pianist. But, one story says, after a musical soirée at Government House in Melbourne the wife of the Governor said to her, "Child, you play well, but you sing better. Someday you will give up the piano for singing, and then you will become famous." This is the sort of anecdote one always hears about the struggling days of great singers. The fact is that Nellie became a singer because she was, as the saying goes, "born to sing." She couldn't escape from what she later called "a natural development."

She had studied with various teachers and now she began to work earnestly with Signor Pietro Cecchi, a retired Italian singer, who was willing to train her for the concert hall and to defer payment until she would earn good money. She couldn't afford another teacher. She had very little money, and her father refused to finance her singing education.

Nellie's first appearance as a professional took place on May 17, 1884, at the Melbourne Town Hall, at a benefit concert for Herr Elsasser (first name forgotten), who in his better days had been conductor of the Melbourne Liedertafel Concerts. When she woke up on the morning of the concert, she thought she had a sore throat. ("How many times since have I suffered from the same illusion," she later wrote. She would have been a bad singer if she hadn't so suffered.)

Afternoon came, and she was more and more nervous. At five she put on her "simple gown of golden satin" and unhappily sat with her Daddy, "wondering why I had ever undertaken this devastating task." (That, too, is not an uncommon thought.) At a quarter to eight she tremblingly stepped into the buggy, and they rode to Town Hall.

The concert, Melba recorded later, was "two hours of a wonderful triumph." Prima donnas are apt to overstate their successes, but in this case the local music critic of the *Australasian* concurred with her opinion, writing in the first newspaper review of the future diva:

> . . . Mrs. Armstrong sings like one picked out of ten thousand . . . The Elsasser concert hall will never be forgotten, on account of the delightful surprise afforded by Mrs. Armstrong's singing, and everybody who heard her will desire to hear her again, and everybody who didn't hear her is at this moment consumed with regrets at not having been present.

It was one of the most prophetic notices of Melba's entire career. She later admitted that the concert made her realize that "there must be something in my voice."

There certainly was.

Nellie Armstrong, it should be remembered, had never heard a famous singer; she had never been to an opera; but she was dimly aware that perhaps Melbourne was not the world's greatest musical city. She had common sense and a sound instinct.

"People," she told her father, "are the same everywhere." They had liked her in Melbourne, and they might like her elsewhere. She decided to work "harder than ever before" and try to go to England.

She signed a contract with a local impresario, George Musgrove, who gave her twenty pounds a week during the concert season. She would sing an average of four concerts a week, earning five pounds a concert, which she thought was terrific. Sixteen years later Melba gave a concert in Sydney for which she was paid twenty-three hundred and fifty pounds. It must have given particular satisfaction (and perhaps a sense of wonderment) to Mr. Musgrove, who was again her Australian impresario.

She would sing wherever she had a chance, but the Australian public wasn't exactly bowled over by her voice. Sometimes "the receipts did not cover the rent of the hall," a situation not unknown to many young artists. But the Australians atoned handsomely for their early lack of appreciation. After Melba became famous in Europe, every young artist in Australia who wanted to go to Europe to make a success there was given applause, good advice and money. "After all," people said, "she might become another Melba — you never know." Most of these artists, needless to say, were never heard of again.

For several months Nellie sang as soloist in the choir of St. Francis's Roman Catholic Church in Melbourne, which must have shocked her father a little. Nellie was fascinated by "the picturesque ritual" and "the romantic traditions" of the Roman Catholic Church.

"She was not much of a churchgoer but she was a deeply religious woman," says Hazelton-Cochrane. "The pageantry of the Roman Catholic Church appealed strongly to her sense of the dramatic. When she sang the prayers in *Faust*, *Otello* or *Tannhäuser* you sensed that she was not merely singing. She was really praying."

A few months later, early in 1886, David Mitchell was appointed Victorian Commissioner to the Indian and Colonial Exhibition, held in London that year. He invited his "lassie" to come along with her little boy.

"I believe that was the greatest thrill of my life," Melba said later, with customary addiction to superlatives.

A last-minute complication arose when Signor Cecchi, who had second thoughts about her ability to make good, suddenly asked for eighty guineas "for services rendered" before she left for England. Otherwise, he said, he would have to seize her trunks. Nellie was desperate. She didn't dare ask her father, who had already paid for her passage. He was a prosperous man now, but still very much opposed to her idea of becoming a singer. She managed to borrow the money from an uncle and a friend, she put it in a purse, went to Cecchi, threw it on a table, and told him what she thought of him. "I honestly believe," she later wrote, "that Signor Cecchi died of apoplexy talking of me and my ingratitude." She never mentioned his name to anyone, and she told her friends in Australia that she later had to unlearn everything Signor Cecchi taught her.

On March 11, 1886, Mrs. Nellie Armstrong sailed for Europe with her father and her little boy. Except for a small group of friends and relatives, no one paid any attention to her departure. There was no excitement at the pier.

It would be a different story one day sixteen years later when she stepped back again on Australian soil under a different name.

⚜ 4 ⚜

"Salvatore, I've Found a Star!"

THE DIRTY WHARVES and gray skies of Tilbury were not an inspiring first sight of England. Mrs. Armstrong's first thought was whether she would "ever be able to sing in such a gloom." But London was different when she arrived there — on May 1, 1886 — a great, noble city. Mrs. Nellie Armstrong of Melbourne, Australia, was fascinated by the people and the buildings, the carriages with their coachmen, the footmen in smart liveries and powdered hair, the shops in Bond Street and the luxury of Mayfair. And the lovely parks of London! Hyde Park was a fairyland, with a sea of yellow, golden, crimson tulips. David Mitchell had taken a small house in Sloan Street. When Nellie stepped over the threshold she sang "a trill of welcome."

She had brought along several letters of introduction and could hardly wait to present them. Within forty-eight hours she was on her way. She knew that everything, her whole future, depended on these letters. Her father had warned her that unless the reports were "exceptionally favorable" he would not allow her to become a singer. She had letters to

Sir Arthur Sullivan, to the celebrated singing teacher Alberto Randegger, and to other prominent musicians.

She was quickly disillusioned. Sullivan received her in his large flat in Victoria Street. He listened to the unknown singer from Australia politely, without obvious interest. Not bad, not bad at all. Naturally, she wasn't ready yet for the D'Oyly Carte's Royal English Opera at the Savoy Theater. But if she studied another year, there might be a chance of giving her a small part in *The Mikado*. And Sir Arthur stepped to the piano and played one of the ditties that were then the rage of London. Nellie almost wept with anger after she left him. And Alberto Randegger, very much in vogue as the fashionable singing teacher of peeresses, was too busy to bother with her: impossible, at this time, when the season was about to start; next year, maybe, he might squeeze in a few lessons. . . .

Years later, both Sullivan and Randegger became Melba's ardent admirers and friends. Melba got angry quickly, but she bore no grudge. Still, she rarely missed a chance to tease the two men for their lapse in vocal judgment.

She took her next letter to the piano maker Brinsmead, who listened to her with a rapt expression and declared, "The timbre of your voice is almost as pure as the timbre of my pianos." It was meant to be a compliment, but Mrs. Armstrong was not elated to be compared to a piece of musical furniture. At least Brinsmead had noticed that her voice did have timbre, which neither Sullivan nor Randegger had mentioned.

The following day she went to see William Ganz. He was a busy man, running a music school, arranging the music for

big dinner parties, and composing light music, which he con-
ducted himself. Nellie had often performed his song "Sing,
Sweet Bird" at concerts in Australia. She now sang it for him.
Before she had finished, Ganz jumped up from the piano.
"I am enchanted. You have a very beautiful voice. I will ar-
range for you a little concert."

Nellie went home "in the seventh heaven of delight." She
had visions of conquering London, of "waking up to find myself famous."

The concert took place at Prince's Hall. It was a foggy day
and the audience was tiny. The critic Herman Klein, a friend
of the de Reszkes, who happened to be there, remembered
her "sweet, pleasing voice, yet insufficiently trained. Her style
was up to the ordinary amateur level, no more." Sir Arthur
Sullivan had not been wrong: Nellie wasn't ready yet for
the stage.

This was the most disheartening experience of all, because
she had expected so much. She had another letter for Sir
Hubert Parry, an important man in musical circles, but he
was too busy to see her. And Carl Rosa, the brilliant manager
of the English Opera Company, whom she was to meet in
Mr. Ganz's house in Harley Street, forgot about the appointment and didn't show up. So that was that.

There was one more letter left. Mrs. Elise Wiedermann-
Pinschoff, wife of the Austro-Hungarian Consul in Melbourne, herself a singer and teacher, was recommending
Nellie to Madame Mathilde Marchesi, with whom Mrs.
Wiedermann-Pinschoff had studied in Vienna. Madame Marchesi, who was living in Paris, was the most famous singing
teacher in the world.

Nellie asked her father to give her one more chance. "Let me go to Paris. If Marchesi doesn't like me, I promise I'll come back with you to Australia and forget all about singing."

David Mitchell didn't very much like the idea of Nellie's going off to Paris, the City of Sin. But he knew what it meant to her and let her go. He even gave her some money. Not too much — but Nellie would soon be back in London, anyway, and then she would be cured of this silly ambition to sing.

Mrs. Armstrong packed a couple of suitcases, took her beloved four-year-old boy, George, and bought a second-class ticket to Paris.

She saw nothing of the boulevards of Paris, the shops in the Rue de la Paix, the beauty of the Champs-Élysées. The legendary magic of the City of Lights was totally lost on her when she arrived in Paris on a lovely day in the autumn of 1886. The only thing on her mind was to be accepted by Madame Marchesi and to study with her. Nothing else mattered. Two hours after Nellie had arrived in a cheap little hotel, she was on her way to Madame Marchesi's house in the Rue Jouffroy.

She rang the bell and handed the precious letter to a resplendent footman. She had to wait ten minutes and was informed that Madame would receive her the next morning at ten o'clock. Mrs. Armstrong went back to her hotel and spent one of the longest days of her life.

Madame Marchesi, a native of Frankfurt am Main, had been a pupil of the great Spaniard Manuel García, one of the most celebrated *bel canto* teachers of all times.

The Garcías were an astonishing family. The father,

Manuel del Pópolo Vicente García, later known as "García the elder," was one of the most successful operatic tenors of his time. At the world *première* of Rossini's *Il Barbiere di Siviglia* in 1816, he created the role of Count Almaviva. When he brought the very first Italian opera company to New York, where he opened the season in 1825 with *Il Barbiere*, he sang Almaviva, his seventeen-year-old daughter Maria Felicita (Malibran) was Rosina, his wife sang Berta, and his son Manuel was Figaro. They also performed Rossini's *Tancredi*, *Semiramide*, and *Otello*.

Their greatest admirer in New York was Lorenzo Da Ponte, librettist of Mozart's *Le Nozze di Figaro*, *Don Giovanni* and *Così Fan Tutte*, who was then seventy-six (having outlived the seven-year-younger Mozart by forty-seven years) and, after a stormy life, had become Professor of Italian Language and Literature at Columbia University. Da Ponte visited the elder García, speaking modestly of "my *Don Giovanni*," and García got so excited that he danced around with the old man and sang *"Finch' han dal vino,"* the "Champagne Aria."

García's children obviously inherited his astonishing gifts as an opera singer. Maria Malibran was the "angelic" prima donna of her era. One of the world's beautiful opera houses in Venice still bears her name. García's younger daughter Pauline, later known as Pauline Viardot-García, studied with the amazing papa and the amazing brother, became a great mezzo-soprano and a great prima donna, and immortal as the unforgettable passion of Ivan Turgenev. She was the first mezzo (some called her a contralto) to sing Gluck's *Orfeo*. Liszt was her piano teacher, and she was admired by Chopin,

Mendelssohn, Schumann, Meyerbeer, Gounod, Flaubert, Maupassant and Delacroix. At the time when Richard Wagner was trying to interest German opera singers in his new work, *Tristan and Isolde,* Pauline Viardot-García sang at sight the part of Isolde in the second-act love duet, with Wagner himself singing the part of Tristan.

So much for the sisters. Manuel García II was born on March 17, 1805, in Madrid. Haydn, Beethoven and Cherubini were still composing. He died on July 1, 1906, at the age of a hundred and one. He was already singing in New York when Beethoven and Schubert were still composing. In 1905, when García celebrated his hundredth birthday, Richard Strauss's *Salome* had its *première* in Dresden and created quite a furor. García grew up with the classicists, saw the romanticists come and go, and knew the modernists. Wagner, Verdi, Chopin, Brahms and Brückner died before him. He met Debussy, Ravel, Mahler, Strauss and Schönberg. He won fame as voice teacher, author of books on singing, and inventor of the laryngoscope. He was fourteen years old when Queen Victoria was born. He was still active as a voice teacher when she died at the age of eighty-three. When García was a boy, Jefferson was President of the United States. While he celebrated his hundredth birthday (driving to Buckingham Palace, receiving the insignia of a Commander of the Royal Victoria Order from King Edward VII, attending a reception at the Royal Medical and Surgical Society, and going to the Hotel Cecil for another splendid reception in his honor), Theodore Roosevelt mediated the Russo–Japanese War.

Melba met García one day in May, 1906, when he lived in Cricklewood near London. She had heard that he was very weak — this was two months before he died. Melba offered to come and sing to him, it might cheer him up. He was very pleased, and wrote her in his clear handwriting, "I look upon your offer to sing for me as a special favor." She went there and gave him one of the finest demonstrations of *bel canto* that he had ever heard.

From Manuel García Madame Marchesi inherited the great traditions of the *bel canto* style — the impeccable technique of "beautiful singing." Melba has called her "the greatest teacher of singing of them all, a marvel of scientific method. . . . There is no other method that can touch . . . [hers] for bringing out the full beauty of the human voice and preserving it for the largest possible period."

There exists a wonderful photograph of the teacher and the pupil: Madame Marchesi, a formidable woman in black, looking like a mixture of Queen Victoria and the Empress Maria Theresa, severe and autocratic; and Nellie, also in black, with her high waist, and a black mesh in her hair, demure and modest, the prototype of Manon or Marguérite.

Among Madame Marchesi's famous pupils were half a dozen who later became prima donnas, including the celebrated "three Emmas": Emma Calvé, a beautiful French woman with a seductive, luscious voice, who had so many registers that the experts spoke of her *quatrième voix,* and who was the most famous Carmen of her generation; Emma Nevada, the great coloratura soprano; and Emma Eames, an American born in China, who later became the ruling prima donna of the Metropolitan until she was dethroned by Melba.

All of them attained the technical perfection that became the trade-mark of the Marchesi school — certainty of breath control, smoothness of scale, finish of style, mastery of florid technique. Madame Marchesi, as every other teacher, received her share of ingratitude. Madame Eames later wrote in her autobiography, "As my voice was healthy, Madame Marchesi did it no harm, but neither did she give me that absolute vocal security which I was to gain for myself later." Such statements from aging prima donnas have a familiar ring. Madame Marchesi's successes far outnumbered her failures.

Exactly at ten o'clock the next morning, Nellie rang the bell of Madame Marchesi's house in the Rue Jouffroy again. This time she didn't have to wait. She met Madame Marchesi, "a mixture of alarm and attraction, standing very upright, dressed all in black, a small, gray-haired figure." Madame Marchesi questioned her "more in the manner of a businessman than of a musician"; told Nellie to get up on a small platform in front of a few other pupils, and asked her what she wished to sing. She seemed a little tired and bored, as if she wanted to get the whole business over.

Mrs. Armstrong said she would like to sing *"Sempre libera"* from *La Traviata*. Madame Marchesi nodded and sat down at the piano. The other pupils went on whispering. Certainly no one in the large room had any premonition of witnessing a historic event.

Madame Marchesi began to play the accompaniment. Mrs.

Armstrong began to sing, watching Madame Marchesi's profile out of the corner of her eyes.

The old lady listened attentively. Suddenly she stopped, turned around on her stool, and said, "Why do you screech the top notes? Can't you sing them piano?"

Nellie was mortified. This was the end. But she was no quitter. As Madame Marchesi now struck a note, Nellie said to herself "This is it" and sang, as softly as she could, the top B.

"Higher," said Madame Marchesi, and struck a high C. Nellie sang the C as softly as possible.

> When I glanced at her [Melba writes] I saw that a little sparkle had come into her eyes. I sang another note, I think it was the top E, still pianissimo, and suddenly, without a word, Madame darted up from her piano and rushed from the room. I was left standing, trembling, on the platform. I wondered whether it was all over.

It wasn't over. It had only begun. Madame Marchesi returned, took her by the arm, and led her into another room, while the other pupils were so surprised they stopped whispering.

It was a small room with a sofa in one corner. Madame Marchesi sat down next to Nellie and looked her straight in the face. In her autobiography Melba calls this moment "the turning point of my life."

"Mrs. Armstrong," said Madame Marchesi, "are you serious?"

There could be various meanings in this question, and Mrs. Armstrong was so dumbfounded that she just managed to give a nod.

"Because," continued Madame Marchesi, "if you are serious, and will study with me for a year, I shall make something *extra-ordinary* of you."

Melba never forgot the way Madame Marchesi pronounced the word — "extra-ordinary," with great emphasis, as if it were two words. Months later Madame Marchesi told her why she had suddenly run out of the room. She had dashed upstairs to see her husband, the Marquis Salvatore Castrone de la Rajata (known for his first Italian translation of *Lohengrin,* to which Richard Wagner strongly objected). The Marquis, a sedate character busy reading his newspaper, found himself being shaken by his wife's grip. Then she snatched the paper out of his hands and exclaimed, "Salvatore, Salvatore, at last I've found a star!"

Singing is a mysterious art. The best teachers know that there exist no fast rules for teaching. Each pupil presents a different problem. Madame Marchesi soon showed Nellie how bad her previous teachers had been.

"Before you start to learn anything," she said, "you will have to unlearn everything you know. You take your chest notes too high and as a result you force your voice."

Madame Marchesi quickly cured Nellie of her faults and began to train her in her own way. She would tell Nellie time and again, "Change to the middle notes on F. Begin the head notes on F sharp. Once on the head notes, always practice pianissimo." It sounds easy, but few, very few, singers are able to do it. Nellie learned it quickly. As a result, her scale, as Sir Thomas Beecham later said, "rippled from low C to top C with never a change of quality."

Madame Marchesi was a wise teacher. She didn't attempt to darken the silver-white timbre of Nellie's medium register but left it bright and glistening. She always told Nellie to cultivate her head tones but never to force them. Nellie spent at least eight hours every day studying music and singing, but she used her voice wisely and very little.

Madame Marchesi was very severe with her. Once Nellie burst into tears, ran out of the room, and decided to leave for good. Fortunately Madame Marchesi came after her.

"Nellie, you know I love you."

More tears.

"All right, Nellie, you've cried enough. Now you will come back and sing as I wish." Which was exactly what Nellie did. She later called Madame Marchesi "my artistic mother." The old lady taught her not only the secrets of *bel canto* but also the facts of life in Paris.

"I had no idea of the dangers and temptations which beset any young woman in Paris," Nellie later wrote her father. "Such things simply did not occur to me." Melbourne had never been like that. For a few months Nellie lived *la vie de Bohème* and enjoyed it. She had rented two poorly furnished rooms in Montmartre. There was an attractive Rodolfo in every café, and some of them looked much better than the average tenor. It was a great time for young musicians, young poets, young painters, young people generally who were in love with life. Manet, Renoir, Cézanne and Degas were around, and so were others who thought they were just as good. Montmartre was one giant *Bal Musette*.

Mrs. Armstrong had little money, but she didn't mind. So many pleasures of Montmartre were free in those days! She would often walk to save the bus fare, and Madame Marchesi said, "Walking is good for your voice." When she couldn't manage, she would borrow a pound or two from two sweet old Irish ladies in the building. She had only one warm winter dress, a monstrosity of thick, blue-and-white striped serge, which she wore day after day. The dress irritated Madame Marchesi, and one day she could stand it no longer.

"Mrs. Armstrong," she said suddenly during the lesson, "you are never to wear that dress again."

Mrs. Armstrong blushed. "I'm sorry. I have no other warm dress."

"Why?"

"I can't afford one."

"Nonsense. You have a rich father. Go buy yourself another dress and send him the bill."

There the matter rested and the lesson went on. When Mrs. Armstrong appeared in the same dress the next day, Madame Marchesi became very angry.

"I told you not to wear that dress any more!"

"But I can't afford another one. It's cruel of you to bring it up again!"

Madame Marchesi had a fit. She couldn't bear to see that dress any more; she wouldn't teach Mrs. Armstrong any longer; and besides, Mrs. Armstrong looked ridiculous.

Mrs. Armstrong burst into tears and ran out of the room. It was a critical moment in the career of the future prima donna. God knows what might have happened, or rather not happened, in the world's great opera houses during the following thirty-eight years if Madame Marchesi hadn't rushed after her.

"Nellie, Nellie, don't run away. I'm sorry. Go to Worth's now and buy yourself the most beautiful dress you can find. I'll pay for it."

It was then that Nellie showed she had the stuff of which an authentic prima donna is made.

"No, dear Madame," she said, with dignity. "Either you will put up with me in this dress, or I cannot come any more."

Madame Marchesi kissed her and both had a good cry.

"I wore that dress for weeks more, day in and day out, and never a word did she say, though I know it must have cost her agonies," Melba later said. Madame Marchesi had become very fond of Nellie. She called her *"l'élève de mes rêves."*

It was not easy to study with Madame Marchesi. Not only did you have to sing her way, but you had to live her way as well. She told Nellie she must give up riding horses, "because it's bad for your vocal cords." Nellie loved horses, but she gave up riding. When Madame Marchesi told her, "A singer never washes her head, she cleans it with tonic and with a fine-toothed comb; if she washes it she can catch cold," Nellie obediently stopped washing her hair and got herself a tonic and fine comb.

It was a hard life, but there were compensations. Once Nellie met Madame Carlotta Patti, the sister of the prima donna, and the idea of meeting someone connected with "the greatest woman in the world" so awed her that she bent down and kissed Carlotta's hand.

About this time she was taken for the first time to the opera. "It seemed to me incredible that so wonderful a place could exist, and when I heard . . . the first strains of the marvelous orchestra, I leaned back in my seat and thought if I could sing on that stage for once, I would die happy."

In Madame Marchesi's house Nellie met the gods of French music — Gounod, Ambroise Thomas, Delibes, Massenet, Lalo. Many famous authors, artists, ambassadors, politicians were regular guests at Madame Marchesi's. Young Mrs. Armstrong would often sing for this sophisticated audience. There was general agreement that the pretty soprano from Australia would have a great future.

Mrs. Armstrong was a very gifted pupil. Madame Marchesi had said she would need a year to make something "extra-ordinary" out of her, but after less than nine months she decided that Nellie was ready to be heard by *tout Paris*. Madame Marchesi was a generous woman who never did anything by halves. She decided to give Nellie a lavish debut. Something special was needed, a conversation piece on a large scale, so Madame had electric lights installed at considerable expense. It was a great success. She was one of the first hostesses in Paris to display the new extravagance. A stage was erected in the large dining room, where Mrs. Armstrong would sing extracts from Herman Bemberg's opera *Elaine*.

A minor problem remained. Madame Marchesi told Mrs. Armstrong she would have to take another name. "Nellie Armstrong" just wouldn't do for a diva. Impossible!

"But why?" Nellie Armstrong wanted to know. "Surely

I shall sing just the same, no matter what I am called."

Madame Marchesi shook her head. "I said, Impossible! It would be a handicap. You don't understand, but I do. Think of a better name."

"Suppose I were to use something in connection with my home town, Melbourne?"

"You can't call yourself Nellie Melbourne."

"No, that's true. Maybe — Melbourna?"

"Silly. That's even worse."

"Yes, that's no good either. Melbourne . . . Melbourna . . . Melba — Melba! How's that, Madame? Nellie Melba?"

Madame Marchesi thought it was a good name. Melba was born.

In her later years Melba often told young people who came to ask her advice that she didn't believe in luck. "I am inclined to distrust any young artist who attributes her lack of success to bad luck. If one is a good artist, one succeeds; and if one is a bad one, one fails. That is the rule I have found in ninety-nine out of a hundred cases."

Melba herself had her share of good luck, but she also had talent and the ability to use her talent in a moment of luck.

She was having her singing lesson one day, studying *"Caro nome"* from *Rigoletto* with Madame Marchesi in the music room. Upstairs, Madame's husband had a visitor, the famous impresario Maurice Strakosch, Patti's brother-in-law and manager, discoverer of several famous voices.

Suddenly Strakosch put his drink down and stared hard at the Marquis.

"Listen! That voice! I must have that voice! I must possess that voice! Tell me, who is she?"

The Marquis, who knew his friend, said the voice was not for sale — a young and inexperienced Australian soprano.

"I don't care," said Strakosch. "She may be young or old, beautiful or ugly. I want that voice." And he rushed down and burst into the music room, where he was pleased to see that the owner of the voice was neither old nor ugly. He was introduced. Melba sang two songs for him. He listened carefully, "his twinkling eyes lifted to the ceiling."

Five minutes later Melba had signed a ten-year contract with Strakosch, starting with "the enormous sum" of one thousand francs a month for the first year, two thousand for the second, and so on.

Melba felt she had arrived at last. The big party at Madame Marchesi's had been a *succès d'éstime;* the deal with Strakosch meant money, a commodity that always impressed her.

A few weeks later two directors of the Théâtre de la Monnaie in Brussels, Messieurs Dupont and Lapissida, heard Melba at Madame Marchesi's and wanted to engage her.

Madame Marchesi liked the idea very much. "Brussels will be a great chance for you, Nellie. I advise you to accept."

"But, Madame, I have a contract with Strakosch."

Madame Marchesi waved the question aside with her long white fingers. Never mind the contract. Strakosch was a great friend of hers. *"On va s'arranger."*

Messieurs Dupont and Lapissida offered Melba three thousand francs a month, and would provide all costumes.

Melba signed "with a hand that trembled with delight."

Madame Marchesi was right. Brussels was a good jumping-off place. Brussels audiences were kinder to foreign artists than were the people in Paris or Vienna. And François Auguste Gevaert, composer and director of the Brussels Conservatory, was a friend of Madame Marchesi and godfather of her daughter Blanche. He would look after Nellie.

Before Melba left Paris there was an unpleasant scene with Maurice Strakosch. He called her ungrateful and Madame Marchesi wicked, and left with dire threats. But Nellie was too happy and inexperienced to worry about legal complications and contracts. She would sing in opera at Brussels, and Madame was going to arrange everything.

The morning after her arrival in Brussels Nellie Armstrong went to the Théâtre de la Monnaie. All around the house she saw big posters, with MADAME MELBA in huge crimson letters, announcing her debute the next week as Gilda in *Rigoletto*. Melba was very excited.

"Why is my name so much bigger than the others?" she asked.

"Because you are the star," said Monsieur Lapissida.

"But I haven't proved myself yet."

He merely shook his head. "You will."

Melba's head was swimming with happiness. She was walking on a cloud. When she went out through the stage door, the concierge gave her a large blue envelope which had just arrived. It contained a court order. In view of her valid contract with Monsieur Strakosch, she would not be permitted to appear at the Théâtre de la Monnaie.

I was in the depths of despair. I went back to see Monsieur Lapissida. He threatened, he entreated, he sent telegrams right and left. He could do nothing. To use force would have caused an open scandal. Only seven days remained before the first night. Unless some miracle occurred, I should not be able to sing at all.

It must have been one of the worst weeks of her life. She was unable to go to the theater. She had drawn the blinds in her room and was lying on her bed. She hardly slept. When she thought of the big posters with her name in crimson letters, she started to weep.

Early in the morning of the Monday before the *première* there was a knock at the door. Melba jumped up. She had had another sleepless night and was exhausted. She walked out and leaned over the banister.

Lapissida stood downstairs, looking wildly excited.

"Yes — yes, what is it?"

He could hardly speak. "Strakosch is dead. He collapsed after a heart attack last night at the circus . . . And I expect you at the theater at eleven o'clock!"

Thursday, October 13, 1887, was a dark, rainy day in Brussels. From her windows in the Rue du Bac, Melba looked at the gray house walls and wet pavement of the drab street. She was lonely and depressed. The short elation that she'd experienced when she came to Brussels was gone, and now there were only doubts and fears. Tonight she would walk out on the stage of the Monnaie in the part of Gilda. She had no stage experience whatsoever. She had stood only once on a stage, at the Paris Opéra, during a short audition. She had sung a couple of arias on the dark stage, with a single gas jet flaring in her face. She hadn't sung well. It had been an unhappy experience.

She was briefly cheered by the arrival of Madame Marchesi, who had come especially from Paris with her husband. Salvatore looked dignified with a big flower in his buttonhole. Madame Marchesi kissed her and they left.

As the afternoon light faded, Melba felt lonelier than ever in her life. She wished her father were here. She thought of Australia, of the gum trees, of Steel's Flats. She dragged herself to the theater, sat down in her dressing room in front of the mirror. She had no experience in make-up. "I knew nothing about anything," she later told her father. She refused to wear the blond wig which the hairdresser wanted to put on. Monsieur Dupont was called. He let Melba display her own hair. It was much prettier, he said.

The endless first act, in which Gilda does not appear . . . Intermission . . . She stood in the wings, lost and miserable. The second act began and her cue came. She walked on stage and heard her voice floating out into the audience "as though it were the disembodied voice of someone else."

She didn't know how she got through "*Caro nome,*" the difficult aria which she had painstakingly studied with Madame Marchesi. Perhaps she sang it automatically. She never remembered what happened. There was applause after the aria, but she thought, "It cannot be for me. They are cheering for someone else."

After the third act she was summoned to the royal box. The Queen of the Belgians told her she had been wonderful. ("My first queen," Melba called her later.) She went back to her dressing room in a daze. Very slowly she began to realize that she was a success. At a supper party afterwards, Madame Marchesi filled her glass with champagne and told Nellie that she had missed two notes in the quartet in the fourth act.

"My face fell, for I was still the student. I had not yet learned to be the prima donna," Melba writes.

She was learning fast. When she woke up the next morning she found herself "famous all over Europe." The Brussels critics raved about her voice, praised her finished technique and exquisite trill, compared her to Patti. *Le Patriote* wrote, "Within two years Madame Melba will be known as La Melba."

Melba lived at the right time. Great composers were writing great operas for great prima donnas.

> I have been most fortunate, for in the operatic roles with which I am most closely identified, I had the invaluable assistance of the composers themselves — Gounod, Verdi, Delibes, Ambroise Thomas, Leoncavallo, Saint-Saëns, Massenet, Puccini.

Composers are hard-working, businesslike people. It takes more than a sudden flight of inspiration to get an operatic score done. They liked Melba because she too was hard-working and businesslike. Prima donnas often like to pretend that they, and they alone, know the authentic secrets of interpretation. Melba didn't have to pretend. She learned the secrets from the composers.

Gounod was the first composer with whom she studied. "To meet Gounod was an adventure," Melba has said. "To be taught by him and to arouse his interest, and I think I may say, his admiration, was a dream."

She went to see Gounod at his house in the Place Malesherbes. He was, in appearance, the perfect composer, with his velvet smoking jacket, flowing bow tie, velvet skullcap. When she entered his study he was writing a letter, and before he got up he took a stoppered bottle and sprinkled sand all over the wet ink. Melba had never seen anything like it. They didn't have such composers in Australia. She thought he was "the very best type of Bohemian," the type she approved of. She might not have approved of the genuine Bohemians, up in the Butte de Montmartre, but — good girl that she was — she never went to their cafés anyway.

She soon learned that there was nothing "Bohemian" about Gounod's methods of work. He was a stern self-disciplinarian, a strict perfectionist who left nothing to chance. While he studied an opera with Melba he would sing the various parts himself and accompany himself on the piano. He was a very gifted actor; he would be Mephisto one day and Juliette the next. He could easily switch from Juliette to Roméo, adapting himself completely in voice and temperament to a different character. He taught Melba to see an operatic character as a human being. Once, for instance, when he explained to her the difference between Juliette and Marguérite (in *Faust*), he said, "Marguérite is a simple peasant girl. But Juliette isn't simple at all. She is *une affrontée* — outraged, insulted."

"Don't forget, Nellie, that it was Juliette who proposed to Roméo, not he to her."

Ambroise Thomas was delighted to give her some pointers

when she studied the part of Ophélie in his opera *Hamlet*. They became friends, and he called Melba *"ma belle belle."* She sang the part in 1888 at the Théâtre de la Monnaie. Thomas was enchanted; he called her "the Ophélie of my dreams." The hard-boiled Paris public agreed with the composer a year later when Melba made her debut at the Paris Opéra in this part. "People would close their eyes happily and feel a thrill of elation when Melba sang the simple notes in her middle voice, *'Je suis Ophélie.'*"

She studied the part of Manon with Massenet, "a charming old man with a passion for flowers and a habit of coining some very pretty phrases."

Massenet, too, was a perfectionist. "He never let anything pass, however slight," Melba remembers. "If he didn't like my singing of a phrase he would go over it a hundred times."

Delibes, who studied *Lakmé* with her, liked her voice so much that he didn't even mind her pronunciation of French — which was then rather atrocious. She was taking French language lessons with the celebrated Mademoiselle Tordeus, and when Melba set her mind to achieve something, she worked hard at it. She studied French six hours a day, between her singing lessons, but never lost her Australian accent, and when she was scheduled to appear in *Lakmé* at the Théâtre de le Monnaie, the directors held a meeting to decide whether it was a good idea to let her sing the part in French. The decision was made by Delibes, who was present.

"Qu'elle chante 'Lakmé' en français, en italien, en allemand, en anglais, ou en chinois, cela m'est égal, mais qu'elle la chante," he said. Other composers have felt the same way

about Melba. They knew that as long as she sang everything would turn out all right.

Saint-Saëns traveled especially from Paris to Monte Carlo to study the title role of *Hélène* with Melba. He had written the opera for her, but it was no success; even Melba couldn't put it over. Saint-Saëns was "one of the most amazingly youthful old men." Melba loved to take long walks with him. Usually a taciturn man, Saint-Saëns would relax in her company, talking about opera, music, and life in general with great gusto. He was an eccentric, disliked parties and crowds, and was eager to play up his eccentricity. One night Melba came to his place to take him to a party. First he refused to go, then he went with her, but halfway there asked her to stop the car and return to his house because he had forgotten something.

He went in, and a minute later came back waving his toothbrush.

"What do you need the toothbrush for?" she asked him.

"I have no house key but I know from long experience that the toothbrush opens the door."

Saint-Saëns made a habit of dropping in unannounced. When Melba was upstairs he wouldn't bother to call her. He would come late in the afternoon when she was resting upstairs before dinner, but that didn't bother him. He would sit down at the piano and start to play in fortissimo. "I had never heard the piano played so loudly and beautifully before by anybody," Melba remembers.

She became very fond of Puccini, who appeared to her "an extremely simple man, a peasant of genius. He was shy and gentle, and rarely talked, except in short staccato sentences, sitting on the edge of a chair. Only at the piano, when he was playing melodies from his operas or just dreaming and improvising, he would get out of himself for a while. Sometimes he would sit down and improvise a whole scene from an unwritten opera, and when Melba asked him what it was, he would give a shrug and say, "Oh, it's nothing." Modern recording devices were not yet invented, which is a pity. Puccini ought to have installed a magnetophone, which is standard equipment in composers' studies today. There must have been more melody and beauty in Puccini's dreamy moments of inspiration than in all operatic music that has been written since his death.

One night in 1893, after Melba had appeared at Milan's La Scala in *Rigoletto*, she was informed that Maestro Verdi was waiting outside her dressing room. He didn't dare come in. Verdi was a humble genius. Melba ran to the door and opened it.

"Maestro, what an honor! And they didn't tell me you were here! Please do come in."

He bowed slowly, almost sternly.

"It was like a tree trying to bend," Melba remembers. "That was the impression he gave me, of some gnarled, wonderful, old tree."

She noticed there was "an impenetrable reserve" about him. But she also saw "his bright eyes, like a boy's, and his eager, restless hands."

For once, the prima donna was hesitant, almost timid. "Maestro, I have a favor to ask of you."

He looked at her sternly. She felt as if she were appealing to a judge.

"Yes?"

"I would like to sing for you my part in *Otello*."

He smiled, very slowly. There was great warmth in his eyes. She suddenly understood the universal human appeal of his music.

"That, Madame, is not a favor," he said. He suggested that she come out to his house in Sant' Agata the following day.

Melba never forgot that lesson — or the lovely country, the long cool room with the sun streaming through the windows. Verdi sat at the piano, playing and playing, until they had finished the whole opera. He insisted on going through even those scenes in which Desdemona doesn't appear.

"He was an inspiring master," she wrote. "He made me feel his phrases as he himself felt them, and he gave to each phrase an added loveliness." It is a perfect description; there is so much beauty in the part of Desdemona, so much love and happiness and sorrow.

All contemporary critics agree that Melba's Desdemona was one of her best parts. She always sang beautifully, but she brought an unusual understanding to the part of Desdemona. People were deeply moved when she said, "*Buona notta, Emilia*," shortly before her final, desperate outburst, before she dismissed Emilia.

"She would give you a stark sense of premonition of disaster," says Hazelton-Cochrane. "She made you feel that she knew she wouldn't live through the night."

Verdi was enchanted, and often nodded his head when

he liked a phrase that she did especially well. When they had finished the whole opera, he leaned back and looked up at her with a warm smile.

"Tell me, with whom have you studied this role?"

"With Tosti."

"Ah!" he nodded. *"Caro* Tosti" . . . I wondered. He is the only man who would have taught you to sing my opera like that." Thus the great genius of opera (who was working right then on *Falstaff,* that masterpiece of masterpieces) praised Francesco Paolo Tosti, long-forgotten composer.

Before Melba went back to Milan, Verdi gave her an autographed photograph. His last words were he hoped to hear her in *Otello* someday soon at La Scala. He took her to the door and said *"Arrivederci"* to her. Turning back, Melba saw once more "the wonderful, gnarled old tree" in the doorway. She waved and he waved back. She never saw him again.

⚶ 5 ⚶

Toujours l'Amour? Toujours l'Argent

ALL PRIMA DONNAS have a healthy predilection for money. The golden-voiced Angelica Catalani, an early nineteenth-century diva, received as much as two hundred guineas for singing "God Save the King," and in one year — 1807 — earned twenty-one thousand seven hundred pounds, or a hundred and eight thousand dollars. Prices were considerably lower than today. (No wonder her voice made them think of gold, twenty-four carat gold.)

We must try to understand the prima donna's materialistic outlook on life. Her artistic life is short, her security limited. A queen keeps her income for life provided she keeps her throne, but a "Queen of Song" loses much of her income when she loses some of her voice. Many divas stop singing in their forties and most in their fifties, and a few have even stopped in their thirties.

Today the prima donna lives under a constant nervous strain. She travels too fast, sings too much, diets too severely, rests too little, and burns out too fast — much faster than the giants of the past. Melba was sixty-seven when she gave her celebrated farewell performance at Covent Garden, when "she surprised and moved her audience with the purity, freshness and beauty of her voice."

The English writer Beverly Nichols, who saw a great deal of Melba during her last years, remembers an unforgettable spring morning in Venice, a few years before her farewell performance.

> The canals were veiled in a haze, and the city seemed poised like a silver bubble between this world and the next. Melba and I were sitting on the steps of an old *palazzo*. She saw a friend passing in a gondola, a pianist, and hailed him, suggesting that we all go to her salon. She wanted to sing.
>
> She sang as I had never heard her sing before. Every trace of age seemed to have left her voice. . . . She sang the Mad Scene from *Lucia*. She had not sung it for twenty years. It is the supreme test — exhausting even for the youngest coloratura. I know all its pitfalls, the devilish little breath-traps in which it abounds. Never, never have I heard it sung as Melba sang it then, at the age of sixty-one, in the middle of the morning, unrehearsed.
>
> One felt there must be some strange harmony between the morning and the song. The mists were lifting from the city, leaving it bright and sparkling; the mists were lifting from her voice, leaving it brilliant and golden. There was indeed a quality of light about her voice. She sang *"Voi che sapete"* from *Nozze di Figaro*. It was like a moonbeam stealing into a darkened room. We were all crying when she had finished. I would give a lot to cry like that again.

Melba's technique was so perfect that she spent only her vocal dividends and kept her capital. She had no illusions about the future when she could no longer sing: A few minor concerts at small fees, attended by faithful old listeners who came mainly to remember their own youth. . . . "Ah, but you should have heard her sixteen years ago!" A lonely life as a struggling singing teacher and a forgotten celebrity. No subsidiary income from record royalties, radio and television appearances. Nothing but the money and jewels she had saved, and her memories.

After Melba's successful debut in Brussels her fees went up with her fame. The Paris Opéra, whose directors had not been impressed by her audition the year before when she would have been glad to sing for a thousand francs a month, now offered her six thousand francs. After Melba became a success at Covent Garden she rarely got less than three hundred guineas (fifteen hundred dollars) for a performance, and as much as twenty-five hundred dollars for singing at a private party. Her concert fees were enormous. Sometimes she would make over ten thousand dollars from a single concert, more than Patti, whose American fees were between six and seven thousand dollars. In her best years, between her American debut in 1893 and the First World War, Melba earned close to a quarter of a million dollars a year, what with opera, concerts, recordings and private appearances in the houses of wealthy people.

When Melba was paid her first "princely" monthly salary of three thousand francs in Brussels, Monsieur Lapissida asked her jokingly whether she wouldn't say "thank you."

"I don't understand," she said, stuffing the money into her purse.

"I've given you more than you earned. You missed two of the stipulated ten performances a month, but we are paying for them too."

The Brussels management was generous to Melba. A few months later, when she was to leave for London to make her debut at Covent Garden, she told her dresser to pack the costumes which they had made for her at the Monnaie. The trunk was almost filled with her costumes for *Rigoletto, Lucia* and *La Traviata* when Melba looked up and saw Monsieur Lapissida's face. He seemed astonished.

"What are you doing?"

"I'm having my dresses packed."

"But they are not your dresses."

Melba was very indignant. By that time she had learned to be a prima donna. "But surely these dresses belong to me."

Monsieur Lapissida shook his head. "They were *made* for you, according to your contract, but remain the property of the theater." And he left.

Feeling "very sad at heart," Melba began to unpack again, when Monsieur Lapissida returned and told her to keep the dresses. He had spoken to the directors. They were making her a present.

On her last day in Brussels Monsieur Lapissida brought her a large leather box.

"A little gift that will be useful in London when you sing in *La Traviata*," he said. The box contained a beautiful set of paste jewelry — necklace, earrings and brooch. The directors had known that she worried about having to appear in London in the decorative part of Violetta with no other adornment than the thin gold necklace that she always wore around her neck in those early days. Twenty years later, when Melba came to New York to appear in *La Traviata* at the Manhattan Opera House, she had so many precious

jewels that Oscar Hammerstein, the producer, provided two
detectives to guard her diamonds.

Fame and wealth came quickly to Melba. She could afford
to buy beautiful things and she received precious presents.
She was given diamonds, pearls, necklaces, automobiles, and
once, in California, she even received free cable privileges
when she met John Mackay, cofounder, with James Gordon
Bennett, of the Commercial Cable Company. He sent her a
large box of orchids with a letter asking her to cable away
as much as she liked. Melba thought it was just another
proof of American generosity.

Later, during a party, a settee on which she was sitting
tipped slowly to one side, knocking down a bronze bust. It
grazed Melba's head and rendered her unconscious for
several minutes. News of the accident spread "like wildfire"
all over the world. She was front-page stuff by that time.
She was rumored to be seriously ill, dead, buried. Cables
began to arrive from anxious friends and managers. Melba,
by that time completely recovered, remembered Mackay's
generous offer and took advantage of it to answer the cables.

Melba's business acumen often startled her friends and
irritated her managers. Her millionaire friends were delighted with it. Alfred de Rothschild, whom she called "one
of the most generous men of our time," was so pleased with
her sagacity in financial matters that he would often give her
a little investment tip. But Melba wouldn't blindly follow
Rothschild's advice. She would investigate, and if she agreed
with Rothschild she would call her broker and invest.

She was very tough with rich hostesses who asked her to dinner hoping she might sing "a little song" afterwards. When a millionairess said to her that after all, it was no trouble to sing a little song, Melba answered that it was even less trouble to sign a little check. She loved the story of Pablo de Sarasate, the great Spanish violinist, who was once asked by his wealthy hostess whether he had brought his violin, and answered, *"Mais non, Madame, mon violon ne dine pas."* Another hostess suggested to Melba's devoted friend Paderewski that he "try out the new piano." Instead of saying that the piano didn't dine, Paderewski shook his head sadly and said, "Impossible, Madame, I've eaten so little."

In Paris an American hostess with social ambitions, Mrs. Pless Moore, invited Melba "to come to a *chic* little supper on Thursday and sing a little song afterwards." "Mrs. Moore," remembers Melba, "was in some ways the most American woman I ever met, and her Americanism was heightened by her determination on every possible occasion to speak French with an excess of gesture and a lack of pronunciation." If Melba were still around, she might find a few other Mrs. Moores today, in Paris and elsewhere.

Melba sat down and wrote a letter to her Mrs. Moore. She would be glad to come; her fee was five hundred guineas. Mrs. Moore wrote back she thought this to be the highest fee that any *cantatrice* had ever asked for. Melba informed her in a charming note that if Mrs. Moore could not afford Melba, she could give her the names of lots of *cantatrices* who would be only too delighted to sing for their supper and a thousand francs.

"Apparently she still wanted me," Melba records coolly. "At any rate, I went. I sang. I got my fee."

She was extremely generous to people she liked — but she hated to be taken advantage of by rich people. Which reminds us of the great Catarina Gabrielli, called "La Coghetta" (because her father had been a cook), who enraged Empress Catherine of Russia by asking three thousand ducats for one concert. When the Empress told the diva that none of her field marshals received as much money, "La Coghetta" suggested sweetly that Her Majesty let her field marshals sing for her. (A few years later Madame Callas was told by an outraged American manager, "Even the President of the United States doesn't make so much money!" — and is said to have answered, "Then let him sing." Certain anecdotes belong to the iron reserve of all prima donnas.)

Madame Melba was just as tough with her managers. In the fall of 1907, Luisa Tetrazzini made an unheralded appearance at Covent Garden. She had been hired while Melba and most members of the powerful "Melba clique" were away, and she made her debut as Violetta in *La Traviata*, a "Melba part." And — she was a sensational success. The critics praised her dazzling coloratura; she looked well; she acted convincingly. The Syndicate which then ran Covent Garden gave her a contract.

The Melba camp was stunned. But as the season wore on, it became apparent that Tetrazzini was no Melba. Some intangibles were missing. Her voice didn't have that "mysterious, thrilling" quality that makes some old people still talk about Melba with misty eyes, while Tetrazzini is widely forgotten.

The Syndicate came to Melba and asked her to sing for a few performances. She accepted. But since she hadn't been given a contract that year, she would have to charge them as much as she got for her private engagements — five hundred guineas a night instead of three hundred, as in her last contract. And they had to pay her five hundred guineas (twenty-five hundred dollars) and smile.

The only way to deal with a tough prima donna is to be even tougher. The genial Harry Higgins, a great friend of Madame Melba, who managed Covent Garden in the early years of our century, once negotiated with a diva better known for her luscious figure than for her thin voice. When she asked a preposterous fee Higgins said, "But dear lady, we are asking you only to sing!"

Hard-pressed managers sometimes try to reduce the overhead of grand opera. They always fail; good opera is very expensive. When Alfred Bunn was joint manager of London's Covent Garden and Drury Lane in the early nineteenth century, he often used his artists for both theaters on the same night. Once the audience at Drury Lane had to be told that John Templeton, the Scottish tenor, was at the moment completing his performance with Madame Malibran over at Covent Garden. "If the audience would kindly permit the orchestra to repeat the overture, no doubt shortly Mr. Templeton will be in attendance."

The audience applauded and the overture was repeated. At last Templeton arrived, bathed in perspiration. He refused to go on until he could get his whiskers and mustache to stick to his face (for which he can hardly be blamed). In the middle of his first aria, however, the mustache worked

itself into his mouth. When he flung it away in a fury, it
clung "like an octopus" to the strings of the first violinist,
"an effect which caused the house to rise in a body and
cheer."

Such desperate efforts of opera managers to balance their
precarious budgets are not restricted to the early age of
grand opera. Hard-pressed managers have tried throughout
the centuries to cut down on expenses and make opera pay;
alas, they have never been successful at it. In his memoirs,
Theme and Variations, Bruno Walter recalls his early days
as *Kapellmeister* in Berlin, when the General Management
of the state opera, Unter den Linden, supplied casts for the
regular evenings at the state opera as well as for light-genre
works at the Kroll Theater (which, incidentally, later became
the temporary home of the German Reichstag after Göring
and his friends put fire to the old Reichstag building).
Bruno Walter particularly remembers a performance of
Rheingold at the Linden Opera in 1901 when he had to stop
after the first measures of the Nibelheim scene, for there
was no sign of either Alberich or Mime.

> A few minutes passed before I was able to start again,
> this time *prestissimo,* for the two dwarfs, confused and out of
> breath, sang their first measures at a precipitate tempo.
> Lieban-Mime had been singing the part of Alfred in the
> first act of *Fledermaus* at Kroll's. The act over, he had been
> driven to the Linden Opera and had hurriedly put on his
> make-up and costume for *Rheingold,* intending to return to
> the Kroll Theater for the final act of *Fledermaus.*

The Edwardian prima donna had an enormous income
and paid almost no taxes, but her expenses too were very

large. When Melba attained world fame and became a popular idol, she had to live on the grand scale expected of her. She would rent large houses in London and Paris, usually with large staffs. Once she cabled from New York to London "for her servants, linen and silver," and set up house there. She had followed Madame Marchesi's advice on sartorial matters and ordered expensive clothes from Worth and later from Reville-Terry. She had new automobiles, gave lavish parties, employed a retinue of personal maids, cooks, secretaries, business managers (but had neither a press agent nor a psychiatrist). She was always besieged by hangers-on, and her name was high up on professional mendicant lists, according to police reports. She was internationally known as a "soft touch." Still, she had no illusions about the evanescence of fame and fortune. *"On les adore quand elles sont belles et on les jette à la voirie quand elles sont mortes,"* Voltaire had said.

Melba would have agreed if she had ever read Voltaire.

Melba earned millions, but she was not an avaricious woman. Unlike other prima donnas, she never wanted "a little more than anybody else." To many a prima donna this tiny difference means more than the entire amount she is getting. (Not long ago a celebrated diva was dropped by the Vienna Staatsoper because she insisted on getting "a little more than any other leading soprano.")

The demands of famous singers are sometimes perplexing. Mademoiselle Regina Pinkert, a Polish soprano who sang with Melba at Oscar Hammerstein's Manhattan Opera House in New York, once refused to accept her salary in dollars and instead asked for gold francs, though no one was afraid of the imminent devaluation of the dollar.

Perhaps the most avaricious of the great prima donnas was Adelina Patti. The flamboyant English nineteenth-century impresario, Colonel James Henry Mapleson, in his *Memoirs* recalls an unforgettable performance of *La Traviata* in Boston's Globe Theater with Patti as Violetta.

Adelina's development from an American child of nature, "half timid and half wild," to a French "*grande dame*," as the famous Viennese critic Eduard Hanslick once described her, would have inspired the satirical genius of Jacques Offenbach if he had lived a little longer. She was now the uncontested Victorian diva, just as Melba later was *the* great Edwardian prima donna.

All the critics didn't agree about Patti; they rarely agree about anything. Hanslick, a virtuoso of sarcastic invective, called her "a musical genius, a beautiful natural phenomenon — perfect, artless, inexplicable." "Madame Patti's offenses against artistic propriety are mighty ones and millions," wrote another master of the verbal stiletto, the erstwhile London music critic George Bernard Shaw. But there was no disagreement among the critics about Madame Patti's propensity for large sums of money, for which she was notorious. She spent the money, too. In St. Petersburg she stayed at the largest hotel, in a suite of twelve rooms with precious furniture, exotic plants and "gilded cages in which nightingales sang for their great rival."

When the prima donna appeared on the stage after the performance, flanked by the Tsar and the Tsarina, a rain of flowers came down on them, which cost the aristocratic

Jockey Club over six thousand rubles. After Patti's benefit performance six generals waited for her in the lobby of her hotel, placed her in a "flower chair," and carried her to her suite while an orchestra was playing.

At least once, Patti was defeated by her greedy nature. After a *soirée* in the house of a Parisian nobleman, the host sent Madame Patti a magnificent diamond ring in lieu of the customary check. The prima donna sent back word that her host may have forgotten to add her salary. The following morning her host sent her a much smaller ring and his apologies. He had indeed made a mistake, he wrote. The small ring was Madame Patti's salary. Would she kindly return to him the large stone, since it was for another diva? Madame Patti had hysterics. She was licked.

At two o'clock, on the afternoon preceding the memorable *La Traviata* performance in Boston, Signor Franchi, Patti's agent, came to collect from Mapleson the five thousand dollars contracted for her services. (Those were the days, ladies! Today's top fee at the Met is a paltry fifteen hundred — inflated — dollars. Even the great Callas never got more than three thousand dollars.)

Mapleson had to admit that he was one thousand dollars short. The agent talked it over with Madame Patti and informed Mapleson that he was a fortunate man. Madame Patti did not wish to break the engagement with him, as she certainly would have done with anyone else under the circumstances. She would take the four thousand dollars and get ready for the performance. She would be at the theater in time for the beginning, dressed in the costume of

Violetta, with the exception only of her shoes. She would put them on just as soon as she received the balance of her payment.

After the opening of the doors Mapleson received another eight hundred dollars, which he gave to Signor Franchi. The agent came back, beaming: Madame Patti already had one shoe on. "Ultimately," Mapleson remembers, "the other shoe was got on, but not, of course, until the last forty pounds [two hundred dollars] had been paid. Then Madame Patti, her face radiant with benignant smiles, went onto the stage; and the opera, already begun, was continued brilliantly until the end."

The fees of prima donnas are often exaggerated by themselves, their managers and the press. Reports of record fees are no more trustworthy than the claims of Hollywood agents. But doubtless the great singers of the past earned more money than the stars of today. Jenny Lind received forty-eight hundred dollars for the season from April 14 to August 20, 1847, "also a furnished house, a carriage and a pair of horses." Opera managers no longer make similar contracts.

Hector Berlioz once calculated that a tenor who appeared seven times a month and made about a hundred thousand gold francs a year was being paid at the rate of one franc per syllable. For instance, in *Guglielmo Tell* a short sentence — "My [one franc] presence [two more] may well seem to you an outrage [eight more]" — would cost the management eleven gold francs. Francesco Tamagno, the robust Italian tenor who was Verdi's first Otello and often sang with Melba, always traveled with a suite of eight relatives, friends and retainers, and by contract was entitled to eight free tickets for every performance. Tamagno was one of the loudest tenors of all times — it was said that his powerful high C's made the chandeliers in Covent Garden rattle — and also one of the highest paid yet stingiest. (Prima donnas are not the only people who care about money.) Before Tamagno sailed for Buenos Aires in 1890, where he would earn a hundred and thirty thousand dollars for forty performances, he insisted on being paid a cash advance of thirty-one thousand dollars in Italy. He got the money. Then a revolution broke out in Buenos Aires. Tamagno refused to go to the Argentine, but he also refused to return the thirty-one thousand dollars.

Tamagno once told Melba that the bills at the Hotel Continental in Paris were too high, and that he sent his shirts to be laundered in Italy. She thought he was joking, but she knew better one day at a dinner in New York when Tamagno amassed salted almonds, chocolates and orchids from the table, explaining to the wife of the Italian ambassador that his daughter was ill at the hotel and he wanted to bring her a little present.

A few days later Melba and Tamagno were invited by Maestro Luigi Mancinelli to lunch at an Italian restaurant in New York. After the main dish, Tamagno called the waiter and asked for a newspaper, in which he carefully wrapped the veal cutlets *alla Milanese* that remained on the plate, telling Melba, "My little dog, he love *costeletta.*"

The following day Mancinelli happened to visit Tamagno at his hotel. It was noon. Tamagno and his daughter were eating lunch in their room.

"You guessed it, didn't you?" Mancinelli told Melba that night. "They were having *costeletta alla Milanese.*"

Melba's friends remember her as always generous. She may have shown Scottish blood in business dealings and she knew the value of money, but she remained openhanded and kind to the people she liked.

"She helped people all her life," wrote the ever-critical Colson. "She helped young people, friends, hospitals, Australian institutions, and frequently gave her services in aid of charities and to help other singers. She could never do enough for those she really liked." There were rumors that "Melba is so mean she sells her autographs." She did, but sent the proceeds with an extra check to local charities. In New York she charged a dollar for her autograph and regularly sent the money to the Blind Babies' Home on Long Island.

Once when she was driving in her new, very expensive car with her lifelong friend, flute accompanist and manager, John Lemmone (who must have played the flute accompaniment hundreds of times while Melba sang "Lo! Hear the Gentle Lark!"), Lemmone said, somewhat wistfully and perhaps without really meaning it, that he wished someday to own such a car. Melba said nothing. When they arrived at her house, she got out and said, "You'd better drive the car back to the garage, John. It's yours." In Australia she heard of an elderly ex-prima donna who had made a tour which was such a failure that the singer had to pawn her jewels to be able to return to England. Melba quietly redeemed the jewels and sent them back to her erstwhile colleague.

Melba's friend Stella Murray remembers a beautiful diamond-studded gold bag which Melba gave to one of her sisters. The sister lost the bag and all efforts to find it were in vain. She was heartbroken. Melba quietly ordered an exact replica at Tiffany's and pretended it was the original bag brought back by an honest finder. "Melba's sister discovered the truth only years afterwards," says Miss Murray.

Among Nellie's Australian protégés was a gifted young painter, whom Melba promised to send to Paris at her own expense with a yearly stipend. The painter, a lonely sensitive boy, had one friend, who died just as the artist was about to sail for Paris. The heartbroken young man started to drink and blamed Melba as responsible for his friend's death. During a long-lost week end he met Melba in the street and screamed at her. She went home and wept.

"The young fool!" she said. "He's so gifted, and destroying himself."

At last the young genius sobered up and was very ashamed of himself. He asked a friend to intervene with Melba. Would Madame Melba — well, would she still pay for his trip to Paris and the promised stipend?

Melba looked astonished. "Of course the arrangement still stands. Send him here. I'm glad he's well again."

Like royalty and billionaires, Melba never bothered to carry money around and often had to borrow half a crown from whoever happened to be around, but she would quickly return the money. One night in Monte Carlo — she loved to

play roulette and she loved to win — she lost everything she
had with her. Looking around for financial assistance, she
saw Baron Hirsch, one of the richest men in England and a
friend of the Prince of Wales. She asked him to lend her
a thousand francs. Instead of diving into his pockets, "as
most of one's friends would have done, he frowned, hesi-
tated, and only after a considerable display of reluctance"
produced a thousand francs, which he handed to her.

Melba was surprised; she knew that Baron Hirsch was a
generous man. The next morning she sent him a check for a
thousand francs with a thank-you note, and forgot all about
it. Two days later a small package arrived from Baron
Hirsch. It contained a lovely diamond brooch and a letter:

DEAR MADAME MELBA,
You are the first woman who has ever paid me back
money which she has borrowed. I am so touched that I have
taken the liberty of buying you the enclosed little brooch,
which I hope you will accept as a token of my admiration.

Melba never again borrowed money in Monte Carlo,
where there is a strong superstitution about it. "It was not
superstition, it was sound common sense," she said.

She loved antique hunting as much as playing roulette,
and was always looking for another Sheraton or Chippendale
in London, or for a Louis XIV bargain in Paris. Hazelton-
Cochrane remembers an afternoon in London when they
walked into an antique shop, where Melba picked up a
lovely piece of Dresden. She agreed on the price and wanted
to give the shopkeeper a check. He shook his head.

"I never take a check from people I don't know."

Melba stood up straight, the great prima donna.

"I am Melba," she said.

"I don't care who you are, Madame. I don't know you and I won't take a check."

Melba was speechless for a moment.

"I thought she would smash the piece of Dresden against the shopkeeper's head," remembers Hazelton-Cochrane. "Fortunately, she was not the smashing type. She counted to ten, quietly put it down, and walked out. She was so angry she couldn't talk for a few minutes.

" 'I didn't go through life giving bad checks,' she said to me bitterly.

" 'No, Nellie. You went through life giving beautiful notes,' I said.

"My answer cheered her up. She laughed and regained her good humor. 'Thanks, Tommy,' she said. 'Come on, let's have tea at the Ritz.' "

And again I saw that magic mist in Tom Hazelton-Cochrane's eyes that all old friends of Melba have when they remember her.

✻ 6 ✻

"You Are Too Innocent, Chérie"

MELBA CALLS the Royal Opera House at Covent Garden "my home," "my beloved Covent Garden." During her reign, which lasted thirty-seven years, she "all but owned Covent Garden," as Colson points out. But it was not love at first sight.

She came back to London in May, 1888, after her triumphs at the Théâtre de la Monnaie in Brussels. She felt lost and let down. Her father had gone back to Australia. She had no friends in London. She was alone with her little son. Most of her "princely" Brussels salary was gone. She took a modest flat in Bayswater, not a cheerful neighborhood even on a lovely morning in May. And her first inside glimpse of the Royal Opera House was a shock.

"As I stepped over the cabbage tops, the fruit skins and the straw, and paused in front of the stage door, I said, 'Surely this is not Covent Garden?'"

They had to persuade her that it really was the Royal Opera House. When Melba went in and asked for Mr. Augustus Harris, the manager, she felt that by some mischance she was standing "in a great fruit store." Many other people have had a similar shock after *their* first glimpse of Covent Garden. It takes time to get used to London's great opera house and to its people, but when you do you discover that London is full of wonderful people and wonderful things, including Covent Garden.

A great deal was going on, on May 24, 1888, the day of Melba's London debut. Queen Victoria had left London and had proceeded to Balmoral. Mr. Gladstone was said to be greatly cheered by the Liberals' victory in Southampton. At Henry Irving's Lyceum, Ellen Terry was to be seen in *The Amber Heart.* Beerbohm Tree was playing at the Haymarket in *Pompadour,* and William Terriss presented *The Bells of Haslmere* at the Adelphi. The St. James's featured Mr. and Mrs. Kendal in *The Ironmaster.* The Savoy had a revival hit, *The Pirates of Penzance.* J. L. Toole was presenting, at his own theater, *The Red Flag.* Edward Terry appeared in *Red Lavender,* and Marie Tempest in *Dorothy,* at the Prince of Wales Theater.

"Niagara" — "the largest picture in the world, with original and realistic effects, and lighted by electric light" — packed four thousand visitors a day. At Earl's Court there was an Italian exhibition. Pablo de Sarasate, the great Spanish violinist, was giving the first of a series of four concerts at St. James's Hall, and Christine Nilsson, the famous soprano, would soon appear there. Sir Charles Hallé announced several chamber music concerts. The front page of the *Daily Telegraph* listed some minor concerts, and several singers announced evenings of popular ballads. Millais was the star exhibitor at the Royal Academy, where John Seymour Lucas and Dudley Hardy were also exhibiting. Sir Arthur Sullivan was writing yet another opera, *The Gondoliers*. Swinburne and Tennyson were still living, and Oscar Wilde, Whistler, Pater, Burne-Jones, Rossetti and Leighton were around. A "commodious sitting room and bedroom, with lights and full attendance" on Bury Street, St. James's, was offered for two guineas a week. Ordinary coal cost from thirteen to seventeen shillings a ton, and the best "Derby Brights" twenty-three shillings. Scotch whisky "of guaranteed age and excellence" was four shillings a bottle — one dollar at that time. Victorian England was not without its merits.

It was Augustus Harris's first season at Covent Garden. Harris's father had been a stage manager at Covent Garden during the regime of Frederick Gye, and his mother had run a theatrical costumer business in Wellington Street. As a boy, Harris had spent his nights backstage at the theater, "while the great prima donnas came and petted and kissed me."

Augustus Harris remained fond of prima donnas ever since, though they no longer kissed him. Some, in point of fact, cursed him. He was only thirty-six when he took over Covent Garden, a genuine opera lover with musical taste, an artistic conscience, and a sound business sense. He knew that without any national or municipal subsidies (which he had no hope of getting) his only chance of producing opera at Covent Garden on a grand scale was to enlist the support of "society" and "the real aristocracy." In this effort he was astonishingly successful.

In his initial announcement Harris said that "at the request of an influential committee" he had taken Covent Garden for the production of Italian opera. "The artists and operas have been selected in accordance with the suggestions of the committee . . ." Lord Charles Beresford was chairman, and Earl de Grey, the Honorable Oliver Montagu, Henry Oppenheim, and A. de Murietta were among its members — "all men of influence and ability, and staunch supporters of the opera. By their hard work, and the efforts of their wives, all the boxes on the pit and grand tiers and a large proportion of the stalls were subscribed for before the issue of the prospectus," writes Harold Rosenthal in *Two Centuries of Opera in Covent Garden.*

Augustus Harris gave London some of its finest opera seasons. He was knighted in 1891 — not for his services to music and opera, but because he happened to be Sheriff of the City of London during the visit of Kaiser Wilhelm II. Such are the rewards of the artistic life.

Much of his success Harris owed to the two leading London hostesses, Lady de Grey and Lady Charles Beresford. Their fondness for opera and for some of its great singers (particularly for "darling Jean" de Reszke), and their friendship with the Prince and the Princess of Wales, gave Harris a certain financial security. He had the patience, the tact and the firmness to handle temperamental tenors and prima donnas, and he knew what the public liked. In his first season he gave the people Verdi, Mozart, Donizetti, Meyerbeer, Rossini, Bizet, Gounod, Boito, Auber and Wagner. The company had distinguished stars — Mesdames Trebelli, Nordica and Albani, the brothers de Reszke, Luigi Ravelli, Jean Lasalle.

To stand up against such competition, Nellie Melba would have to be very, very good.

She had been recommended to Augustus Harris by Madame Marchesi. He had gone to Brussels to hear her, was very impressed, and offered her a contract for Covent Garden. She had hoped to make her debut as Gilda in *Rigoletto,* as in Brussels, but Harris informed her regretfully, that Madame Albani had "exclusive rights" to the part of Gilda. Melba would appear in the title role of *Lucia di Lammermoor.*

Everything went wrong. The orchestra was "half-asleep," and the audience, which filled only half the house, was bored to tears. "It certainly was not a Melba night," the diva later remembered. "There was a general air of apathy over the stalls and boxes. It is true that those who were there were wildly enthusiastic, but there were so few they hardly seemed to count."

The "wild" enthusiasm was perhaps more the young diva's fancy than plain fact; there is no evidence of it in the newspaper reports. It was one of those dull, mediocre nights that are routine (and the curse) in every opera house on earth. So many divergent experts and artists — poets, dramatists, composers, conductors, coaches, singers, musicians, dancers, painters, designers, technicians, producers and extras — are involved in an operatic production that its standards are often precarious. Rarely are all the elements of opera production — the words and sounds and lights and voices — fused into an exciting work of art. Gustav Mahler said, during the years when he presided over the "golden age" of the Vienna Court Opera, that one fine evening a week was a pretty good average.

Melba had had only one hasty, slovenly orchestra rehearsal. Unknown singers are rarely given extensive (and expensive) rehearsal time. Melba had never seen a performance of *Lucia* in London. A short announcement in the papers said that Madame Melba, an Australian singer who had had some success in Brussels, would make her debut in *Lucia*. Most of the first-string critics had more important things to do that night than attend the debut of a young Australian who had only sung a few times on the Continent.

There was applause after the Mad Scene, which cheered up Melba for a while, but when she read the papers the following morning she broke down and cried. She was always easily discouraged. The critics completely ignored her singing and praised her acting, in expressions which, Melba later admitted, "were too generous. . . . In those days I couldn't act." Even in later days some of her best friends didn't claim that she was a great actress. "Her acting never got much beyond the rudimentary stage," writes her friend Colson. "To express a mild emotion, such as Juliette's love for Roméo, she would raise one arm. To express extreme passion or violent despair, she would raise two."

Yet somehow all the London critics were unanimous in their praise of Melba's acting ability. The *Pall Mall Gazette* called her acting "accomplished," the *Observer* praised "her genuine dramatic instinct," the *Standard* "her capacity as an actress," the *Daily Telegraph* "her dramatic ability in the

Mad Scene." *The Times* wrote that "Madame Melba availed herself of the dramatic opportunities"; *Vanity Fair* stated that she displayed "emotional power as an actress," the *Morning Advertiser* called her "intelligent dramatically," the *Lady Pictorial* praised her "strong dramatic instinct," the *Musical Standard* her "dramatic power." It might have been quite encouraging had she been an actress, but she happened to be a singer; and no one was in the least impressed by her vocal achievements.

It was a dark hour for Melba, and it wasn't much brighter a few days later when she sang the part of Gilda in *Rigoletto*. Madame Albani had graciously permitted Melba to sing the part (she must have been convinced the "young Australian" was no competition for her; by the time she knew better it was too late). Again the house was half empty, and a thick cloud of apathy hovered over the auditorium. The performance, Melba said later, was of a much lower standard than the one in Brussels. Everybody was half-asleep or wishing he were elsewhere. Mr. Harris was sympathetic. "If any foreign singer appeared and sang half as well as Melba, the English connoisseurs would show unrestrained enthusiasm," he said to a friend. "In a little while they will clamor for Melba, and, by gad, they will have to pay for her."

Mademoiselle Bauermeister, "first among the secondary singers" at Covent Garden, told Harris, "Melba has gold in her voice and one day will put gold in your pockets."

Augustus Harris gave a deep sigh. At the moment he could offer Melba nothing better than the small part of Oscar, the page in *Ballo in Maschera*. Melba's answer was to pack her trunks and go back to Brussels.

They loved her in Brussels. At the end of her second season there the subscribers presented Melba with a beautiful diamond "as souvenir of their affection and admiration." In two seasons she had progressed from a paste necklace to a genuine diamond. At her farewell performance she received over sixty bouquets from delirious, heartbroken admirers. The King of the Belgians awarded her the gold medal of the Brussels Conservatory. It was Melba's first decoration. At the end of her career she had more medals than the average four-star general.

It all sounds wonderful, but life in the tight little world of opera was not always unmitigated bliss in those days for an English-speaking singer. The great American voices had not yet been discovered. Italian and German artists dominated the field, and foreigners would often italianize their names. Opera was rarely performed in English. Melba would always sing either in Italian or in French (though, whatever she sang, she never quite lost her Australian accent). In an Italian company she would be surrounded by Italians, in a French company by French singers. On the rare occasions when she ventured into Wagnerian territory — which really remained no man's land to her — she would be surrounded by Germans. At Covent Garden, for instance, the chorus was made up of foreigners, and the leading conductors, Mancinelli and Randegger, were foreigners.

In London it was an asset to be a foreigner, but in Paris, where Melba made her debut at the Opéra on May 8, 1889, as Ophélie in Ambroise Thomas's *Hamlet*, it was a terrific drawback. Wherever poor Melba sang in those days, she was always at a disadvantage.

She was terrified of her Paris debut. The Paris Opéra is much larger than the Théâtre de la Monnaie. The French critics were known to be severe. The audiences were said to be blasé. Melba didn't know that the critical, xenophobic operagoers in Paris were also alert and intelligent. At that time there was a great understanding of good singing in Paris. The people knew a good singer when they heard one.

After the Mad Scene in *Hamlet* Melba had a triumph "which literally moved the audience to a frenzy." The *Figaro* critic showed more astuteness than his London colleagues. He noticed "the exceptional quality of that sweetly timbred soprano voice, equal, pure, brilliant and mellow, remarkably resonant in the middle register . . ."

Melba was recalled three times after the fall of the curtain. The *Figaro* man calculated this was "the equivalent of seventy-five recalls in Italy, at the very least."

It was a triumph at a time when the Paris Opéra had far greater prestige than today. Jean and Édouard de Reszke sang there, the great basso Plançon, the baritone Lasalle. The Opéra was the hub of the glittering "society" of Paris. "It was practically a necessity to have a box at the Opéra, much as in London it was a necessity to have a house in the country as well as in town," Melba observed matter-of-factly. She had learned to take "society" in her stride.

During the intermission, Christine Nilsson, the great Swedish soprano, came into Melba's dressing room and cried, *"La vieille Ophélie salue la jeune Ophélie,"* one of the rather rare expressions of prima donna-ish magnanimity in operatic history. Ambroise Thomas, the composer of *Hamlet*, came with Maître Gounod, the very best type of Bohemian, and both were "almost overcome by emotion." The anonymous "Gentleman from the Orchestra," whose contributions always followed the music critic's review in the *Figaro*, noted that Melba "breathed the perfume of romance without which there can be no true Ophélie and had the aristocratic grace which befits the fiancée of a king's son." Though some critics had reservations about Melba's foreign accent, she had become in one evening the ruling prima donna of the Paris Opéra.

She appeared later in *Rigoletto* and *Lucia*. The performance of *Lucia* had its dramatic moments, on stage as well as backstage. During the first act Emile Cosira, the tenor, suddenly lost his voice. For a while Melba sang his recitatives as well as hers. (Caruso once sang the "Coat Song" in the last act of *La Bohème* at a performance in Philadelphia for the bass Andres de Segurola, who had suddenly lost his voice. "Stand still and move your lips," Caruso told him and sang the bass aria with his back to the public. Most people didn't notice the switch. Caruso later recorded the aria privately, but ordered the master record destroyed, saying, "I don't want to spoil the bass business.")

Melba carried on bravely for herself and the tenor, but when it was time for a duet, she couldn't sing both parts. Even a celebrated prima donna has only one voice at a time. The curtain came down. There was bedlam backstage. The house was packed, and there was no understudy available. Suddenly Melba remembered that she had given two tickets to a colleague, the tenor Pierre Emile Engel, who had been her partner at her Brussels debut and had often sung with her in *Lucia* at the Monnaie.

They found Monsieur Engel in a box. He was "exceedingly calm and exceedingly businesslike" — qualities that always impressed Melba, because they are rare in the emotion-filled atmosphere of grand opera. Monsieur Engel bowed. He was deeply honored and would be perfectly delighted to sing, at a certain price. Naturally, he expected that they would also give him a contract to sing in the next three performances. Melba thought they would have given him a contract "to sing for the rest of his natural life," had he asked for one, so great was their predicament. Monsieur Engel dressed in an incredibly short time and the performance was saved after a delay of only twenty minutes, and brilliantly concluded.

"And now all of Paris with its marvelous people was before me," Melba remembers. Paris acclaimed the new prima donna with enthusiasm. It was no longer the poorly furnished rooms in Montmartre and taking buses to Madame Marchesi. She rented a charming apartment at 9 Rue de Prony, near the Parc Monceau. Little George, who was at school in England, came to spend his vacations with her. Madame Marchesi and Sarah Bernhardt were neighbors. Gounod's house in the Place Malesherbes was just a few blocks away. Melba decorated her apartment in the style of Marie Antoinette and Empress Josephine. She met everybody who was anybody. The most exciting of "the marvelous people of Paris" was Sarah Bernhardt, then at the height of her fame and eccentricity. Melba later said that of all voices she had known none had ever the same effect on her as the voice of the *grande tragédienne.*

Sarah Bernhardt was then having a *succès fou* as *La Dame aux Camélias.* Madame Marchesi took Nellie to meet the Divine Sarah at her home. Perhaps Madame harbored the secret hope that Melba might learn a little from the great actress.

When they arrived at Sarah Bernhardt's house the *tragédienne* was still dressing; she was always late. The visitors were taken into the drawing room, which, Melba remembers with her usual frankness, "was calculated to amaze people far more sophisticated than myself." The large room gave the impression of a circus tent rather than the *salon* of a theatrical star, with "heavy stuffs hanging over the ceiling, drooping down and catching the dust, skins of animals on the floor, heads of animals on the walls, horns of animals on the mantelpiece — stuffed tigers, stuffed bears, even a stuffed snake." Side by side with this menagerie were busts of the divine Sarah, pieces of tapestry, easels, plants, a large goldfish bowl, and some horrible bric-a-brac.

The *grande tragédienne* made a formidable entrance, which left the young prima donna speechless. Sarah jumped up to a box in the corner and sat down on it, waggling her legs like a schoolgirl, talking rapidly, with violent gestures. Did Melba like Paris? Did she like Marchesi? ("This," reports a shocked Melba, "in front of Madame Marchesi's astonished face!") Did she like the men of Paris? Above all, did she like Bernhardt? Had she seen Bernhardt in *La Dame aux Camélias?*

Suddenly she leaped down from her box and said, "You

sing like an angel. I want to teach you how to act." Madame
Marchesi beamed. Sarah Bernhardt started to go with Melba
through the part of Marguérite in *Faust*. She had never
played the part herself, and had heard *Faust* only once in
her life at the Opéra. But unlike Melba she was a born actress, and she proceeded to give Melba some of the best
advice the prima donna ever got on acting. Sarah knew all
the subtle touches of gesture, the imperceptible movements
of eyes and hands, the almost inaudible modulations of the
voice.

"It was an inspiration," Melba remembers, "and also very
practical and essentially useful."

Sarah Bernhardt played for her the scene when Valentin
curses Marguérite as he dies. "He curses you. He tells you
you have sinned with Faust and your white hands will never
be called upon to spin any more. Now, what must you do?
You must hide your hands behind your back, terrified,
ashamed, as though you wished that you might cut them
from your body. Like this, see?"

And Bernhardt whipped her hands behind her back, staring at Melba with such an expression of torture in her eyes
that Melba was haunted by the memory for years whenever
she stood on the stage and heard Valentin sing, "*Sois
maudite!*"

Sarah Bernhardt was a smart actress. "You must not
imitate me," she said. "Do it your own way. Be yourself.
Be natural."

"Alas," writes the irrepressible Colson, "Melba was never
able to call up a look of tragedy more intense than that of
the lady who has forgotten the name of the gentleman who

takes her out to supper." Melba admired Bernhardt and often went to see her. Once she was so overcome after a performance of *La Dame aux Camélias* that she took off a string of pearls from her neck and clasped them around the throat of the great actress.

When it was time to leave, Sarah Bernhardt gave Melba her photograph inscribed, *"A la plus charmante femme, à la plus delicieuse artiste; à la voix de pur cristal, la plus vive sympathie."*

Sarah Bernhardt was utterly unmusical. She had nothing against music, it didn't bother her, but she never noticed it. Music was just noise to her, though everybody said she had that musical "golden" voice. Sarah had no use for any language except French, dismissed England as impossible, Australia as barbaric, and America as "the worst of all, because you are so uncomfortable there." Opera bored her but she did go to hear Melba as Juliette. Afterwards she came into Melba's dressing room, seated herself on the dressing table, and told Melba that she made up her face like a schoolgirl.

"You have no idea how to do these things. You are too innocent, chérie. Take a lesson from me, the wicked one!"

Thereupon the wicked one took the innocent face in her hands and proceeded to apply deft touches of rouge and blue pencil, powder and lipstick, forbidding Melba to look in the mirror before she had finished. When it was over, Bernhardt jumped down again, clapped her hands and said, *"Voilà!* Now you may look, *ma jolie petite!"*

Melba was astonished at the transformation which Sarah had effected. She liked herself as she looked in the mirror, and she wished Sarah could always do that for her. The next day Monsieur Pluque, the *maître de ballet*, gave Melba the address of a beautiful *danseuse* who was an expert in the art of make-up.

When Melba decided to do a thing, she didn't stop until she was satisfied that she knew everything about it. For a month she went every day to the beautiful *danseuse*, experimenting with grease paint under different conditions. She learned to make up differently according to the size of the theater. She learned the cardinal rule: that the audience, no matter how near, must never see the faintest trace of cosmetics.

"Modern actresses will claim this is impossible," Melba writes. "But people who say such things are merely ignorant of one of the first principles of dramatic technique. My dancer was quite right. If make-up is applied properly it should remain invisible, whether you are in the first row of the stalls or in the back of the gallery. It is merely a question of knowing how to do it."

Years later Melba and Sarah Bernhardt performed together one night at a private party in the London town house of Lady George Cooper in Grosvenor Square. "She had inherited a huge fortune from her uncle, known as 'Chicago Smith,' so money was no object," noted the cynical Colson (and went right along to the party). Money surely couldn't have been an object. The great Melba and the Divine Sarah each got twenty-five hundred dollars. Jan Kubelik, the famous Czech violinist, the French actor J. Coquelin, and others were also engaged.

The *pièce de résistance* was Murger's poem, *"La Ballade*

du Désespéré." Herman Bemberg had written the music, and played the accompaniment on the piano. Critic Colson played the violin obbligato. Melba sang the part of Death knocking at the door of the Poet, whose part was recited by Sarah Bernhardt.

The day before, they all met for a rehearsal at the Hyde Park Hotel, where Sarah Bernhardt made her headquarters. Melba came first, punctual to the minute, as usual, well-dressed and fresh as a daisy. Bernhardt, as unpunctual as always, had completely forgotten about the appointment and was still asleep. When she appeared at last, she wore a greasy old dressing gown and down-at-the-heel slippers. This shocked Melba, an early riser, who always put on a dress for breakfast and very much disliked the gown-and-slipper habit of celebrated artists.

Bernhardt's hair was straggling in wisps from some lace head-covering and her face bore traces of last night's make-up, but all distressing details were forgotten the moment she began to speak. It must have been wonderful to hear those two great voices together, Sarah's golden voice and Melba's silvery one. Sarah's saying, *"Qui frappe à ma porte à cette heure?"* and Melba's singing, *"Ouvre. Ton nom? Vite, ouvre-moi."*

Sarah Bernhardt never stopped acting. Melba went to see her years later at her Paris house. The great *tragédienne* was performing her last part — the part of a dying woman.

She gave a great performance. She was lying in bed, propped up against the pillows, and though the body was nearly gone, the radiant spirit was still there.

"Ah, Melba!" she said, clasping Melba's hands. *"Tu as toujours ta voix d'or. Ma voix d'or n'a plus besoin de moi, car je meurs."*

Great dialogue, great delivery. One can almost hear the words, *"cars je meurs,"* "for I am dying," in the ringing, sonorous tones of the great actress. Her lips were scarlet, her cheeks were rouged, she wore a fair wig. Bernhardt was dying in a part worthy of her and she had made up well for it.

But she broke down when Melba kissed her good-by. Sarah clung to her feverishly, pathetically. For a moment she forgot to act. She was terrified to be left alone, afraid to die.

Melba remembers that she left at last and went into the next room, pausing for a moment to pull herself together. She knew she would never see Sarah again, and she thought of all that Sarah had been and had had, the fame and the glory and the triumphs and the men — and all was gone now.

Outside a friend was waiting. She looked at Melba curiously. "Why, Nellie, what have you been doing to yourself?"

Nellie looked into her small mirror. Her cheeks were covered with rouge — Sarah Bernhardt's rouge. Melba shuddered and rubbed her cheeks with her handkerchief, but Sarah's rouge wouldn't come off.

7

Command Performance

AFTER HER UNHAPPY DEBUT in London Melba had vowed that she would never return there, "and when I make that kind of vow to myself I usually keep it." But on the night of June 15, 1889, she appeared at Covent Garden as Juliette in the first French-language performance of Gounod's *Roméo et Juliette*. Both the cast and the audience were exceptional. On the stage Melba was surrounded by Jean and Édouard de Reszke and Mademoiselle Mathilde Bauermeister, who had made her debut in 1869, had sung over a hundred large and small roles and been called by G. B. Shaw "probably the most indispensable member of the company." She had also accurately predicted Melba's ultimate success. The house was sold out, the Prince and Princess of Wales were in the royal box, and everybody who was somebody in the fashionable world of London was present.

It was a big night for the music critics and a bigger one for the society reporters, who worked overtime noticing that "Lady de Grey had brought those five lovely women, the

Duchess of Leinster, the Duchess of Sutherland, the Countess of Warwick, Lady Dudley and Mrs. Cornwallis-West . . ."
There was also the Duchess of Devonshire, notorious for her
sharp tongue, Lady Cynthia Graham, Lady Helen Vincent,
and "all the best-known men in London."

"There was that indescribable atmosphere which one
senses on a big night at the opera," Biographer Colson remembers wistfully. It was the first "Melba night" at Covent
Garden, and it was all the doing of Lady de Grey.

Melba had packed her trunks and left London after her
unfortunate debut at Covent Garden, where she had been
"shabbily treated by audiences and critics." As we have
seen she had gone back to Brussels, where they were glad to
have her. One morning, a few weeks later, she had been
sitting at breakfast in her small house when she received a
letter in a strange handwriting. Melba was intrigued. "Letters were rather luxuries in those days." She opened it
eagerly. It was from Lady de Grey, asking whether she
would sing the part of Juliette next season in a new production of *Roméo et Juliette* at Covent Garden.

Melba had never met Lady de Grey, and she had "not
the faintest intention" of returning to London. She replied
to Lady de Grey that she deeply appreciated her kindness
but felt she "had been so badly treated in London on her
first visit that she had detemined never to venture on a
second." (The uncrowned Queen of Song already expressed
herself in a way which reflected her exalted position.) She
sent off the letter and thought no more about it.

Another letter from London came by return mail. Lady

de Grey explained that the Princess of Wales (later Queen Alexandra) was "most anxious" for Melba's return. The Princess had been present at that unfortunate *Rigoletto* performance and had been deeply impressed by Melba's voice.

> I know things were badly arranged for you before [wrote Lady de Grey]. But if you come back I promise you that it will be very different. You will be under my care, and I shall see that you do not lack either friends or hospitality.

"So, after all, somebody had been there who appreciated me," Melba later said with satisfaction. She had her principles, but she also had common sense. She knew that Lady de Grey's summons was like being asked to a command performance. She immediately sat down and wrote back to Lady de Grey that she would be "only too happy" to return for the next season.

Lady de Grey was infatuated with the crazy and wonderful world of grand opera. She was the greatest patron of opera during the closing days of the Victorian era and during the Edwardian epoch. At Covent Garden she exercised "an enormous influence, both in front of the house and behind the scenes," writes Harold Rosenthal, the historian of Covent Garden. Lady de Grey later married the Marquess of Ripon, who was a member of Covent Garden's board of directors. Her brother-in-law Harry Higgins became chairman of the board of the Syndicate that ran the opera house.

Gladys de Grey was a beautiful, swanlike Renaissance figure, very sure of herself and serenely indifferent to other people's opinions about her. She had wealth and social position, beauty and impeccable taste. Best of all, she had intelligence and wit. Melba said that Lady de Grey was "perhaps the last of the women able to hold a *salon*." Obviously Lady de Grey's magic personality succeeded in blending the most different people into a harmonious whole. Everybody was welcome in her house who wasn't a bore, from the Duchess of Leinster, who always fascinated Melba "with her marvelous sapphires around her neck, holding her head like a queen," and Lady Dudley "with her lovely turquoises, so numerous that they seemed to cover her from head to knees" — what a splendid way of getting dressed! — to Oscar Wilde and Sir Arthur Sullivan. Lady de Grey and her friends would congregate in Monte Carlo in wintertime, and there Sir Arthur would often take Melba to the roulette tables of the Casino. He was only forty-seven then, but Melba noticed that "his hand was already so shaky that when he stretched it out to play roulette the money would fall on the wrong numbers." The croupiers were kind to the great gambler (maybe they liked *The Mikado*) and gave him time to push the coins into place.

Melba was a passionate gambler herself. "We had lots of fun together at the gaming tables of Monte Carlo," Mary Garden writes in her memoirs. "Melba would win a few francs and you would have thought it was a million dollars."

One day Melba and Lady de Grey went to the Casino and sat down at a roulette table on either side of a bearded Frenchman, who became very annoyed when the two women on his right and left were winning while he lost all the time. At last he got up and said loudly enough to be overheard, "What can one expect when one sits between two cocottes?"

The two "cocottes" were delighted by the compliment and convulsed with laughter. Lady de Grey said later she had never been so flattered in her life. It is not unusual for a cocotte to be taken for a lady, but it doesn't often happen the other way around.

Lady de Grey and Lady Charles Beresford, another famous opera hostess, "demanded" the engagement of Jean and Édouard de Reszke in 1887, and of other great singers. Fortunately they knew something about voices. There have always been people like Lady de Grey, everywhere and at every epoch — aristocrats, princes of the Church, or simply wealthy people who loved opera — who kept composers from starving, paid for the deficit of bankrupt opera houses, gave parties for temperamental divas, appeased offended tenors, and generally kept the complicated machinery of grand opera smoothly running. They serve over and above the call of fashionable duty and should be decorated with the (as yet nonexisting) Legion of Operatic Merit.

Grand opera is the most complex and most expensive of all dramatic arts. It has always depended on the support of wealthy enthusiasts, or of opera-minded governments dispensing taxpayers' money. No opera house on earth ever makes a substantial profit. There are hosannahs when it breaks even during a season, as Covent Garden did a few times under Harry Higgins and Neil Forsyth, during the "golden" Melba-Caruso days.

Today all opera houses in the Communist countries are handsomely supported by the state. Budgets are often secret but subsidies are sometimes high. Vienna's Staatsoper runs up a considerable deficit although it is always sold out; of the six million dollars of taxpayers' money a year which small Austria puts up to subsidize its state theaters, the Staatsoper gets the lion's share. All opera houses in West Germany are subsidized by the state or by a municipality. Milan's La Scala receives not one lira subsidy from private patrons, since such gifts would not be recognized as deductible by Italy's income tax collectors. Only half of La Scala's expenditures are covered by ticket sales. The fifty-percent deficit is cheerfully made up by the city administration of Milan, through a small tax on movie tickets and other entertainment, and by the provincial government, through a tax on the national football pool.

By comparison, the Metropolitan, which is often on the brink of financial disaster, tries to get money from rich opera lovers or not-so-rich radio listeners. Covent Garden now gets just enough from the Arts Council to support a short opera and ballet season, but there is always some sort of financial crisis. Obviously Lady de Grey would be very useful if she were still around.

When César Ritz opened the Carlton, he asked Lady de Grey to help him launch the place, and the expense be damned. That suited Lady de Grey well. She rented London's Lyric Theater for a night and brought the entire cast, scenery and orchestra of André Messager's *Véronique* from Paris, where it was then a big hit. She invited all her friends from the *première* (she had enough of them to fill the house) and afterwards for supper at Monsieur Ritz's new Carlton. The expense must have been damnably high, but the Carlton was well on its way.

Music and especially famous musicians were very much in vogue with the leading hostesses of Victorian and particularly of Edwardian London. King Edward VII and Queen Alexandra were fond of opera. The pleasures of cocktail parties, *après-ski dances* and fast automobiles were not yet discovered. People didn't constantly talk about leisure; they *had* leisure and enjoyed it. Composers were popular matinee idols, provided their music was not too "heavy." Bach was considered extremely boring and Wagner was impossibly dull. On the other hand, Gounod and Verdi were "just divine." Minor composers, such as Herman Bemberg and Francesco Paolo Tosti, who wrote light melodies were extremely popular with the leading hostesses.

Lady de Grey used to say that a symphony concert or a string quartet bored her to tears, but she rarely missed a performance at Covent Garden and showed the usual symptoms of operatic intoxication, such as a slight fever and violent palpitation in moments of supreme bliss — a pleasant affliction from which so many of us suffer happily. It was no secret that Lady de Grey "ran" Covent Garden. When she and Melba became great friends, they probably "ran" it together. Exactly to what extent Melba was involved in the invisible but omniscient management of the opera house is still a mystery, and a part of the Melba legend which is often reiterated and just as often denied.

Lady de Grey kept her promise. Prior to the *première* of *Roméo et Juliette* word went out you-had-better-be-there. The critics were given to understand that Madame Melba was now *persona gratissima* in some Very High Circles. Whether that impressed them is doubtful, but at any rate the operatic climate this time was quite different from Melba's previous appearances. She was no longer an obscure young singer from faraway Australia who had sung in some second-rate Continental houses. She was basking in the bright sunshine of royalty.

"English critics," writes Mr. Colson, "like to be very sure that an artist is to be reckoned with before expressing any very decided opinion about him. So do the English people, and that is why in England, once you've conquered the affections of the public, you can go on singing until you are a hundred years old and completely gaga."

Not only in England. How often have I seen bewildered listeners at the Vienna Staatsoper who would ask their neighbors why on earth they were applauding a tenor or a soprano whose voices were completely gone, and were told, in tones of injured feelings, "Maybe — but you ought to have heard them twelve years ago." Several years ago Maria Jeritza, then well past her sixtieth birthday, returned to Vienna to perform two of her greatest parts, Tosca and Salome. The Viennese forgave the vocal calamity and reveled in their memories of their beloved prima donna. Madame Jeritza had a great and, everybody agreed, well deserved success.

Such loyalty to his former goddesses is a touching, endearing trait of the genuine opera lover, who never forgets his former loves. "Every generation of operagoers sighs for the memorable singers of the past, and it is therefore tempting to infer that the Golden Age of Opera is a perennial myth," writes Desmond Shawe-Taylor. At the Metropolitan Opera House, Milan's La Scala, and Germany's leading opera houses audiences have shown less sentiment for the heroes of their past. There they applaud a singer only as long as his or her voice lasts. Very cold-blooded people.

"The remembrance of the past is infinitely more agreeable than the enjoyment of the present," wrote Lord Mount-Edgecumbe in his *Musical Reminiscences,* which covers the years from 1773 to 1823. He might have written it today. Opera lovers are hopeless nostalgia addicts. I remember with great warmth the "golden" voices which I heard during my carefree young days in the Vienna claque. It is sometimes agonizing in reappraisal to hear these voices on recordings and to realize that they were merely gold-plated. There were great natural voices among the giants of the past — especially among the great tenors, who have become rare nowadays. But it was a golden age of great voices rather than of great opera performances. In his *Chapters on Opera* Henry E. Krehbiel reports that during the first season at the Metropolitan in 1883 "the instrumentalists made a sad mess of the orchestral score." We read that "Madame Sembrich ended a dazzling feat of vocalization to the discordant scrapings of half a dozen fiddlers." For a *Carmen* performance at Covent Garden in 1890 the program lists three conductors: Mancinelli conducted the first and last act, Bevignani the second and Randegger the third. (Two years ago the Metropolitan did almost as well when it consumed three Tristans during a performance of *Tristan und Isolde,* a different one in each act, and all three had lost their voices at the end. Opera management is not a business for people with weak nerves.)

The great singers of the past were mainly opera singers. They knew their trade and worked hard at it. Thirty appearances during the short Met season was not unusual for Melba. Caruso once sang fifty-one performances. But sloppiness prevailed, novelties were suited mainly to the wishes of the stars, little money was spent on good orchestras and first-rate conductors. Maurice Grau, the manager of the Metropolitan, paid Caruso twenty-five hundred dollars a performance, but saved on good conductors. "No one ever paid a nickel to see a man's back," he would say. Maybe the golden age of opera wasn't even gold-plated.

After Melba's waltz song *"Je veux vivre,"* in *Roméo et Juliette* there was "a tempest of applause." (All contemporary critics agreed that Melba sang this song better than anybody else on earth.) At the end of the performance she received several ovations. Almost all the critics who a year ago had ignored her voice praised the purity and sweetness of her tones. The *Standard* noted, with a faint hint of reproof, that "the few embellishments which she introduces are almost invariably in good taste." (It was a few years before Melba wrote in her essay "On the Science of Singing" that "the singer's mission is . . . not to embellish the composer's message with extraneous ideas.")

The lone dissenter was the able publicist and young music

critic of the newly-founded *Star,* who wrote under the pen name of "Corno di Bassetto":

> Madame Melba may thank her stars that she had so good a Roméo (Jean de Reszke) to help her out in the last two acts.
>
> At one or two points in the Balcony Scene she sang with genuine feeling, and in the tragic scenes she was at least anxious to do her best. In the first act, however, she was shrill and forward. The "waltz ariette" was coming out with great confidence and facility which, I think, Madame Melba mistook for art. Her fresh bright voice and generally safe intonations are all in her favor at present.

It was a typically Shavian comment, which piqued Melba's drawing-room admirers in high places. Similar Shavian sallies appeared during the following five years in the pages of the *Star* and later, under his own name, in the weekly review the *World.* G. B. Shaw had wit as well as knowledge of opera; his reviews were readable and funny, and at the same time critical and erudite (although he was mainly interested in promoting the Wagnerian cause). He admitted that the performances of *Roméo et Juliette* with Jean de Reszke and Melba "seem sure of a place in the front rank of my operatic collections," but ridiculed Augustus Harris for failing to put on *Tristan* and the *Ring* with Jean de Reszke. When Harris finally presented the *Ring,* he opened the tetralogy with *Siegfried* instead of *Rheingold,* under the young conductor Gustav Mahler, because the great *Wagnertenor* Alvary insisted on making his London debut in his *Glanzrolle!*

Shaw constantly complained that there was no effective direction at Covent Garden, and that the company had five leading tenors and no stage manager. "For want of a stage

manager," Shaw wrote, "no man in *Les Huguénots* knows
whether he is a Catholic or a Protestant." Seventy years after
these reviews were written they still make wonderful
reading.

In spite of "Corno di Bassetto's" acid comment on Melba's
early performances, she soon became the established prima
donna *assoluta* at Covent Garden, taking over the crown of
Patti. A few weeks after the memorable *Roméo et Juliette*
performance, she sang in her first command performance at
Covent Garden, in honor of the Shah of Persia. It was
noticed that His Majesty was extremely bored by the whole
affair, except by the tuning up of the orchestra, which interested him very much. At a state dinner the Shah amused
himself by throwing peach stones at the satin dress of the
Princess of Wales, who later complained about it to Melba.

The following year Madame Melba was commanded to
sing to Queen Victoria and the German Empress in Windsor.
The former Helen Porter Mitchell had arrived in the
charmed Inner Circle.

It was Melba's first appearance before the formidable
Queen and she was excited. Only three years ago Mrs.
Nellie Armstrong, a little known singer from Australia, had
studied with Madame Marchesi in Paris. Now Madame
Melba was on her way to Windsor Castle with Jean and
Édouard de Reszke, two of the world's most famous artists,
and with Francesco Paolo Tosti, who was going to accom-
pany them on the piano.

The de Reszkes, for whom a command performance was
nothing new, were "in their usual high spirits," and Tosti,

who was almost always in high spirits, looked resplendent in his long black cape which, Melba noted, "always aroused the curiosity of the crowds." Composers still dressed and looked the part.

Only Melba was nervous, drumming her fingers on the windowpanes and clearing her throat.

"*Qu'est ce que tu fais?*" said Tosti. "*Tu n'as pas peur, toi?*" Yes, she was a little afraid.

There had been some mistake about the train, and no carriage was waiting in Windsor Station to meet them. They had to hire a four-wheeled rickety old cab. When they arrived at the Castle, they were taken to a small anteroom. The performance had been commanded for four o'clock, but by a quarter past four no one had appeared to take them to the Presence.

"I hope they know that I'm singing at Covent Garden tonight," said Melba.

At half-past four a courier appeared and told them there had been a delay because the German Empress, who was a guest at Windsor, had gone out for a drive and had not returned. Queen Victoria would receive them now alone.

They were ushered into a large room. Melba saw a tiny figure in black, attended by her ladies in waiting. The Queen shook hands with them one by one, looking them straight in the eyes. "I had a dim sense of a picture come to life, so like was she to her portraits — the smooth silvery hair, the heavy eyelids," Melba remembers.

The Queen asked them a few questions about their careers. Then there followed an uncomfortable silence. Melba could hear the glass-incased clock on the mantelpiece ticking off the seconds. It was a quarter to five. Melba kept thinking of her performance at Covent Garden.

Queen Victoria broke the silence.

"The Empress is very late. I think we will begin."

She returned slowly to her chair, sat down, and waited, looking at them.

They sang — solos, duets, and finally the trio from the last act of *Faust*. Tosti played the piano. It was growing dark, and the clock on the mantelpiece struck half past five. Melba could almost hear the crowd shuffling outside the gallery at Covent Garden. Obviously the ladies in waiting had forgotten to inform the Queen that Melba was singing that night.

At that moment the door opened and the German Empress came in. Melba sighed with relief. Now they would be allowed to go.

But, to her horror, Queen Victoria smiled graciously at the Empress.

"What a treat you have missed! We must have more for you."

At that point Melba almost opened her mouth to inform the Queen that she was singing at Covent Garden at eight o'clock. Jean de Reszke nudged her and gave her a warning sign.

"With a sinking heart," Melba returned to her singing and once more they went through the entire program, but at a much faster pace. "The trio from *Faust* must have sounded almost like ragtime," Melba said later.

It was now ten minutes past six. Melba was "absolutely desperate." She managed to whisper to Miss Minnie Cochran, a lady in waiting, that she *had* to get back to London at once, would it be possible to be dismissed? Evidently the message was conveyed to Her Majesty. After a few gracious words and the offer of refreshments in another room, they *were* dismissed.

As they were about to leave, Miss Cochran handed each of them a little parcel. Then they were taken back to the station, "with mingled emotions," this time in the royal carriage. Fortunately a train just steamed into Windsor Station, and they got in, sat down, and opened their parcels.

"You show yours first," Tosti said to Melba.

"No, you show yours," Jean said to Tosti.

Finally they compromised by opening their parcels at the same time. Melba's contained a little brooch of pearls and rubies, Jean's gold links, Édouard's gold and platinum links, and Tosti's a gold pencil.

Melba arrived at Covent Garden while the first act of *Rigoletto* was already in progress. There was pandemonium backstage, and Augustus Harris was tearing his hair. Melba ran to her dressing room, dressed hurriedly, put something on her face and ran out on stage. She had delayed them by fifteen minutes, which was a major crime to her punctual soul. And "it was a very hungry Gilda who was singing that night!"

To be summoned to sing before Queen Victoria was the cherished goal of all artists who sang at Covent Garden. Madame Nuovina, a Belgian soprano better known for her friendship with Casimir Périer, Carnot's successor as President of France, than for her voice, had been engaged by

Augustus Harris. (It was rumored he hoped to add the French *Légion d'honneur* to his foreign decorations.) Madame Nuovina was no success as Gemma in Frederic Cowen's opera *Signa,* and after the *première* was taken ill "with the usual soprano indisposition," producing a doctor's certificate that she could not sing for ten days. In reality she wanted to appear in the "Melba operas." Augustus Harris had a hard time finding a substitute for the second performance of *Signa.* A Miss Gherlson, so unknown that even her first name has remained obscure, took over Madame Nuovina's part.

Then word came that Cowen's opera had been commanded by Queen Victoria for a Windsor Castle performance. Madame Nuovina recovered miraculously. She sent off a letter to Harris saying she was "not quite so ill as had been feared" and would be very pleased to sing before the Queen. Her cold was "not so bad," perhaps the doctor had "inaccurately diagnosed the matter."

Harris didn't bother to answer. More letters and telegrams arrived at his office. At last Harris wrote to her, "The young artist who came to my rescue so gallantly at the eleventh hour must go to Windsor."

Madame Nuovina sent a final telegram:

FAITES-MOI JOUER A WINDSOR ET J'ARRANGERAI QUELQUE CHOSE BON POUR VOUS AVEC CASIMIR PÉRIER. NUOVINA.

Madame Nuovina had underestimated Augustus Harris. Miss Gherlson sang at Windsor Castle before the Queen. Madame Nuovina never appeared again at Covent Garden during the Harris regime. Harris did not get the *Legion d'honneur*.

Melba sang many times before Queen Victoria. She took part in several state concerts in the ballroom of Buckingham Palace, "cheerless affairs," according to Colson.

> Her Majesty sat alone in front, in a gilt chair, and around her were grouped the Royal Family and the Court officials. Behind them were row upon row of the elite of the aristocracy, the men in Court dress or uniform, the women in their very best clothes, wearing all their family jewels, many of them in the most lumpy and hideous settings. No applause was permitted unless Her Majesty gently gave the signal, and then it was discreet, to say the least of it. What an atmosphere to sing in! The program generally consisted of classical arias and selections from the older Italian operas, varied occasionally by violin or piano solos, or performances by the Court orchestra. The influence of the "ever lamented" still pervaded the solemn assembly, and I think that the august old lady, as she sat there, tired, stiff, and formidable, thought wistfully how music had degenerated since "Dear Albert" had left for a higher sphere — where he would most assuredly be asked to direct the celestial concerts — and how poor was this musical fare compared with the solid slabs of oratorio which "our dear Mr. Mendelssohn" had been wont to set before them in the forties. But she was Queen of England and Empress of India, and the arts, however unimportant, must be encouraged. And in giving these dreary concerts she sincerely felt that she was doing all that was necessary to encourage them.

Actually, Queen Victoria in her early years was very fond of theater and music. Both she and her husband, the Prince Consort, were enthusiastic operagoers and her writings at that time contain many references to *Norma, Anna Bolena* and *La Sonnambula,* her favorite operas, and to Malibran, Grisi and Jenny Lind, her favorite singers. During a concert of Jenny Lind, Queen Victoria became so excited that she threw her flower bouquet at the feet of the diva. She studied singing with "my good Lablache," the noted bass Luigi Lablache, who had been the first Don Pasquale. "Dear Albert" played the piano and composed a little. In the first year of her reign Queen Victoria paid a state visit to Covent Garden, which didn't turn out too well. An enormous mob packed the cheaper seats, "causing such tumult, fainting and screaming that a great number of women had to be lifted over the boxes in an exhausted condition."

A few years later, in 1852, Louis Spohr's opera *Faust* was performed at Covent Garden "at the urgent wish of the Queen," but was a failure, dull and heavy. At another state visit of the Queen to Covent Garden, where she wanted to see *The Magic Flute,* the Grand Foyer was turned into her receiving room. "At each extremity crystal curtains, intermingled with ruby drops, most brilliantly lighted up with gas, were suspended, and large mirrors were placed in every panel."

It must have been a splendid sight, but the behavior of the audience didn't quite live up to it. Operagoing was highly fashionable. The auditorium remained lighted during the performance, so that the society people could view each other in their gowns and jewels. There was much coming and going during the first act and after the intervals. It was as bad as it still is at the Metropolitan, where some of my finest moments are always spoiled by people stepping on my toes.

The Queen would often arrive after the performance had begun, and the performance would be interrupted, the audience would rise and cheer, and the national anthem would be played. Queen Victoria had the good sense to suggest later on that it was unnecessary to play the anthem every time she entered the theater but only at the beginning and the end of each season. This custom still remains at the Royal Opera House. Throughout the performance the audience often chattered away. People stopped to listen only when their favorite prima donna was singing, and as soon as Patti and Melba had finished their arias, they would resume their conversation.

Across the Atlantic things were just as bad. "The annual dispute as to the rights of man to talk in an opera house has broken out with customary severity," the *New York Times* wrote in an article about the tribal mores of the Metropolitan Opera House audiences in 1890. "People sometimes bear a sudden outburst of sibilant sounds not in the score. These are admonitory hisses of the three-dollar men and women who sit in the orchestra stalls and grow weary under the constant down-dropping upon their heads of diamonds of speech from the thirty-two-hundred-dollar ladies and gentlemen in the boxes."

It came as something of a shock to Melba that she was not asked to a command performance of *Lohengrin* on the eightieth birthday of Queen Victoria. Jean and Édouard de Reszke, Nordica and Schumann-Heink were the wonderful cast. The Queen, who heard the opera for the first time, found it "the most glorious composition" and the singing of the two brothers "beyond praise." But Melba sang at the state performance at Covent Garden on June 23, 1897, to mark Queen Victoria's Diamond Jubilee. She sang with the de Reszkes the third act of *Roméo et Juliette*, before what must have been one of the most gorgeous audiences of the century that was coming to an end.

Command performances became more cheerful affairs when Edward VII ascended to the throne. The King wasn't musical in the strict sense of the word, but he loved opera and its prima donnas. He was a great admirer of Melba. During his happier years as Prince of Wales, Melba met him constantly at parties given by Lady de Grey, Lady Charles Beresford, Sir Arthur Sullivan and Alfred de Rothschild, and besides they met at week-end parties and race meetings. He often gave her the impression of "a happy schoolboy," though there were evenings when he was tired and "showed his disapproval of anyone who annoyed him." At Covent Garden he once spotted a hapless wood-wind player in the orchestra who wore a black tie instead of a white one, and sent an equerry to express his disapproval. He could be quite sardonic in his disapproving moods. At a party in Lady de Grey's house, Melba saw an American heiress sweep down "almost to her knees, rather in the manner of a leading lady in a musical comedy," when she was presented to the Prince. He looked at her calmly and said in a particularly penetrating voice, "Have you lost anything?"

One night Sir Arthur Sullivan gave a supper party at

which the Prince was present. Melba and the baritone Eugene Oudin were asked to sing a duet from *Roméo et Juliette*. While they sang, the Prince sat on a sofa and was talking "in an audible but subdued loud voice." Melba noticed a dangerous glitter in Oudin's eyes and "began to feel a little awkward" herself, but at the end of the duet the Prince paid them a charming compliment and indicated he had been obliged to discuss "affairs of state."

Melba was devoted to the Prince. She would sing for him whenever he desired. Once during lunch at the home of Sir William Gordon Cumming, with the Prince of Wales, Lady de Grey and the Duchess of Manchester, a message arrived for Melba from Augustus Harris asking her to sing at Covent Garden that night because another diva had become indisposed.

"Certainly not," said Melba, sure to be overheard. A prima donna always says no when she is asked to sing for another prima donna.

Then the Prince smiled at her across the table.

"I am going to Covent Garden myself tonight. Please, Madame Melba, send back another answer."

Needless to say, Melba obliged. Opera managers everywhere would be glad to get help from somebody like the Prince, especially around noon when singers call up to say they have to cancel that night.

Melba's friendship with the Prince of Wales almost came to an end when she was summoned to sing at a state concert in Buckingham Palace and was forced to cancel her appearance owing to a sudden attack of laryngitis. A week later Melba was at Lady de Grey's house talking to Charles Beresford, when the Prince of Wales was announced. He looked all around the room, bowing to his friends one by one, but when his eyes reached Melba, he glanced at her coldly and then looked away. Not a smile, not a hint of recognition.

"I felt absolutely miserable," Melba later said. "I had to sit down on a sofa and wished I could sink through the floor. Had it not been for the fact that the Princess of Wales her-self sent for me and talked to me for several minutes, I be-lieve I should have died."

Melba had a bad night. The next morning she rushed to Lady de Grey's to find out why she was in disgrace.

Gladys shook her head. "Well, Nellie, I'm afraid the Prince has heard that you were enjoying yourself on the Thames the very night when you should have sung in Buckingham Pal-ace. He is naturally very angry about it."

Now it was Melba's turn to get angry. The whole thing was a mean intrigue, a disgusting lie.

"Why, I've been ill in bed, hardly able to talk."

"Can you prove it?"

"Of course. Dr. Semon was attending me. He will give me a certificate. It's silly, Gladys. After all, I'm no longer a schoolgirl."

"Leave it to me," said Gladys de Grey. "Don't worry."

"I'm not worried. I am angry," said the prima donna.

Poor Gladys de Grey now had two angry shining lights, but she managed somehow, and a few days later Melba was summoned to Marlborough House at four in the afternoon, and shown at once into the Prince's suite.

According to Melba (there exists only her account of what happened) the Prince bowed stiffly.

"You wished to see me, Madame Melba?"

"Yes, sir. I am unhappy, terribly unhappy. You cut me at Lady de Grey's the other night."

He looked away and frowned. "Why didn't you sing at Buckingham Palace?"

"I was ill, Sir."

"Are you quite sure?"

And like a schoolgirl, the great diva drew out her doctor's certificate and held it before him.

The Prince began to smile. "Oh, I don't want to see that."

But he hadn't reckoned with the indignant prima donna. She told him she had been ill, lying in bed, unable to speak. "Surely, Sir, you couldn't imagine that I would do such a terrible thing?"

She may have said more, but she didn't record it. At any rate, the Prince laughed and shook her hand, and they were "friends again."

They remained friends until the day of his death in 1910. That day in May Melba was to give a concert, but when the sad news came she broke down, cried "for many hours" and had to postpone the concert. She sensed that they had lost more than a King.

It was a wonderful era while it lasted. "What an amazing gallery of fine men and noble women the Edwardians were," Melba wrote in her autobiography. "Not only the men who were born to greatness but also those who achieved it. They had a glamor about them which is sadly lacking today."

A tendency towards eccentricity has always been a lovable English trait, and the Edwardians were master eccentrics.

There was Alfred Harmsworth, later Lord Northcliffe, an admirer of Melba, who often would call her up before breakfast to ask whether he could do something for her and be quite hurt when she had no special request. Lord Northcliffe once fired the music critic of his *Daily Mail*, who had written a malicious review of Melba in *Roméo et Juliette*.

"I was at Covent Garden last night with Lady Northcliffe," he said. "You sang beautifully. His criticism was unfair. I'm not going to have that sort of thing in my papers."

And there was Lord Mount Stephen. Melba was fond of him because he reminded her of her father. The same wry Scottish humor, the same directness, and his success story from poor country boy to chairman of the board of the Canadian Pacific. Like many people who made their money, Lord Mount Stephen tried to hold on to it. He was fond of bargains. When he saw a beautiful diamond necklace in Christie's, he went in and asked the price. "Too high," he told them gruffly, "but if you can get it for five thousand pounds less, I'll take it."

It was the sort of thing millionaires liked to say. He walked out and forgot all about it.

A few weeks later Lord Mount Stephen was informed by Christie's that the necklace was now five thousand pounds less, and his. He was stuck, and he didn't like it. His wife already had a diamond necklace. He paid for the necklace and angrily put it away in a dispatch box. There his wife found it a few months later.

She called up her friend Nellie. "I asked him why he hadn't told me about the necklace. You should have seen his face. He had to give it to me. What else could he do?"

By way of saving face, Lord Mount Stephen made the condition that his wife must not wear both necklaces at the same time. But Lady Mount Stephen loved to show off her jewels.

"She had a charming way of dragging them rather diffidently from their boxes and holding up diamonds and pearls and emeralds to the light, as a child would hold up a new toy," Melba remembers.

Melba loved jewels; she was particularly fond of pearls that were as perfectly matched as the tones of her scale. She sympathized with Geant Mount Stephen, who would wear both necklaces when she was in a "naughty mood," sitting at her end of the table "like a glittering Christmas tree." Sooner or later her husband would notice it and get very angry. No one cared because he got angry too often. He even got angry when she bought new soap plates.

And there was that great Edwardian, Lord Sandwich, "who might have stepped out of the pages of Thackeray." He was one of the most delightful and worst-tempered people on earth. When he was Melba's partner at a game of croquet in Hinchingbrooke and Melba was chattering with some women, Lord Sandwich shouted, "If you would stop talking for two seconds, you might perhaps sometimes go through a hoop."

No one ever talked that way to the ruling Queen of Song. She was so astonished that she actually stopped talking. They lost the game. Lord Sandwich ran across the lawn, seized the balls and furiously threw them into the lake. Half an hour later he took Melba on a tour of Hinchingbrooke as though nothing had happened.

Another eccentricity of Lord Sandwich's was his punctuality, worse even than Melba's. None of his guests dared come for dinner one minute past eight. And he was particularly annoyed when the women wore hats during lunch. Melba had been informed of His Lordship's little idiosyncrasies, but sometimes she would forget. Once she was out for a walk with several women. They came back just as lunch was served. Rather than arouse Lord Sandwich's wrath by being a minute late, they went into the dining room with their hats on.

Lord Sandwich was already at his end of the table "with an expression of deep gloom on his face." He took a sweeping glance at the women in their hats, turned to his butler, and told him in a loud voice to bring him his hat. The impeccable gentleman's gentleman nodded gravely and went to the door.

"*You* put on your hat too!" Lord Sandwich said.

"Yes, sir," said the butler, as if this were the most natural thing on earth.

"And," His Lordship shouted, "the footmen will also wear their hats!"

Melba wasn't sure whether she should laugh or take no notice, but the atmosphere around the table was "one of deep gravity," and so she chose the latter course. The butler appeared in a smart grey Homburg and was followed by two sheepish-looking footmen, one wearing a slouch hat, the other a cap. Lord Sandwich was handed a tweed cap on a silver tray. He put it on, tugged it over his eyes, and glared fiercely in front of him.

Supreme indifference to other people's opinions was the outstanding trait of the Edwardians. Lady Charles Beresford, next to Lady de Grey the most enthusiastic dispenser of operatic patronage, would appear at Covent Garden in a tea gown and a tiara, because she happened to like the combination. Another prominent Edwardian, Cecil Rhodes, whom Melba met at Alfred de Rothschild's house, relapsed into gloomy silence during the whole dinner while he sat next to Melba. Suddenly he boomed into her ear, "Madame Melba, is it the art or the applause that appeals to you most?"

Melba was angry. "After his long silence the question was positively extraordinary," she said later.

Rhodes turned away, mumbling he'd been wrong. Then, his hand up to his mouth, he said in a loud whisper, "I apologize. After all, it's the power we like — yes, the power."

Melba never forgot his words.

One of her great friends was Alfred de Rothschild, who loved opera but often fell asleep during a performance and began to snore in a different key. Sometimes Alfred would call up Melba. He'd heard that she was giving a party tonight, he was sending her something — fruit or wine or orchids from his hothouses, or an immense chocolate cake made by his celebrated chef. Colson reports that Alfred de Rothschild had the engaging habit of inviting his lady friends to lunch at the dignified Rothschild offices in the City and slipping a hundred-pound note in the folds of their napkins. He was a generous man.

Alfred was perhaps more fond of prima donnas than of opera. He had been a friend of Patti's and helped her to

invest her considerable earnings, and afterwards he became
a great friend of Melba's and gave her financial advice. She
impressed him with her excellent business sense. Famous
singers refused to accept a fee when they sang in his house,
which gave Alfred de Rothschild a feeling of special pride.
They knew that he would later send them a present that
was worth much more than their fee.

Melba complained that staying with Alfred de Rothschild
at Halton was "extremely luxurious and extremely strenuous." After teatime the guests would be taken in little pony
carriages to see "Alfred's little circus," his collection of
animals from all parts of the world. Melba noticed that the
animals loved their master, "possibly because his pockets
were always full of sugar and apples and carrots."

"The Edwardians were individualists," Melba wrote.
"They had a character and a personality of their own, and
they let you know it. . . . Nowadays people are made after
a pattern — dressing alike, talking alike, walking alike, and
even thinking alike."

Melba wrote this in 1925. Things, it seems, were almost as
bad then as now.

When Melba went to Dublin in the summer of 1900, to
sing at a charity concert of the Royal University Hall, she
spent a few days in the "less respectable" parts of the city
looking for bargains. She was accompanied by Lord Coventry, a fellow antique connoisseur. Both were well known
locally, and their appearance made the prices of old china
and grandfather clocks go up automatically. The day before
Melba's concert, they decided to put on old clothes and dis-

pense with the viceregal carriage which they had been using.

They set out on foot, called a jaunting car, told the driver to go to a certain address, and leaned back, congratulating themselves on their clever idea, and dreaming of all sorts of bargains.

Then the driver, a cheery, red-faced fellow, looked over his shoulder.

"Fine afternoon, M'Lord," he said.

Lord Coventry glanced uneasily at Melba.

The driver turned around again and said, "That's a grand concert you'll be givin' tomorrow, Madam." Melba thanked him for the compliment, somewhat unenthusiastically. The ride ended with the driver asking Melba for a couple of free passes. When they entered a dark store, Lord Coventry was hopeful again.

"It's difficult enough to see the *bibelots,* let alone the customers," he said.

The proprietor advanced toward them in the dimness and said, "Well, Your Lordship, I'm glad you've brought Madame Melba too."

Then they gave up. When they returned to the Lodge where they were both staying as guests of Lord Cadogan, they couldn't remember the password and were stopped by a sentry — the only person in Dublin who did not know who they were. They had to wait a long time there until they were rescued by an aide-de-camp.

Melba calls the short and happy reign of King Edward VII "an immense week-end party in which everybody was intent on getting the most out of life." After the severe strain of Queen Victoria's last years "everybody was getting more youthful." The caricatures of the young men in *Punch* who behaved strangely gave way to cartoons of smoking women and "modern" girls. No longer was the same importance attached to fine points of social etiquette. "There were riotous house parties in which everybody seemed to live in a permanent state of high spirits."

It was an age of extreme extravaganza. Melba liked the comforts of wealth without being impressed by riches, and she loved the great balls at Devonshire House, where "the staircases were massed with orchids, the stream of people glided up and down like a glistening snake and the great families of Europe were gathered together in an immense procession of magnificence — Bourbons, Marlboroughs, Romanoffs, Rothschilds."

It was a splendid age of lovely women and lavish men. At a party which Hector Baltazzi, a rich man, gave after winning the Derby, each of the guests found a pearl in his soup plate. The flowers alone cost over ten thousand dollars. Melba went to parties that were "Arabian nights." It was not unusual to spend fifty thousand dollars on a big party, and thousands of pounds on a wager. Melba once had lunch with her friend Hwfa-Williams and two other men on a wet day. After lunch Hwfa-Williams bet three thousand pounds, then fifteen thousand dollars, on which of two drops of water would first reach the bottom of the windowpane.

"These Edwardians," writes the ubiquitous Mr. Colson, "were gay, carefree, charming people. They only asked to be amused at all costs, and regardless of cost. Then men raced, shot, gambled, made love; and the women raced, danced, dressed, gambled, patronized suitable charities, and were made love to. The last distraction was then, as now, the most popular. . . ."

Melba, never a puritan, enjoyed the story told her by a certain great lady of her acquaintance, who once showed her a wonderful pearl necklace.

"What lovely pearls, dear," Melba said. "If they were mine I would be afraid of losing them. Don't they keep you awake at night?"

"Not now," the lady said. "They did — before I owned them."

Ladies who had divorced their husband were looked at askance. If their husbands divorced them, "they ceased to exist."

It was a gay time. In the morning the men would walk in frock coats and silk hats, and the women would drive in the park in carriages with coachmen and footmen with powdered hair. Sunday was still a big day in London. After church, people would walk in Hyde Park, the women in long dresses and large picture hats. Young men hoped to be asked to somebody's house for lunch. (They might be asked by Melba who always had a weakness for good-looking young men.) Or they would go to the Carlton or to Prince's. In the afternoon people would go to musical parties. On Sunday evening the happy few who had been invited would drive down to Lady de Grey's Coombe Court, where Lady de Grey "held court." Royalty would be there, prima donnas, famous composers. Melba might even volunteer to sing.

Yes — it was a wonderful time, and Melba was its uncrowned queen.

※ 8 ※

Melodrama in Milan

MELBA, having already conquered Brussels and the Paris Opéra, was now the uncrowned Queen of Covent Garden and had also signed a contract with the Metropolitan Opera House in New York. But before going to America she decided she would have to succeed at Milan's La Scala. Then, as the prima donna *assoluta* of London, Paris, Brussels *and* Milan, she could not fail to take New York by storm.

No great prima donna whose repertory consists to a large extent of the great coloratura parts in Italian opera feels she has really arrived unless she has made her success in Italy's greatest opera house, one of the world's great musical theaters — the Teatro alla Scala in Milan.

Italy is the birthplace of opera in the modern sense of the word. It all began around 1590 in Florence in the *Camerata,* a group of artists, musicians and scholars founded by Conte del Bardi, who called music *"la forza di movere l'affetti,"* "the force to move the feelings." The first opera, Jacopo Peri's *Dafne,* was performed in 1597 in the palace of Jacopo

Corsi, a local aristocrat. There were no sets and no curtains in the Renaissance hall. But the performance made history.

After Peri came Giulio Caccini and Claudio Monteverdi of Cremona, a widely unrecognized genius, who reformed the orchestra and created *Orfeo*, the first music drama, in which he developed the synthesis of word and tone, of drama and music. Pergolesi, Puccini, Paisiello, Cimarosa carried on in the great tradition, and then came Rossini, Donizetti, Bellini, Verdi and Puccini.

Italy is also the birthplace of *bel canto*, that great style of singing, and for centuries Italian singing was synonymous with great singing. The original prima donna was Italian, as the name implies. Frederick the Great once said he would rather have an aria neighed by his horse than sung by a German prima donna.

By the time Nellie Melba appeared, the hegemony of the great Italian voices was no longer universal. Italy still produced the best tenors and some excellent baritones, but few great women singers. Melba was Australian, Nilsson Swedish, Calvé French, Eames and Nordica American, Sembrich Polish, Albani Canadian, Mary Garden Scottish, Destinn Bohemian; Milka Ternina, Elena Gerhardt, Lilli Lehmann and Schumann-Heink were German. It was a bitter pill for the *aficionados* of Italy, where grand opera is almost a national religion and La Scala a national shrine, "the first opera house on earth." In the opinion of the people of Vienna or London or New York, however, the same distinction goes to their respective opera houses.

"There is no second opera house in the world," Toscanini once told a friend of mine. "There are only first houses."

The Maestro, incidentally, left no doubt that he considered La Scala the world's first opera house.

Melba's debut at La Scala was as melodramatic as an early Verdi opera. Even before she arrived in Milan, the city's operatic cliques had declared open warfare on her for committing the unpardonable sin of making her success elsewhere before coming to Milan. The usual whispering campaigns were started by jealous competitors. There has always been more intrigue in the small, emotionally supercharged world of opera than at the court of the Borgias.

At the popular artists' hangouts around the Piazza alla Scala it was whispered that Melba's voice was "plain as a steam whistle." She "never learned to sing." She was "ordinary looking." Some said she had no love life and others said she had too much. The erotic exploits of a prima donna fascinate her audience as much as her staccato runs. Some said that Melba's debut at La Scala would be a sensational fiasco. Others said she should have stayed away altogether. There was no need for an Australian nightingale. A few weeks ago Patti had given a series of triumphal performances. On February 9 Verdi himself had appeared at the *première* of *Falstaff*. There had been wild ovations for the old genius. The *aficionados* had expended their last reserves of enthusiasm. Everybody said that Melba had a nerve to attempt her debut as Lucia, one of the most difficult parts!

As the time of the performance approached, the opposition took on such proportions that the Italian impresario advised

Melba's manager that she had better give up the idea of singing at La Scala. He suggested she make her Italian debut in Venice, where the emotional climate would be less hostile.

Melba shook her head. No, she was going to Milan. "I love a good fight," she said. She was a gambler. The year before she had signed a contract with the Metropolitan. On August 27, 1892, the house burned down. Henry Abbey and Maurice Grau, the managers, told her she would be legally justified in demanding her whole salary. She told them she hadn't sung and didn't expect to get paid.

It was a noble gesture, but she was in trouble. She had just two hundred pounds in the bank and no prospect of an immediate engagement. She had been told that Grau was on a holiday in Nice and she went there. "I went with two maids instead of one, and took the best possible rooms in the best possible hotel. What would have happened but for a stroke of luck, I don't know. Probably I should have languished in a debtors' prison."

Perhaps she helped her luck a little. She met Grau, who asked her whether she would like to sing in Nice that season. Melba said, "Oh, well, I wouldn't mind," but she thought that all artists had already been engaged.

"I'm sure they will be delighted," Grau said. "I can get you four thousand francs a night."

"I wouldn't dream of singing for less than five thousand," Melba said indignantly.

She got the money. "I often think it was five thousand francs' worth of bluff," she told Hazelton-Cochrane many years later.

Milan was another calculated risk, and she regretted it bitterly. When she arrived there in March, 1893, several letters "in a strange, spidery handwriting" were handed to her as she entered her hotel. The anonymous letters contained specific threats: Melba would be poisoned; the elevator in her hotel would crash to the floor; if she dared venture out into the street "a stiletto would be waiting for her on more than one dark corner."

It was all in the best melodramatic tradition of the Italian *verismo,* where everybody lives, loves and perishes with great gusto, but it was not agreeable for a young, rather inexperienced singer who faces the nerve-racking ordeal of singing, in a new place, a very difficult part — and before one of the world's most difficult audiences. It was getting so bad that the management asked the police to look after Melba. She felt terribly lost. As a rule, prominent local musicians would come to pay their respects to a visiting prima donna, but in Milan only one braved the trend and came to see her. He was Arrigo Boito, the composer and librettist of Verdi's *Otello* and *Falstaff,* and he offered her "the tribute of his admiration."

For the first time in her life, Melba's "pluck" deserted her. She would touch no food until her faithful secretary, Miss Louie Mason, had tasted it. She refused to leave the hotel. She wouldn't go near the elevator. More anonymous letters arrived, but no one at the hotel seemed to remember who had delivered them. It was real Maffia stuff and Melba's nerves cracked. The day before the performance she told Miss Mason she was going to leave.

"Even if I come through alive, I couldn't give my best under the circumstances."

Miss Mason resolutely shook her head. "You can't quit, Nellie. It wouldn't be like you. You've got to stay and face the music."

"I don't mind the music," Melba said miserably. "It's these terrible letters."

They argued. Miss Mason, "whose like I have never since found in the whole world," didn't give in. If it hadn't been for her resolute secretary, Melba might have packed her bags and run away, which would have been fatal for her career, for she would never have completely recovered from her moment of weakness.

And so the next evening a terrified prima donna walked down the stairway of the hotel, shunning the dangerous elevator, and was driven under police escort to the theater. Sinister shadows seemed to be lurking everywhere, particularly in Melba's imagination.

In *Lucia di Lammermoor* the heroine appears only twenty minutes after the curtain has gone up. Melba never forgot those twenty minutes; it must have been a perfect nightmare, and even many years later she often talked about it to her friends. She was standing behind the wings, listening to the harp playing Lucia's solo, her heart throbbing, her hand clutching Louie Mason's, wondering "whether these notes should prove to be the last I sung." Melba liked to project the serene impression of a sober, businesslike artist, but the truth was that she was a melodramatic, highly impressionable prima-donna-at-heart.

Her cue came, and she walked out on stage. She looked around the auditorium, which usually was not her custom. It seemed to her that the audience had turned away from her; she thought she "could only see their backs."

"So startling was this that I almost forgot the phrase I was singing," she writes.

She noticed that some people turned to their neighbors and kept talking, demonstratively ignoring the stage. She saw the audience "turning gradually in my direction, which my quickened imagination distorted into something ominous." Later she found out that many seats in the boxes of La Scala don't face the stage and their occupants are always half-turned away. That gave her the impression that the box-holders literally "turned their backs" on her "simply because they were determined not to listen to my singing."

Much of the drama took place only in Melba's mind. But there was an eerie, hostile silence among the three thousand people in the vast auditorium. And from the gallery came a few hissing sounds.

It is moments like this which make or break a prima donna. *"C'est presque toujours avec son sang et ses nerfs que l'on remporte de pareilles victoires,"* Victor Maurel, the great baritone, who was Verdi's original Iago and Falstaff, wrote later to Melba.

Melba had the *sang-froid* and the steady nerves. She closed her eyes for a moment, and took a deep (and invisible) breath, lest the three thousand experts might criticize her breath control.

"How I ever sang my initial *récitatif* I do not know to this day," she later said. It was a terrible ordeal, but a brief one.

Doonside, Richmond, Melbourne, where Helen Porter Mitchell was born.

Nellie Melba's bedroom at her home in Paris: luxury, autographed pictures on the walls, and two telephones.

David Mitchell, Melba's father —
"somebody whom one loves very
much."

With Madame Mathilde Marchesi,
"the greatest teacher of them all."

Melba with her only son,
George Armstrong.

"My song-bird has flown again." Car-
toon in Australian newspapers afte
Madame Melba had gone back t
Europe in 1903.

"Singing for the Gramophone was no rest cure," Melba said in 1910. She got
fifty thousand dollars for one week of recording.

"Rosina"

"Ophelia"

"Violetta"

"Mimi"

"Marguérite"

"Manon"

"Juliette"

"Aïda"

The "Queen of Song" returns to her native city, Melbourne, in September 1902.

"Home, Sweet Home." Back to Lilydale, Australia, 1902.

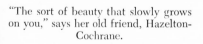

"The sort of beauty that slowly grows on you," says her old friend, Hazelton-Cochrane.

"Nellie was a queenly woman."

After the aria wild shouts of *"Brava! Brava!"* echoed all over the theater. By the time she was halfway through the Mad Scene she had the entire audience under her magic spell. They couldn't resist the seductive timbre of Melba's voice, her pure intonation, her finished art of modulation. After the Mad Scene the ovation lasted for over ten minutes. And when the curtain fell at last, and she was back in her dressing room, worn-out but happy, she thanked God — and Louie, "who made me stay to face the music."

The next morning Aldo Noseda, the critic of the *Corriere della Sera*, wrote about Melba's true, genuine success that almost no one had expected. "The people who went to La Scala last night felt sure they were to mingle in the holocaust of the diva Melba and the complete annihilation of *Lucia*." When they realized that "their anticipations had melted away in the light of reality, they seemed as stupid as an elephant before a corkscrew. . . . Madame Melba won a great battle yesterday. Many are the stars who have fallen on the stage of La Scala. . . . Who else now, may we ask, can sing like Melba?"

❦ 9 ❦

Life Is a Fantastic Joke

HERMAN BEMBERG was one of Melba's closest friends. He is almost forgotten today as a composer but was very fashionable at her time. Massenet once paid Bemberg a serious compliment: "It's a good thing for us composers that Bemberg was born rich. He doesn't *have* to compose."

Bemberg was the son of a wealthy Argentine banker and a French mother who was a gifted amateur singer. Young Bemberg showed great musical talent, played the piano very well, worked with Bizet and Henri Maréchal, and at the Paris Conservatoire studied composition with Gounod and Massenet. Once he was awarded the Rossini Prize for composition. His opera *Elaine* (which he dedicated to his friends Nellie Melba and Jean de Reszke) was quite popular in France and England, where Melba, Jean de Reszke and Pol Plançon appeared in the *première* in 1892 at Covent Garden but had no success two years later in New York with the same cast. After the second performance at the Met, *Elaine* was withdrawn. Bemberg's *Le Baiser de Suzon* was a failure despite its clever book by Jules Barbier, who wrote the books for Gounod's *Faust* and *Roméo et Juliette* and for Offenbach's *Tales of Hoffmann.*

Barbier adored Melba. "*Que célébrer en vous?*" he once wrote her. "*La beauté, la voix, l'âme? Toutes les trois ensemble en adorant la femme.*" Bemberg's *Salome* preceded, but did not survive, Strauss's *Salome.* In France, Bemberg is remembered for some charming songs which Melba would often sing at concerts and parties, sometimes accompanied by the composer on the piano.

Bemberg was a Parisian Oscar Wilde — handsome, witty, charming. He had plenty of money — too much for his own good, some people said. His parents had a beautiful house in the Avenue de Bois de Boulogne. Bemberg was the companion of all great prima donnas of his time, and also one of their sternest critics. He once told Calvé after a Covent Garden performance as Carmen — her most celebrated part — "I wish, Emma, that I could hear you sing Carmen again."

"But I sang tonight and you were there!"

"I said, I wish I could hear you *sing* Carmen again," Bemberg said. Madame Calvé didn't speak to him for the rest of the evening.

Bemberg was popular with society in Paris, which, Melba said, "is amused by brains rather than birth. . . . It was his brains that most appealed to my democratic Australian character, and his irresistible sense of humor." Bemberg treated life as an immense, fantastic joke. He was the perfect companion for Melba, who always loved fun.

She never forgot the day when she first met him. She was sitting in her salon in the Avenue Victor Hugo — it was

shortly after her Paris debut — when very slowly and softly
the door opened. She was going to get up and shut it when
a magnificent bouquet of orchids was pushed through the
crack. Orchids didn't grow on trees, even for prima donnas.
Melba, always a horticultural enthusiast, was delighted.

"*Qui êtes vous?*" she cried.

The door was opened a little wider. "A very handsome
young man" advanced toward her, got down on his knees
and said, "Only Bemberg."

It was the perfect entrance for the lifelong French farce
which she and Bemberg were to play. Melba began to laugh
and told Bemberg to stay for lunch. He was an amusing
guest.

"It was noon," she remembers, "and I went on laughing
the whole afternoon and most of the evening until midnight"
— when Bemberg finally took his leave. For a first visit, he
had stayed a little long; but Melba didn't mind. She always
had a good time when Bemberg was around.

Bemberg dressed in the style of a Frenchman, and sometimes created astonishment among his sartorially impeccable
friends in London. When Melba took a house on the Thames
for the summer and invited him down, "and don't bother to
bring town clothes," Bemberg appeared in a glaring blazer
and ready-made flannel trousers which split after he had
worn them a few hours, but he was not in the least concerned about that. Like many Frenchmen of his era he intensely disliked sports. Once he accompanied Melba to
Wimbledon but couldn't stand it, and spent the rest of the
afternoon sulking in his car. He said he was sick and tired
of seeing "nothing but tennis balls."

During the performances of his opera *Elaine* at Covent Garden Bemberg regarded Melba's dressing room as his personal domain and would leave his hat and coat there. It was a small, crowded room, but Melba suffered in silence for a long time. Then, during the third performance, she found his top hat, coat and umbrella on the only chair in her room, and decided to teach Bemberg a lesson. She cut his hat almost completely around the brim, covered its inside with black grease paint, cut his umbrella so it would fall to pieces when it was opened, and as a finishing touch placed two raw eggs in the pockets of Bemberg's overcoat.

At the end of the performance the composer came for his things, telling Melba hastily that Lady de Grey and some very important people were waiting for him. Lady de Grey later said that Bemberg arrived with a black face, and when he took off his hat it fell down at her feet. "Nobody enjoyed my little prank more than Bemberg himself," Melba writes with her usual self-deception. Perhaps Bemberg had pretended to be amused but he was only waiting for his chance to pay her back.

The chance came on April Fools' Day — always a major holiday in Bemberg's private calendar. In the afternoon a huge box was delivered for Melba. She opened it happily. There was a piercing noise; a large turkey pushed out its head and bit her finger. Soon another box arrived. This time Melba was more cautious. She asked the Baron de Saint-Imand, who had come for a visit, to open the box. The Baron, a gallant, pompous, old-fashioned nobleman, was glad to oblige. He opened the lid and a large rabbit jumped out, "regarding the Baron with quivering nostrils." A card fell out of the box which turned out to be the card of Baron de Saint Imand.

"Ma carte! C'est une infamie!" the worthy nobleman shouted. In vain Melba tried to appease him. He was insulted, and vanished "in a cloud of indignation."

That night Melba had Lady de Grey for dinner with Bemberg and his friend, Comte Charles de Mornay, who had contributed his share of high jinks by sending Melba two dozen letters in Russian, Spanish, English, French, German and Chinese, all bearing mythical elaborate crests on very cheap notepaper and containing marriage proposals from legendary noblemen, including one Charles de Mornay. As the four of them sat down for dinner, the maid came in looking confounded.

"The cakes, Madame — they keep arriving. I've paid for them, because the bill was always attached, but we have nineteen now. What shall we do with all the cakes?"

Melba glared at Bemberg, who pretended to study the ceiling.

"Put them anywhere," she said to the maid, as if she were getting dozens of cakes every day. "On the floor, in the cupboards. . . . And if more should arrive, don't bother to pay for them."

A few minutes later the maid came in again.

"The cakes, Madame. They still keep arriving. There is no more room on the floor. What shall we do?"

Melba noticed that Bemberg was watching her with great interest. She played her part well.

"Give them to the concierge. Give them to all concierges in the street. There are plenty of concierges in Paris."

Later in the evening, when they went to the theater, the usherette at her box was almost in tears. Two crates of oranges had been delivered at the box. What should she do with them?

"Take them home and eat them," Melba said.

The next day she received payment for the money she had spent on the cakes. Payment was made in "a huge sticky mass of one-centime stamps, so large that I could have papered my bathroom with it."

Melba had her revenge on next year's April Fools' Day. It was then the custom in Paris, "where baths are not such common luxuries as in England or America, for those in need of a bath to hire it." Melba gave orders that a large bathtub be sent to Bemberg once every quarter of an hour beginning exactly at eight o'clock in the morning, until noon. At that time a *professeur de mémoire*, "a gentleman of exceedingly determined disposition," called upon Bemberg, at Melba's orders, to teach Bemberg a first memory lesson.

Poor Bemberg, deluged with bathtubs, was visibly distraught. He swore he had never wanted lessons. The *professeur* protested grimly: Why, Monsieur Bemberg had even forgotten that he himself had sent for a teacher? That only showed how much he needed him! . . . Bemberg arrived in the afternoon at Melba's house, "almost in tears, absolutely disgusted." And she had the last laugh; he had to pay for the baths, and for the professor.

Quite obviously, Melba's idea of a joke was not subtle. Hazelton-Cochrane says, "I'm not so sure about her sense of humor. I thought she had only a sense of fun." Beverly

Nichols remembers that "a man slipping on an orange gave Melba more pleasure than a sparkling witticism." When a visitor who had brought his silk hat into her drawing room — a fine Victorian touch, reminding the gentleman that he was there solely by permission of the lady and must be ready to leave at once — by mistake sat down on it, she was very much amused. And she adored Charlie Chaplin. He once took her to dinner at the Raymond Hotel in Pasadena, pretended to have forgotten his wallet, and paid the bill with a heap of silver dollars that he collected out of all his pockets, performing one of his early slapstick pantomimes. Melba claims that Chaplin offered her a small part in one of his pictures, but perhaps it is just as well that she never did it. It is hard to imagine her as a movie star.

A worthy member of Melba's fun-loving crowd was Francesco Paolo Tosti, the popular composer of light melodious pieces — "Mattinata," "Serenata," "Addio" — still played in France by café and shipboard orchestras. Tosti was an enthusiastic *bon vivant* and originator of funny stories. Melba had met him at Lady Randolph Churchill's in London. They became friends, and Tosti studied several operatic parts with Melba, particularly her Aïda and Desdemona in *Otello*. He was a welcome visitor in her home in Paris. Once when he had not showed up for some time Melba went to his house. Madame Tosti was in tears: Ah, Madame Melba must not go up. Poor Tosti had lost his front teeth! He wished to see no one, *absolument* no one. *Ah, c'est épouvantable!* But it would have taken more than Madame Tosti to keep Melba from going up. She found the great *boulevardier* visibly depressed, looking very unlike his usual cheerful self minus his front teeth. She told him to go to the dentist and have "some nice false ones" made.

Tosti shook his head resolutely.

"I can't. That would give me the fever." He made Melba think of the many Frenchmen who are afraid to drink water because "water makes frogs in your stomach."

Tosti once nearly caused Melba and Caruso to disgrace themselves when they appeared in *La Bohème* at Covent Garden. He sat in the front row, looking extremely dignified in full evening dress. (He had gone to the dentist after all for some nice false ones.) In the second act Caruso suddenly whispered to Melba, "For heaven's sake, look at Tosti!"

Melba did, and "only by exercising an almost superhuman self-control" was able to keep a straight face. Tosti had attached to his mouth a white handkerchief so that it looked like a long, ludicrous moustache, Colonel Blimp style. He puffed out his cheeks and stared at Melba and Caruso with great goggle eyes, "an expression of the utmost solemnity on his face."

Tosti often accompanied Melba on her trips. One night in Venice, after a strenuous season in Milan, they had dinner together. It was a wonderful night, "with the moonlight silvering the roofs of the palaces," and Melba and Tosti decided to go out on the Canale Grande and give a little concert. It was the sort of night, Melba says, that would move even the dullest soul to "some sort of poetry."

A harmonium was lowered into a gondola and Ambroggio, the gondolier, pushed off the steps of the hotel. In the middle of the canal the gondola stopped and Melba began to sing. She sang only Tosti songs, such as "Mattinata" and "Serenata," and the composer accompanied her. "Never shall I forget the marvelous feeling I had as my voice echoed over the water in that city of dreams."

In no time gondolas drifted towards them from all sides out of dark canals, their lanterns faintly gleaming. (That was before the romantic atmosphere of Venice was ruined by the noise of many outboard motors). After the song, people cried "Brava, Melba!" and "Bravo, Tosti!"

They were going up the canal. Melba sang another song, and the chain of gondolas followed. Melba thought that "half of Venice" was listening. Windows were opened in the mysterious, old palazzi, and people stood in dark streets and waved at her, and after each song there was wild applause. Melba sang her way through the canals, a Pied Piper of *bel canto,* until she returned to her hotel at midnight, exhausted but happy.

Melba does not mention another Venetian *al fresco* performance which was less successful. She had been asked to sing in an open-air concert on the Grand Canal for some charity. Wearing a magnificent ermine cape, she floated off from the Grand Hotel on a large raft which had been hired for the occasion. The gondolier had advised her to launch the raft properly and to sing on the Guidecca. But Melba knew better. She would anchor just outside the church of Santa Maria della Salute, the most prominent location in Venice.

Unfortunately she was just beside the landing stage of the *vaporetti.* In her *Memoirs,* Olga Lynn describes the commotion:

> . . . Instead of the voice of the divine Melba all we heard was a dreadful cacophony of hoots and bells and gongs, as

Venice went about its noisy every-night life. Even when the gondola of Melba's friend, Lady Susan Birch, caught fire from its Chinese lanterns, the splendid ermine-wrapped figure could still be seen (although not heard!) to sing in spite of the fact that all attention was now concentrated on Lady Susan's catastrophe.

Melba, with her wonderful ability for deceiving herself, had not noticed that for once she had not been the center of attraction. She discovered the awful truth only when she reached her hotel and found her Cockney maid sitting there, although she was supposed to have stayed at the concert until the end.

"Why didn't you stay out there?" Melba wanted to know.

"I couldn't 'ear a word," said the maid tersely, "so I came 'ome."

When Melba and Tosti happened to be together at Henley, Tosti suggested that they try their successful Venetian experiment again, this time with the English setting of the Thames.

"I was a little doubtful for I knew the English temperament and Tosti didn't," Melba remembers.

It was a glorious night in June. The river was covered with small boats. They went out in two punts tied together, with a harmonium in one of them. Again Melba sang, enjoying herself. The last note died away. There was silence. Not a cheer, not a single burst of applause. The apathy was positively chilling.

"What's the matter with them?" Melba whispered. "Am I singing badly?"

"*Cara* Melba," Tosti said, "you've never sung more divinely."

They drifted to another part of the river and tried another song. No one followed them. There was utter silence again. Afterwards they gave up and punted home.

A few days later a friend asked Melba, "Were you singing on the Thames the other night?"

"Yes."

"I knew it! I was there. The people around us were absolutely entranced."

Melba never again gave a free concert on the Thames. The joke had been on her, and she didn't like it. The gift of laughing at oneself is rarely the outstanding trait of a great prima donna.

Melba met Oscar Wilde one evening at Lady de Grey's house in Paris. She came into the salon and there was "a large, heavy-jowled man of a sallow and unhealthy appearance, clad in a frock coat, with a large bunch of violets in his buttonhole." Melba soon learned that while Wilde was talking, the rest were supposed to be silent. No one minded, though. "One felt it would be almost an impertinence to interrupt," Melba writes. She was fascinated by Wilde. "We do not seem to breed that type in Australia." But behind the brilliant wit of the reconteur she saw some strange, macabre side which always made her a little uneasy when she was alone with him. She was a sensitive woman.

Wilde often came to Melba's house. Brilliant men really enjoyed Melba's company. She was amusing, a good listener, and had a clever way of drawing them out. Wilde never bothered to have himself announced but Melba always knew that he had been there. There would be a heap of cigarette butts in the fireplace. Wilde had his pockets stuffed with cigarette cases. Once Melba counted six of them, in gold, silver and leather. He would light a cigarette, take two nervous puffs, throw it away, and light another a minute later.

He admired Melba. "Ah, Madame Melba," he said once. "I am the Lord of Language, and you are the Queen of Song. I suppose I shall have to write you a sonnet." He never wrote it, though; Melba suspected, quite rightly, that Wilde "used to reserve his best stories for the public."

Oscar Wilde once told Melba something that bothered her for years afterwards. "I was telling my little sons stories last night," he said. "I told them of little boys who were naughty and made their mothers cry, and what dreadful things would happen to them unless they became better, and do you know what one of them answered? He asked me what punishment could be reserved for naughty papas who did not come home till the early morning and made mother cry far more?"

Melba met Wilde for the last time three years after he had been released from prison. She was walking in Paris. Suddenly she saw a shabby man, his collar turned up to his neck, a hunted look in his eyes. She didn't recognize him and wanted to pass.

He stopped. "Madame Melba — don't you know who I am?"

She stared at him.

"I'm Oscar Wilde," he said. "And I'm going to do a terrible thing. I'm going to ask you for money."

"I took all I had from my purse, about ten louis, and he quickly took it, almost snatched it, muttered a word of thanks and was gone. I never saw him again."

❧ 10 ❧

A Tear in Her Voice

ONE EVENING in the spring of 1890 Melba met Louis-Robert-Philippe, Duc d'Orléans, in the house of a mutual friend in Paris. They fell in love at first sight, violently.

Melba was thirty-one then, a beautiful woman with "an aristocratic charm," very gay, capricious and vivacious. She was sitting on top of the world, the young prima donna of the Brussels Monnaie Théâtre and of the Paris Opéra. She was getting ready for her second debut in London under the auspices of Lady de Grey. For the first time in her life she had almost everything a woman wants: success, her own money, beautiful clothes, and the admiration of attractive men. And now she had love too.

"Melba was no Puritan," writes Colson. "She was young and liked the company of her men friends. People began to talk, as people will always talk when a young and pretty woman who is a celebrated operatic star, separated from her husband, is in question."

Of the many attractive men Melba had met Philippe

d'Orléans was certainly the most attractive. He had been born in Twickenham, England, in 1869, the eldest son of the Comte de Paris. He was ten years younger than Melba, but she was always attracted by younger men, and the Duc was handsome and brilliant. History had surrounded him with a romantic glow. He was the Pretender to the throne of France; he came from one of the noblest French families. In her romantic imagination Melba could see him sitting on his throne, a more exciting king than she had ever met in grand opera. He could have walked straight out of *Lohengrin,* armor and all. Prince Charming with a touch of d'Artagnan and the Count of Monte Cristo all rolled into one . . . He would have been a nobler king than some of the real ones she knew.

The Duc was devoted to her. There had been other men in her life, sometimes for a very short time. Melba never makes mention of any of them in her autobiography. This was not the era of nauseating public confessions. The Edwardian prima donna did not commercialize her intimate life and kept her bedroom memories to herself, God bless her. In her late years, when old age and the touch of resignation which is sometimes confused with wisdom had mellowed Melba's outlook on the joys and sorrows of life, she would discourage curiosity even among her closest friends. She was not a cold woman but she had discipline.

"Nellie handled her private life with the poise of a great lady," one of her oldest friends says. "We would often die with curiosity but no one would have dared ask her a question. She had a wonderful way of getting rid of people when she expected company that we were not supposed to know of. She would say, 'What are you doing tonight?' which was our exit cue. Dear Nellie was a gentlewoman."

Another friend told me: "I once had a terrible row with Nellie on the Riviera. She had been seen constantly with a man there. People talked and I opened my mouth. I told her she was still married though she certainly had no husband. Nellie got mad and gave me a piece of her mind, and she gave it to me straight. When she got mad even with her best friends, she would let them have it! Afterwards I never said anything again. Melba simply wasn't the sort of woman who talks interminably about her romantic days when she gets older. She didn't have to escape into the world of her youth, because her entire life was full and rich. She had, of course, her moods of nostalgia and moments of depression, but who hasn't? At any rate, Melba kept them to herself."

And another: "Melba never talked about the men in her life but we knew when she was getting involved. In those times her voice had an incandescence and she would sing with much deeper feeling. She had, as the French say, 'a tear in her voice.' On such an evening people would go home after a Melba performance with great warmth in their hearts though they couldn't explain what had been different. It was simple: Melba was in love, and she made everybody fall a little in love with her. Of course, all of us knew about the Duc d'Orléans and none of us talked about him. He was the only man in her life who was really important. I am sure she never forgot the Duc. It was *La Traviata* all over again — the beautiful woman who loses the man she loves because his family steps in. A corny story, and one of Melba's most famous parts — on and off stage."

During that happy spring of 1890, Melba and the Duc were inseparable. "What attracted the Duke in Melba was her *joie de vivre*, boyishness, overflowing health, and her indifference to the conventions which had hemmed him in ever since he was born," writes Colson. "And to her this fascinating Prince Charming seemed a being from another world."

Melba had grown up in a young country without rigid conventions. She was all her life supremely indifferent to other people's opinions of herself. She was in love and she was being loved, and she didn't give a damn about what people were saying. She was seen with the Duc everywhere in Paris and London. Queen Victoria was mostly now in retirement, and Prince Edward was beginning to be the influence on art and morals. But, naturally, the scandalmongers and gossip writers got busy; a great diva's private life is not entirely her own. Both her admirers and her detractors are curious about her romantic moments; some great prima donnas are now better remembered for their scandals than for their coloraturas. People are always most interested in things that don't concern them.

It got so bad that Melba and the Duc decided to disappear for a while. They traveled all over Europe and finally showed up in Vienna, which was then the capital of a great empire and one of the most charming and most musical cities in Europe, full of that exhilarating gaiety and wine-women-and-song atmosphere that has survived to this day only in the Viennese operetta.

It must have been a wonderful time for music lovers. Brahms and Bruckner were living in Vienna. Johann Strauss was the city's beloved "waltz king." The Court Opera, which Melba had long wanted to hear, was under the great Hans Richter who had worked with Richard Wagner in Bayreuth. There was music in the air wherever you went.

Vienna was a perfect city for people who loved life and were in love. Melba and her Duc went riding in the Vienna Woods or walking where, not so long ago, Mozart, Beethoven and Schubert had walked. They danced at the Prater and heard Johann Strauss perform his waltzes at the Volksgarten. The Duc d'Orléans was incognito, but no one in Vienna cared, anyway. The Viennese were used to glamorous romances and traditionally discreet about them. Their own Hapsburg archdukes were always involved with pretty prima ballerinas and great ladies of local society in *liaisons dangereuses*. Risqué stories about the goings-on in the *chambres separées* of the Hotel Sacher are still — two generations later — the favorite topics of some Viennese weekly papers and lending-library best sellers. The unforgotten archduke who late one night came down the stairway at Sacher's wearing absolutely nothing except his shoes, saber and shako is one of the more innocuous characters of those very, very gay nineties in Vienna.

Melba and the Duc spent their evenings at the Hofoper, and there fate caught up with them in the person of the celebrated Belgian tenor Ernest Marie van Dyck (whom Sir Thomas Beecham later called "the best third-act Tristan,"

giving van Dyck high notes for musicality, power and endurance). Van Dyck knew Melba from Brussels. During a
performance of *Lohengrin* in Vienna, this tenor happened to
stand behind the curtain, at the end of the first intermission,
looking through a small hole into the auditorium. He was
surprised to see Nellie Melba. He was even more surprised
to see the elegant man next to Melba in the box: The Duc
d'Orléans . . . here in Vienna, incognito, with Madame
Melba. *Oh là là!*

Van Dyck was endowed with the opera singer's addiction
to gossip. He sensed a real sensation and called a local news-
paperman who happened to be backstage.

"I've got quite a story for you." He drew him to the curtain. "Look at the fourth parterre box on the left side, and
tell me the names of the couple."

The journalist shook his head. "Who are they?"

"She's Melba."

"Nellie Melba, the coloratura?"

"Exactly. And the man with her is the Pretender to the
French throne."

After the performance, sitting at a restaurant, the journalist met Madame Blanche Marchesi, the daughter of Melba's
teacher. Blanche was married and lived in Vienna at that
time. He told her about Melba and the Duc and said he'd
written a little story for tomorrow's *Wiener Tagblatt*.

Blanche Marchesi is said to have pleaded with the journalist to kill the juicy bit of gossip, but she may not have
pleaded too hard. The two ladies didn't exactly love one
another. Blanche — also a singer and in some ways more
gifted than Melba — was jealous of her mother's favorite

pupil. Blanche herself might have become one of her mother's most famous pupils; she was a very musical artist and a great interpreter of French *chansons* and German *Lieder*. Singing *Lieder* is perhaps the most difficult test of great singing; only artists who have voice and musicality, perception and style, can do it. Blanche Marchesi sang in English, French, German and Italian. An excellent stylist, on the same program she was able to sing a Scarlatti aria, a Schubert *Lied*, the Troubadour songs of Provence, and a couple of English Tudor songs. Unfortunately her talent and musicality were greater than the power and range of her voice. And she wanted to sing opera — for which she just didn't have enough voice. Melba had neither the musical intellect nor the accomplished taste of Blanche Marchesi, but she had a wonderful voice, perfect technique and a simple sense of drama — enough to make her a great prima donna. Blanche Marchesi would speak contemptuously of Melba's limitations, of "her lack of artistic subtlety," her utter inability to sing a simple German song; Madame Melba, in turn, would say "in that kindly, slightly patronizing way in which celebrated singers speak of each other," that poor Blanche was really so gifted — too bad that her voice didn't match her talent. If she would only realize that there were things that were just beyond her . . . Why did she want to sing Elsa in *Lohengrin*, and even Isolde, when she didn't have the voice?

At one time Blanche Marchesi claimed that she had been kept out of Covent Garden by "the cabals of the Melba clique," but as usual these accusations were vehemently denied by Melba's friends. There is little doubt, though, that Madame Marchesi must have been secretly delighted with the Viennese journalist who had found out about Melba and the Duc d'Orléans in Vienna.

It seems that Madame Marchesi "couldn't reach Melba that night" because she didn't know where Melba was staying. However, the next morning Melba is said to have visited Blanche, gay and radiant with happiness. Blanche was indignant; she had something of the strict morality of the French *petite bourgeoise*.

"You'd better pack up and leave at once," she said to Melba.

"Why?"

By way of an answer, Blanche handed her the *Wiener Tagblatt* with the little story in it.

"Oh," said Melba. That was all she said. She knew there was no point in arguing with Blanche Marchesi. She walked out of the room, and several hours later she and the Duc had left Vienna.

But bad news traveled fast, even in those leisurely days. The story reached Paris and London. Melba's absent husband was duly informed, "and once again tried to stir up trouble," Colson reports, harking back to the first time, after Melba's debut in Brussels, when her name had suddenly became famous all over Europe, and her husband suddenly showed up one afternoon at the apartment where she was having tea with the painter Wauters. There was a stormy scene, in front of four-year-old George. Armstrong threatened he would make life impossible for Melba. He said if she attempted to sing at the theater that night, he was going to make trouble for her. Melba went to her friends Dupont and Lapissida, the directors of the Monnaie, explained the situation, and asked them for help. She must have succeeded: there was no scene that night. A few days later, Armstrong left Brussels. Melba's friends assume that she made him an allowance for life on condition that he would leave her alone. She never mentioned her husband again to anyone. He later died in British Columbia.

"He sort of faded away," says Hazelton-Cochrane.

Melba and the Duc remained friends for years. When the Orléans family was banished from France, the two saw each other elsewhere. Once, when they were in Germany, Melba bet Philippe that she could get him across the French frontier and back without trouble. She hired a carriage, dressed up the Duc in the livery of a coachman, and he drove her to the border. The border guards were charmed by the great prima donna and paid no attention to her coachman. The couple had lunch in France and returned to Germany in the afternoon.

As time went on, they saw less of each other, but talk of their romance didn't die down and was largely responsible for much of the contemporary Melba legend and for the romantic halo that surrounds the prima donna. The great diva and the Pretender to the French throne "who were denied the happiness of a simple, married life" were a godsend to the Sunday supplements. THE DUKE AND THE DIVA — DON'T MISS NEXT WEEK'S INSTALLMENT! Women cried as bitterly while they read the unhappy Melba love story as they did during the last act of *La Traviata*. When Oscar Hammerstein tried to get Melba to join the cast of his new Manhattan Opera, "Madame Melba had no wish to come to the United States at all," writes Vincent Sheean. "Her romance with Philippe d'Orléans may have been partly responsible for her reluctance to revisit America." That was sixteen years after the wonderful evening when they had first met. Romantic legends never die.

Despite the predictions of the Sunday supplements, there never was a chance of marriage. Melba still had a husband, though she was separated from him; and even if she had been legally free she could not have become the wife of the Duc d'Orléans, who was bound by the rigid religious, political and social conventions of his position. He was, after all, *le Roi* to a small but very influential segment of the French nation. On November 5, 1896, he married — very properly — the Archduchess Maria Dorothea Amalia of Austria. There were no children. He died in 1926 — five years before Melba.

When Melba returned from Vienna to Paris, there was a tearful scene at Madame Marchesi's house. Melba's teacher, whom she loved and respected like a mother, argued strongly against Melba's emotional attachment. There were a lot of attractive men, she said to Nellie, but there was only one career and Nellie would be foolish to jeopardize her sympathies in England where Queen Victoria had still the last word. London was not Gay Paree. Melba must not compromise her aristocratic patrons at Covent Garden.

"Don't be a fool, Nellie. There will be other men in your life. Why, someday you may decide to get married again."

"I'll never marry another man. Never."

Madame Marchesi had been right once again: there were other men in Nellie Melba's life. But "infatuations rarely lasted very long with her," notes Colson, and Melba's friends agree. In fact, the infatuations of her admirers usually outlived hers. Sometimes she had a hard time getting rid of her boy friends. Once she was pursued by a particularly persistent Italian who threatened to kill himself with a dainty, mother-of-pearl pistol. Melba simply took the pistol away from him. His father later came to see her and made an unpleasant scene. She was disgusted. In her tidy scheme of things, romance had its definite place — like everything else. She owed her public a certain amount of romantic speculation; but, as she said to a friend, "enough is enough."

Melba never remarried. She had many suitors and turned them all down. Poor chaps, some of them were quite heartbroken. They didn't know how lucky they were. Who, I ask you, would want to go through life as "Mister Melba?"

No, the life of the husband of a celebrated prima donna is not exactly a bed of roses. He must remain anonymous. He is expected to talk exclusively of his wife. He must entertain her admirers and appease her managers. It is up to him "to arrange about the bouquets, the wreaths, the recalls, and toward the end of the season he may have to present his wife with a set of diamonds 'on the part of the subscribers,'" H. Sutherland Edwards wrote in 1888. Not much has changed since then. It's an expensive life. The husband of a diva I knew used to sell the flowers which his wife had received from admirers to second hand florists.

Ernesto Nicolini, the husband of Adelina Patti, once was sent out by his wife to measure the letters on the posters outside the opera house — because Patti had a contract that "the name PATTI must be in letters half as big again as those of all other singers." Nicolini discovered that Madame Nevada's name was a fraction bigger than permitted; all the posters had to be cut. Nicolini should be forgiven, however — he was a tenor himself. An Austrian named Nikolaus, who later changed his name, Nicolini was an expensive husband. Patti had had to pay 250,000 francs to her first husband, the Marquis de Caux, to get the tenor.

Berlioz writes that a prima donna's lovers and husband make fine *claqueurs,* "husbands being even better than lovers. Lovers are usually afraid of ridicule; they are also secretly afraid that too marked a success will add to the number of their rivals. Besides, they are not interested financially in the triumphs of their mistress; but the husband, who holds the purse strings, who knows what a bouquet tossed at the right moment will bring in, and likewise the value of a nicely protracted salvo, of a contagiously contrived excitement, of a recall timed just right — for these, the husband alone dares to avail himself of his aptitudes. . . . The husband who is a man of taste, who remains quietly in his seat during an entire act, who does not even applaud the finest efforts of his better half — such a man does not exist as a husband, unless his wife has the fidelity of an angel."

The prima donna's husband is his wife's sounding board, tryout listener, benevolent critic, nursemaid, opiate, press secretary, *chef de claque,* father confessor, manager, chauffeur, amateur psychiatrist, and sufferer from her moods. He must be on hand when she goes through one of her tantrums, but should stay discreetly in the background during her moments of triumph. He is the nondescript person who protects the prima donna against the too violent enthusiasm of her admirers, kindles the too lukewarm attitude of the people around her, organizes the distribution of her autographs and collects her press reviews. He must have the credulity of a child, the stamina of an athlete, the persuasion of a politician, the aplomb of a banker, the cheerfulness of a master of ceremonies, the *sang-froid* of a racing driver and the patience of a saint.

Even during the prima donna's two hundred and seventy-ninth performance as Mimi or Manon or Gilda, or — God help you — Elektra, he must be there, on his house seat in a front row, radiating enthusiasm, confidence and stoicism even in moments of impending disaster. When the prima donna goes through a vocal crisis the husband must convince everybody including himself that she has never been in better form. When he is unable to appease his wife in her difficult moments he is said to be a mouse, and when he speaks up strongly for her interests against managers he is said to be a meddler. In at least one instance the husband of a contemporary diva, an important music executive in his own right, has severely repudiated the critics who did not write about his wife the way he would have liked. The poor man is always wrong no matter what he does. He must plant rumors, but, like a perfect spy, he must never get caught. And in this age of disrespect and bad manners he is expected to behave like an old-fashioned cavalier, twenty-four hours a day.

Our sincere sympathy goes out to him. No wonder he has to have some fun to keep from going crazy! The husbands of three great prima donnas — Catalani, Mara and Schröder-Devrient — played cards for high stakes, losing the money as fast as their wives made it.

The prima donna's husband has his problems even after his death. Giglia Nordica, the former Lillian Norton of Farmington, Maine — a nineteenth-century prima donna Italianized her name for the same reason that some twentieth-century prima ballerinas Russianized theirs — who sang the *hochdramatisch* Wagnerian parts of Isolde and Brünhilde that Melba wanted to sing all her life, was married to one Frederick A. Gower. Gower later lost his life while attempting to cross the Channel in a balloon. The poor man must have tried to get away as high and far as possible from the high-voltage, high-dramatic complications of life with a Wagnerian heroine.

When Madame Nordica wanted to remarry twelve years later, persistent rumors claimed that Gower had been seen alive and happy in various parts of the world. Nordica, a resolute Isolde type, got remarried just the same. She had shown the same unflinching spirit when she declared at a rehearsal with the Boston Symphony that they played "like the Kalamazoo band."

❆ 11 ❆

Dear Nellie Was a Giant

SINGING IS a competitive business. The people who live in
the supercharged atmosphere of grand opera with its
often exaggerated, distorted emotions have to be ego-
centrics to survive. When you have to prove yourself time
and again in front of three thousand critical listeners under
trying conditions, your nerves either break or you wind up
thinking of yourself as a superman or a superwoman. Inevitably many opera singers talk about themselves all the time,
even in their sleep, often to the detriment of their vocal cords.

Melba was an exception. All her friends remember that
you could spend a long evening with her and never guess
that she happened to be a singer, in fact the world's most
famous singer. She rarely spoke about herself; she never
talked shop; she would never clear her throat, hum "mi-mi-
mi" or display the usual idiosyncrasies of a singer that get on
everybody's nerves.

"Nellie never had exalted ideas of being the good Lord's
chosen instrument and having a mission from Him," says
Hazelton-Cochrane. "She knew she had a beautiful voice

and perfect technical equipment, and she was determined to make the best of it. She had inherited a healthy dose of common sense from her father. She disliked pretense of any kind. I remember we once went to a concert of Madame Schumann-Heink's in Paris. Madame Schumann-Heink was known to pay little attention to her dress. It was afternoon, and Melba gasped when Schumann-Heink appeared in a big evening dress. Melba was fond of Schumann-Heink and worried that the super-critical Parisians might scoff at her. And then Schumann-Heink began to sing — something by Mozart. After the aria the people rose to their feet and cheered her. Melba was very pleased. 'There you are,' she said to me. 'They know about singing. They've forgotten everything but her wonderful artistry.' "

In her early years, when success came quickly — perhaps a little too quickly — Melba made the usual beginner's mistakes. She once sang the difficult part of Desdemona in Verdi's *Otello* after a mere four days of study, which is a credit to her musical alertness but not to her artistic conscience. She pulled off a similar *tour de force* when she performed the part of Elizabeth in *Tannhäuser* after seven days of study. In both cases she paid for her foolishness.

She had a prodigious memory. The American baritone David Bispham, who often appeared with Melba, writes in his *Recollections:* "Her memory enabled her to sing a role without an error which she had sung only once, and that six years before!"

The art of singing has always been a mystery even to those who practice it. The singer's chosen instrument, his voice, is of a mystifying nature. In the technical sense the voice consists of the parts of the body that convert breath into sound. It is a combination wind-and-string instrument, potentially the most beautiful and expressive instrument, and certainly the most difficult to master. This instrument is made up of the vocal cords and certain bony cavities in the mouth, throat and nose, called resonators. The cords are comparable to the strings of a violin and the resonators to its body. But the singer — and that is one of the things that make his art so tricky and mysterious — has nothing tangible that can be compared to the violinist's bow. It is only his breath, controlled by various sets of muscles, that can produce sound from his instrument. Thus, where a violinist draws his bow across the strings to create a series of sound vibrations that are relayed to the body which gives them carrying power, the singer must rely on his breath to create in his vocal cords vibrations that can be magnified by the resonators. Nor can the singer see the instrument he is performing on, or manipulate it as other musicians can theirs. Furthermore, although any competent doctor can inspect a patient's vocal cords and resonators, not even a skillful laryngologist can tell by examining them whether that patient has the equipment of a good singer.

And here the mystery deepens. While most people's vocal cords and resonators look much the same, it seems to be a fact that some individuals are born with fundamentally fine voices and others are not.

Less mystifying is the fact that no matter how superior a would-be singer's natural voice may be, he will never become a truly great artist until he acquires a thorough knowledge of technique. Anyone endowed with a voice and average intelligence, and a willingness to persevere, can do this, but then another elusive element enters the picture. For the ability to employ a knowledge of technique with maximum effectiveness is something else again — something that in any one era only a handful of men and women in all the world possess. Thousands of singing teachers spend their lives trying to instruct tens of thousands of pupils in the art of accomplishing this feat, but it is almost freakishly rare for a pupil to find a teacher who understands how to go about solving this problem. Much of the trouble lies in the peculiar nature of the voice as a musical instrument. The movements of a violin teacher's arms, hands, and fingers as he plays his instrument can teach the aspiring violinist a lot if he observes them carefully; the mechanics of technique are there for anyone to see. But even if the singing teacher's own technique is above reproach, there is little that a pupil can learn about it by watching him sing. Nor can the singing teacher always perceive precisely what is physically wrong with the way a pupil is handling his voice and make specific suggestions for correcting it.

Madame Marchesi was a godsend to Melba. When Nellie Armstrong came to her, Madame Marchesi knew almost at once what was wrong with her pupil's voice. "I personally consider Madame Marchesi the greatest teacher of them all," Melba said. She was often appalled by the injury which she saw done to promising voices of young singers through ignorant tuition. "We would not accept tuition in architecture, chemistry, or law from any casual dabbler in these professions, but we welcome the gospel of vocalization from

people who have not even a perfunctory acquaintance with
the science of singing," she once wrote.

It is sometimes said that every singer has three different
voices — head, middle, and chest — and in a sense this is
true. Actually, however, nobody has more than one voice.
When there are audible "breaks" in a singer's voice as she
progresses from her lowest tones to her highest, it is because,
no matter how diligently she has studied the theory of singing, she has not acquired complete control of her breathing
support. Ideally, the tone should "dance" on top of the
breath as a ball dances on top of a water jet. When the jet
gets lowered, the ball sinks. When the breath support is un-
sure, and the tone no longer dances on top of the breath, an
audible break occurs. In most cases this break happens
where the voice shifts from chest register to head register.
The ideal goal is a smooth transition that will assure a uniform quality of tone, and will also eliminate wear and tear
on the voice.

Melba had attained that perfect technique. It was said
that her tones were as even as a perfectly matched string of
pearls. She had no register problem. Sir Morell Mackenzie,
eminent throat specialist, thought Melba used "the same
register throughout her voice." He should have said that
Melba's transition was so perfectly smooth that no one could
say where her chest tones ended and her head tones began.
Melba herself said she carried her chest register up to F and
made the change from chest to head tones on the F sharp,
"half a tone beyond the usual limit." During a musical libel
suit heard at the Royal Courts of Justice in London, in
February, 1908, Dr. Milsom Reese, a famous throat special-

ist, whose patients included most of the great European and American singers of his time, was called to testify as an expert on the unusual retention of an unimpaired singing voice. He defined it as "the result of elasticity in the ligamentous portion of the vocal cords."

"The most elastic vocal cord today is Madame Melba's," said Dr. Reese. "She makes use of the anterior portion of the cord, and that accounts for the lasting quality of her voice. She knowingly uses head notes instead of chest notes. It is an automatic process. A scale can be sung by putting the full tension on the reeds, or varying from the long reed to the short. There is no other singer with more resonance and less nasal quality."

Still another baffling aspect of singing is the act of breathing itself. Italian singers long ago came up with two pointers on the subject: "To breathe well is to open up the bottom of one's throat," and "Sing above, not with, your breath" — the little ball dancing on top of the water jet.

What the Italians neglected to add was any practical advice on how to open the bottom of one's throat and how to sing above the breath. Melba knew the mystery. In her essay "On the Science of Singing" she particularly emphasizes the need for correct breathing, "a singer's greatest technical essential":

> Great success in singing is impossible unless the vocalist thoroughly understands breathing, attack, the use of the registers, the structure and functions above the voice box, and the relation of chest expansion to the production of tone. . . . It is impossible to demonstrate in song the beauty of a singer's voice without proper breath control. Tone, expression, resonance, phrasing, all depend on proper breath-

ing. Exhaling is more difficult than inhaling and conse-
quently calls for the most careful practice.

She warned her students from over-practicing. "Practicing
the high notes in fortissimo is one of the most pernicious
customs of vocal study," she would say. "If a singer sings
the upper register in private very softly, in pianissimo, he
will find that the forte will speedily respond when public
performances demand it."

Melba's essay is the result of a lifetime of experience and
abounds with practical advice and sensible hints. She knew
all the tricks of her trade. She would often jump the fraction of a beat in order to make a careful attack on the note,
but despite such slight jumps she always stayed in rhythm.
"Be careful where you stand," she would say to a young
singer. "A carpet under your feet will affect the sound of
your voice. So will a hat on your head which muffles the
sound of your voice and makes you sing like in a pillow. Be
sure to have no flowers around you because they take away
from you much needed oxygen."

> The timid singer [she writes] should take a few deep
> breaths before her first entrance on the stage or concert
> platform, and choose as an opening number music that is
> free from exacting initial bars.

Melba knew the fundamentals of good singing instinctively. She knew the importance of a healthy voice in a
healthy body. Her gospel was "to give the body ample
exercise and the voice an ample rest."

> Many students in their eagerness for musical headway
> entirely neglect their physical welfare and forget that plenty

of fresh air, simple and nourishing food, and eight or nine hours of sleep are necessary for most young singers.

Melba practiced what she preached. She loved good food but she liked a healthy voice even more, so she sensibly though not always happily sacrificed her epicurean tendencies for the sake of her career. Occasionally she had a little trouble in keeping her figure. She loved a good dinner and would console herself with feminine self-deception that her masseuse would take off the extra weight the next morning. The masseuse did not always succeed.

Melba loved to take her friends out to restaurants. In London her favorites were Leoni's Quo Vadis, in Dean Street, where she always ordered Poulet à la Sicilienne, and Quaglino's in Bury Street. When Mario Gallati (of the Caprice) was manager of the Ivy, he often served Melba — whose healthy appetite did not decrease with age. One day in 1924 Melba called him up in the morning to book a quiet table. She came for lunch with Giacomo Puccini.

"Melba was sixty-five, a formidable woman of royal grandeur," Mario remembers. "Puccini looked very ill. It was their last meal together. He died a few days later in Brussels."

In one respect, Melba was more fortunate than today's crop of prima donnas. People didn't mind their divas' being what the Viennese vaguely and charmingly call *vollschlank*, "full-slim." Today a prima donna is expected to be as svelte as a Hollywood star. Her strenuous dieting often ruins her strained voice.

Melba's day started early. "We often wanted to stay up

late at night, but she liked to go to bed at ten," says Stella Murray, an English singer who was one of Melba's few protégées and pupils after the First World War. Melba was a very good teacher though she lacked the patience to be a great teacher. Miss Murray continued:

"She would be gruff and strict but she was wonderful teaching you diction, phrasing and elocution. I don't think that she ever sang a wrong note. But she was also very difficult; you were never quite relaxed in her company, you were always on your best behavior. When she got up from the piano and slapped down the cover, that was that. She would say, "Go, all of you, I must rest," and you would go. No matter what she did, she was the great prima donna, every moment of her life, even in the privacy of her home. She would get up around seven in the morning, and usually had her breakfast in her bedroom. Very simple — tea and toast. She followed that routine even when she had sung the night before and stayed up late. By nine she would come out of her bedroom, immaculately dressed. Often she would wear a hat. Sometimes she wore a hat at home all day. She was a tidy, methodical woman. I've never seen her hang around in a dressing gown and slippers. She was very strict with us younger people concerning our appearance. She insisted that you wear the right dress at the right time."

Elena Danieli, an American mezzo-soprano, who was another protégée and pupil of Melba in those years, remembers one day when Melba wanted to take her to lunch with several friends. All the women had white gloves except Miss

Danieli, who couldn't afford them and wore old black ones. Melba gave her an imperious stare.

"Why didn't you bring your white gloves?"

"I haven't got any."

"Then you will not come with me." Miss Danieli got no lunch that day. She bought a pair of white gloves the next day.

At nine in the morning Melba's secretary would bring the morning mail, and for an hour or so the diva became the efficient executive, dictating letters, talking to her manager and banker, looking after contracts and investments. Around ten she would be at the piano (she had three, a fine Mason and Hamlin and two Steinways) either alone or with a *répétiteur*. There are singers who need hours to properly warm up their voices and do their vocalizing exercises before they sing at night. Melba's vocal equipment was so perfect and her voice so properly placed that she needed a very short warming-up time.

"Melba was blessed with faultless breathing, secure intonation, good nerves and retentive memory," according to Miss Danieli. "She didn't have to labor for every run or trill. When she studied with Madame Marchesi she had learned the importance of scales, solfeggios and the proper vocalization. After the age of forty she wisely saved her voice as much as possible. I have often been in her dressing room shortly before she went on stage. She would sing a couple of scales and then she would walk out there and sing like an angel."

Melba wrote:

On the days when I sing in opera or concert I run through a few scales in full voice during the morning, and if I cannot sing top D perfectly I consider myself out of form. [The range of her voice was three octaves, terminating on the high F sharp.] Just before going on I try my voice again for a few seconds to warm it. . . . The general muscles of the body become slack in the case of students who spend half the day or more sitting or standing by a piano, wearing out their physical and vocal resources.

Lunch would be light and easily digestible — a grilled steak, a little chicken, salad, fruit. No salt, no wine, no rich dessert. On special occasions she would indulge in some chocolate cream (she just loved chocolate in any form) or in one of the desserts that have assured Melba's gastronomic immortality.

After lunch she would go for a short walk and then rest. "When I am singing in the evening, I do not dine but have a very light repast consisting of either fish, chicken, or sweetbread, with a baked apple and a glass of water at five o'clock, and I always find myself very hungry for supper when I get home from the opera or concert."

She would always arrive at the theater two hours before the performance, and took great care in her make-up. "Detail, detail, detail is the cardinal rule for an artist," she would say. Most of Melba's rules make a lot of sense and are religiously followed by a great many celebrated singers today who have, unfortunately, neither her voice nor her technique.

Sometimes she would go through her part, word for word and note for note, and then she would take a short rest in her dressing room before she was called on stage. She carried no mascots with her and had no superstitions; sometimes, when something went wrong, she would swear in a mild Australian way, but she never stayed mad for any length of time and her hairdresser and wardrobe women adored her. Her contract often stipulated that she had to be paid in cash before the curtain went up, but she left these matters to her manager; she would not touch a check or money before a performance — perhaps that was a kind of superstition.

In her later years Melba would avoid the temptation of a heavy supper after the performances which had been a pleasant habit when she was young. "Eat a raw apple and a slice of brown bread, and you will wake up the next morning feeling fit as a fiddle." It must have been difficult for her, because she came home very highly strung when she had sung and needed hours to unwind.

Intimacy is the enemy of illusion. As a young opera enthusiast I once fell madly in love with a beautiful, celebrated prima donna. I was twenty-one, about half her age, but those things happen, and not only on the stage in *Rosenkavalier*. Actually I was never as lucky as the seventeen-year-old hero in that wonderful "comedy for music" by Strauss and Hofmannsthal which, as you may remember, begins on the morning-after in the bedroom of the charming Marschallin, who is at least twice his age.

My adventure began, and ended, rather ingloriously in the kitchen of the prima donna where she'd taken me for supper one hour after her performance. She was a little hoarse from singing and I from shouting *"Brava!"* She was hungry; I was ecstatic.

My prima donna had a beautiful home with a large drawing room (I didn't see her bedroom, but I'm sure it was as sumptuous as the one shown in *Rosenkavalier*), yet for some mysterious reason she preferred to have supper in the kitchen. I wish I could report we had iced caviar and chilled champagne. It was only cold cuts and warm beer. My diva loved cold beer, but had to warm it up because of her larynx.

It was a chilling experience and left me with a permanent disinclination toward post-performance supper with an admired prima donna. I have no desire to see my operatic goddesses one hour later. Perhaps I am an incurable romanticist.

Nellie Melba, however — of that I am quite sure — would not have disappointed me one hour later. She would have been the prima donna *assoluta* off stage exactly as she had been on stage a short while ago. After the last admirer had left her dressing room and the last autograph had been written at the stage door, she would go home or to a hotel, with the cheers still ringing in her ears, and the excitement ebbing down slowly in her heart. As she entered her drawing room, where her friends were waiting, they would clap their hands and raise their glasses to her, and Melba might have a little champagne with them.

It would be the very best champagne [says Hazelton-Cochrane]. Nellie always needed a long time to unwind after a particularly big night. She would be in high spirits. Sometimes we would be at the Savoy and the orchestra would play one of her arias and she might even sing for her supper.

Few men are heroes to their valets, but Nellie Melba was a prima donna to her maids . . . She was a queenly woman.

When Melba didn't sing and stayed at home, she would have a late dinner, eight o'clock, "and there is nothing to distinguish it from the same meal in the average household," she notes, with uncharacteristic lack of precision.

Her friends disagree with her modest statement. "Melba served wonderful food in her home," says Hazelton-Cochrane. "In the morning she would have a long talk with her cook. She took great pleasure in surprising her guests with their favorite dishes and kept book on her menus. You would never get the same dish twice in a short time. She showed the attention to detail in culinary matters that you would expect from a favorite client of M. Escoffier. Nellie knew nothing about *grande cuisine* and running an elegant house when she first came from Australia, but she learned fast. She had a lovely rose garden in England, which took some daring. She would spend hours with her Italian gardener, telling him what she wanted. She loved flowers but tolerated no flowers on her dinner table. She was a born hostess and managed her large staff efficiently. You enjoyed dining with her because she loved to eat. One of her favorite dishes were Plovers' Eggs à la Muscovite — hard-boiled, garnished with caviar on tartled crusts. And she loved grouse and pheasant and partridge."

Should this have been Melba's idea of dinner "in the average household"?

Unlike many famous artists, Melba didn't think that the parties given for her were her due, like fees and applause.

She would always return people's hospitality on the same lavish scale.

> When she was coming to England from abroad [writes one of her biographers, Percy Colson] she would cable her great friend, Lord William Nevill, and ask him to find her a house and servants, and stock it with everything necessary. She gave him *carte blanche* and never questioned anything he spent. If she took a particular fancy to any of the servants, she would take them back to Australia, and she remembered many of them in her will.

She would give wonderful parties at 30 Great Cumberland Place which she often rented from her friend Hwfa-Williams and later at a delightful house in Old Queen Street, Westminster. Hazelton-Cochrane remembers a magnificent reception which Melba gave at the occasion of the state visit of President Loubet of France in London:

"The house was decorated with thousands of pink malmaisons, her favorite flowers, and with thousands of red roses. She sang the Bach-Gounod "Ave Maria," and was accompanied by Jan Kubelik, her harpist friend Ada Sassoli, and Landon Ronald on the piano, the conductor who was one of her protégés. The party lasted all night and there was plenty of champagne. The Prince of Teck, the Duchess of Devonshire, the Duchess of Abercorn, the Duchess of Marlborough, Lord and Lady Savile, Lord Sandwich, Alfred de Rothschild, Lady Cynthia Graham, Count Mensdorff (the Austrian-Hungarian ambassador) and dozens of others were there. Yes, dear Nellie knew how to give a party."

Melba ran her business affairs with the same efficiency with which she managed her private, artistic and social life.

Her managers were often irritated because she was tough
to deal with, but they respected her because she was absolutely dependable and always kept her word. Her friend
Haddon Chambers, the writer, said, "If Nellie had taken it
into her head to set up a bonnet shop, she would have become the first milliner in Europe." In any army Melba would
not have remained a private for long and she would probably have wound up as a general. Like all efficient people
she knew her own limitations. She knew almost nothing
about cooking but tried to get the best chef she could find.
She had vague ideas about interior decorating, so got
prominent decorators to advise her and followed their suggestions, sometimes with touching naïveté. One of them
had advised her to buy the bed of Louis XVI, the Dauphin,
in which Melba slept for years. But she was prouder of the
autographed photographs of her friends — kings, composers,
artists — which were all over her drawing room. She didn't
trust her own judgment in clothes but knew the importance
of being well dressed. People expect their prima donnas to
look like fashion models, only more so. As soon as she could
afford it, she began to buy her dresses at Worth's in Paris,
and later she had them designed by her friend Reville-Terry.

It was Jean Worth who made her realize that for a great
diva it was almost as important to look well as to sing well.
Jean looked like a Frenchman with his little beard and
polished manners; Melba found it difficult to believe that
his father had been a Manchester boy with a broad North
Country accent. Papa was still wandering around the salons
in his black skullcap, making occasional suggestions, but
she thought Jean was the greater designer. "Had he written

his memoirs," Melba once said, "he would have had some very sensational things to tell." . . . including some about Madame Melba, perhaps. Jean Worth would place the tips of his fingers together and half-close his eyes as he examined critically the figure of some woman "in need of clothes," and thirty seconds later he would know exactly what dress she ought to wear. Melba's favorite color was pale blue.

Melba's old friends still remember some of the Worth dresses she wore, "dreams of beauty." He made many of Melba's opera costumes. A great prima donna wouldn't wear a costume which belongs to a theater and is also worn by other singers. Melba always wore her own costumes, which made traveling a cumbersome business. During a trip from Boston to Liverpool, her trunks got flooded in the hold of the Cunard liner *Saxonia,* and her furs, her private and theatrical wardrobe, "the result of years of trouble" were lost. Melba cried for ten days, not for her wardrobe but for her piano scores of *Aïda, Rigoletto, Faust, Roméo et Juliette, Hamlet* and *Lakmé,* elaborately marked by Verdi, Gounod, Ambroise Thomas and Delibes.

Today most stage designers insist that the prima donna must wear the theater's costumes, which are designed to harmonize with the colors of sets and decorations. But Melba lived in the era of the prima donna and she always had her way. For her part as Elsa in *Lohengrin* Jean Worth designed "an exquisite coat of gold, hand-painted and sewn with jewels." (It was this coat which attracted the curiosity of the Russian border guards who spread it on the snow for closer inspection and trampled all over it.) It must have been quite a garment. When Melba appeared in St. Petersburg before the Tsar and the Tsarina and afterwards was summoned to the Tsar's box, the Tsarina took the coat into her hands and stroked it gently. "How lovely it is," she said.

Melba always felt "like a million pounds" when she came back to London with a new collection of Worth dresses, but toward the end of her life she said to a friend, "When I look at the rather faded photographs of myself in those days, I can hardly keep from laughing at the fantastic fashions which we used to think beautiful."

Melba never had many sincere and intimate women friends. She always preferred the company of men. Her efficiency and energy, businesslike nature and embarrassing punctuality, her passion for facts rather than fancies didn't endear her to women. They found dear Nellie perhaps a little too formidable for their taste. When Melba didn't like people she would treat them with utter disregard. She would tell a woman bridge partner, "You are more dangerous than either of your opponents," though she was not a good bridge player herself. She disliked gossip and had no patience with the vague chatter of many women. She would not commiserate with women who came to her with tearful tales of men, children or servants. Archbishop Corrigan of New York once mentioned Melba's "persistent disregard of those nuances of diplomacy which I have always understood to be essential to the structure of operatic fame."

Beverly Nichols calls her "brutally straight." Once in Australia he told her a lie about an unpleasant newspaper criticism in order to save her pain. She found out the truth and told him he must never do that again. "I want facts," she said. Afterwards he always gave her the facts. "She faced them without flinching, however disagreeable they might be." Nichols often heard her say, "I am an honest woman," with what he calls "a faintly plebeian accent" which he found very attractive. "Melba was, in fact, a woman of the people with a supreme natural gift, a wonderful physique, and a character of steel." When Clara Butt left for a concert tour of Australia and asked Melba for advice as to whether public taste had improved there, Melba, who had just returned from Australia, said, "No — just sing 'em muck." Somehow the Australian newspapers found out about her opinion, and there was a terrific uproar in her homeland. Melba was furious about the indiscretion but didn't deny it.

Melba's energy sometimes frightened her friends. Agnes Murphy, the prima donna's reverent biographer, claims that Melba liked to read biography, history, American short stories, and "the more pretentious popular fiction," and lists as her favorite authors Jack London, Balzac, Shakespeare and Omar Khayyám, but Melba's friends tell me that they never saw her sit still with a book. Hazelton-Cochrane thinks she didn't read much because she was always too busy. She didn't write long letters but would dash off imperious notes with recommendations, wishes, demands, orders.

"She would have people for lunch or tea, and then she would be on her way to dinner or the theatre. The car was always out there. She would be asked to open an exhibition or be the guest of honor at some social function. She lived like a queen. But no matter how busy she was she was always cheerful, light-hearted and fun-loving. When you started to tell her of your troubles, she would say, 'Don't be a fool, don't fuss!' She was never moody or depressed. In her younger years, I'm told, she rarely showed any nervousness before a performance. Some people said she was much too serene, a real artist should be more involved. Later on, when she was not so sure of her voice any more, she was nervous but she wouldn't let other people feel it. Certainly not the ones who couldn't defend themselves. Melba could be awfully rude to another prima donna, but never to her hairdresser."

The "woman of the people" had a way with emperors and kings. In St. Petersburg she enchanted the Tsar, who gave her an exquisite bracelet made of engraved diamond cubes and large pearls strung together on a slender platinum-and-gold chain. When King Oscar, the last ruler of both Norway and Sweden, heard Melba at the Royal Opera in Stockholm, "the smiling giant" rose twice during the performance and bowed to her from the royal box, which created confusion among the audience. Some got up and others remained seated. Etiquette does not provide the answer for such a dilemma. After the performance, Melba was told to be at the royal palace the following morning at ten. She was ushered through endless suites of drawing rooms until she arrived at a small room, "furnished in the simplest possible taste."

The King greeted her in Italian, perhaps because Melba had sung in Italian the night before. When she told him she was Australian, he said, "Then we must speak in Australian." Both laughed and the ice was broken. He said he was going to give her the order "Litteris and Artibus."

"Won't you pin it on for me, Sir?"

"Of course, I will. Lend me a pin."

"I'm afraid I have only a hatpin."

"Fancy a woman without a pin!"

Fortunately the groom-in-waiting was able to supply a pin. The King pinned the order on her breast and kissed her on both cheeks.

Three years later Melba sat in her Paris home when her butler rushed in, crying there was a lunatic at the front door. "An enormous man of incredible height who demands to see you, Madame. He says he is the King of Sweden."

It was "the smiling giant" and he was "absolutely dying for a cup of tea." He stayed more than three hours and wound up singing duets with her. He had a fresh sweet tenor voice.

"You will be Melba," he said, "and I shall be Jean de Reszke." Melba knew quite a few tenors with illusions of grandeur who considered themselves kings and acted that way, but she had never met a king who dreamed of being a tenor.

One day in 1900 Melba had an audience with Emperor Franz Josef I of Austria-Hungary. In Schönbrunn Palace she was led through so many anterooms, gilt corridors and immense salons that she was "quite tired" by the time she stood before the Emporer, "a dignified, sad, old man in a black coat standing very erect with his hands behind his back." To Melba, always a keen observer, "the whole room seemed filled with sadness." He smiled at her but she sensed that "here was a man who had endured terrible suffering."

He too gave her a medal and said she had done a great deal for him last night at the Hofoper.

"Don't you know, Madame Melba, that I have not been to a theater for years?" And after a pause, "Not — not since the Empress was assassinated."

Melba was unable to speak. Her eyes were filled with tears.

The Emperor gave her a sad smile. "You have sung me out of my retirement. I shall never forget that. It was a very great effort, but I'm glad I made it."

Melba's meeting with Kaiser Wilhelm II of Germany was not so pleasant. During a performance of *Lucia di Lammermoor* at the Imperial Opera House in Berlin the prima donna was informed by a nervous manager that she would be summoned to the Imperial Box after the third act. She received the announcement with great serenity which astonished the manager. He didn't know that by now Melba had collected an impressive array of emperors, kings and queens.

"Incidentally, Madame Melba," said the manager, "have you any scent on your handkerchief?"

Now it was Melba's turn to be astonished. "Why do you ask?"

"His Majesty intensely dislikes perfume. Please remember that most distinctly."

("It struck me as very odd," Melba later commented. His Majesty was off to a bad start, so far as the Queen of Song was concerned.)

At the close of the third act, she went to the Imperial

Box, her hair still disheveled from the Mad Scene. The
Kaiser was standing up "in a glitter of ribbons and medals,
a very imposing sight."

The Kaiser talked to her for a minute or so in perfect
English. Unfortunately he made a criticism of Melba's performance. The Queen of Song, taking on her most imperial
air, thanked the Kaiser for his advice and added she "would
not dream of criticizing his government."

The Kaiser abruptly turned around, said briefly, "Good
evening," and walked to the door. The situation was saved
by the Empress, a charming, sympathetic woman, who remained talking to Melba for a while. Then the Emperor in
the doorway turned around and impatiently flicked his
fingers to signal the Empress to come with him. Melba
thought she saw a look of unspoken apology on her tired
face. "She followed him obediently, in the manner of a
puppy dog."

H. E. Wortham, a friend of Percy Colson's, described
Melba's only venture into politics, which occurred a few
years after the First World War. Lord Apsley — whose
mother, Lady Bathurst, was a friend of Melba's — was standing as one of the Conservative candidates for Southampton,
previously held by the Liberals. Some bright Conservative
Party light discovered that Melba happened to be giving a
concert in Southampton the night before the election. Perhaps she might be induced to say a few words in favor of
the Conservative candidate — she might come to a meeting
in the dock quarter after her concert and make a short
speech?

Melba at first wanted to have nothing to do with it, but let herself be persuaded by Wortham, the only condition being that the whole thing must be kept a secret — otherwise it might have a bad effect on her concert audience at the Town Hall.

On the day of the concert Wortham went to call upon Melba at four o'clock in the afternoon in the home of friends with whom she was staying. He found the diva eating "an unappetizing rice pudding — her regular diet, she explained, when she was working." The day was gloomy and so was Melba. She had heard rumors that word had got around the dock quarters she was going to show up there tonight. Had anyone spilled the secret?

Wortham called for her again after the concert, which was "a triumphant evening." She had had to give four encores. But later on in the car "her wrath fell upon her accompanist for having accompanied her in 'Home, Sweet Home' without the music." This she never had allowed and never would allow. Then her foot knocked against something on the floorboard.

"What's this?"

Wortham explained it was a bottle of champagne.

"I never touch it," she said, crossly.

The dock quarter lay in grim murkiness. The car pulled up at an elementary school where the election meeting took place. No one was there to receive them. A room that had space perhaps for a hundred school children was crowded with twice as many tough, brawny dockers. They jeered as Melba appeared and made jests as she walked slowly toward the teacher's rostrum. The atmosphere was quite different from the mood at the Town Hall a few minutes ago.

If Melba was wondering about the fickleness of popularity she gave no indication. "Her Australian blood was up and she meant to see this thing through." Amid catcalls, whistles and shrieks she was introduced by the chairman. She rose and began to speak. "She was fluent and vigorous," remembers Mr. Wortham. "I forgot exactly what she said — that shows it was all the better as a political speech."

The hostile audience was determined to howl Melba down. And she was just as determined to be heard. Once or twice she quieted them with her powerful personality until some of the rowdier spirits began shouting again. They were clearly old hands at the game.

Someone yelled, "Give us a song, old gal!"

Melba lived up to the challenge. "If I do, will you give me your vote?" she retorted.

Howls and shrieks were the answer. The uproar continued until she went to the light upright piano in the corner of the room. Suddenly there was complete silence. And as she sang "Home, Sweet Home," there was no other sound in the room except the wheezy action of the piano under Melba's fingers. When she finished, there were deafening cheers. The room rocked with applause.

But once she went back on the platform pandemonium broke out again. It became clear that the meeting would have to be broken up forcibly. Melba managed to reach the door, with some difficulty. "In the car a shaken prima donna confessed that she did not think she would care for politics. Tears were not far below the surface."

At Conservative headquarters she was triumphantly received by the Duke of Northumberland and other Conservative bigwigs. They told her that her appearance had been a brilliant success for the Party: all the rowdies and breakers-up, the toughest hecklers and wildest radicals, had gone to her meeting in the dock quarters hoping she would give them a song "for free," so meanwhile the fourteen other Conservative meetings in Southampton had been held in perfect quiet.

Twenty-four hours later the results were known. The Conservatives had captured both seats.

But though she was efficient, direct and businesslike, Melba was very much a woman, quite emotional, full of feminine paradoxes. She was a devoted mother to her son George and spent much time with him when he wasn't away in school. People who didn't know her thought she was "cold," but her friends knew better: Melba was too disciplined to show her feelings in public.

Once her car knocked down and killed an old man in a street in Paris. Melba's nerves were shattered for weeks. She canceled all engagements, and although her driver was exonerated of any guilt and she gave a lot of money to the family of the victim, she went on brooding for months.

"Nellie was very emotional, though not in the outward, Italian way," says Hazelton-Cochrane. "Very logical one moment and very illogical the next. She loved the music of *Aïda* but disliked to make up in dark as Aïda. She said because of the arduous make-up she later didn't sing the part; she couldn't forget a critic's advice that she should do away with the hideous black ropes that served for hair. Any unkind criticism made her very unhappy. She wasn't fooling us, though. The part of Aïda had always been too dramatic for her voice."

Much malicious gossip followed her because of her alleged meanness in money matters. She hated being exploited and had no use for the usual hangers-on who congregate around famous people. She was ruthless to people who were in her way or had incurred her wrath, but generous and kind to her friends and protégées. One of them was Elizabeth Parkina, a gifted young coloratura from Kansas City, where Melba sang with Miss Parkina, and played the accompaniment for her protégée's first number. "She was kindness itself, and whatever success I have made I owe entirely to her," said Miss Parkina, who had been billed as, but didn't become, "a second Melba." A New Zealand soprano named Irene Kinsley, who wanted to sing in opera, once came to ask Melba whether she should accept a music-hall contract because she needed the money for her singing education. She sang an aria for Melba, who threw the unsigned contract into the fireplace and made arrangements for Miss Kinsley to study singing at Melba's expense.

After lunch in the modest apartment of yet another protégée, Elena Danieli, Melba noticed there was not enough china. She walked over to Gorde's in South Audley Street and sent Miss Danieli a complete set for twelve people. "We are still using it," says Madame Danieli.

"Melba would show her affection in unexpected ways," says Stella Murray, a close friend of the prima donna. "Once we lunched with a handsome young peer who was always in trouble financially. He was very depressed that day, and

Melba soon found out that he needed money. After lunch she gave him some. 'I thought I'd better do it before he asked me,' she told me later. At that time she was giving me a lesson every day. When she was to go to France, she said to me, 'What am I going to do with you? I can't leave you here. I'll take you along to the Riviera and will give you a lesson every day.' I was overwhelmed by this unexpected generosity and broke into tears, and Nellie Melba, who liked to appear serene and cool, also started to cry. Melba was loyal to her old friends, and always had the same people for her birthday party on May 19th. She lived in a lovely house then, filled with beautiful things, but we knew better than to talk about it. If you said you liked a vase or a painting, she would give it to you at once."

Melba was made a Dame Commander of the Order of the British Empire (D.B.E.), an honor corresponding to knighthood, in 1918 — not for her artistic achievements, but because she had raised more money for war charities than anybody else in Australia.

Melba took up war work with typical gusto. She knitted enthusiastically and sent thousands of letters with autographs that were sold for the benefit of the soldiers. Once, after one of her innumerable charity concerts, she sold a flag worth a guinea for two thousand guineas. Her friends called her "The Empress of Pickpockets." At a large party where she saw many rich people she would approach them asking them to give everything in their wallets before looking inside to see how much they had. She never had an outright refusal, but once encountered "a certain amount of difficulty" in persuading a man who discovered two hundred-pound notes in his pocketbook whose existence he had completely forgotten. She collected over half a million dollars in Australia, which she handed over to the Red Cross.

> Melba enjoyed the war years [writes Colson]. She was rich, famous and intensely alive. She could be hail fellow well met, enjoying her enormous prestige. And whether knitting, or travelling, or giving war concerts, or entertaining, she lived every minute of her life, enjoyed it all, singing, eating, drinking, dancing, with full-blooded joy. Her health was perfect.

Her friends didn't think she was very pleased with being a D.B.E. "She had moved too much among those whose titles and orders *really* counted for something to set much value on such a petty distinction," says Colson. Dame Nellie makes no mention whatsoever of it in her autobiography.

A while ago, six Australians sat in their club in Melbourne. Among them were a prominent conductor, a well-known singing teacher, and other musical experts. All of them had known Nellie Melba for half their lives.

Somebody said Nellie had been dead almost thirty years. The name brought a mist to the eyes of the six men.

"Ah! Melba was a giant," said the first man.

"Yes," said the second. "Dear Nellie was a giant."

"That's the only way to express her," said the third.

The others agreed in silence.

☙ 12 ❧

New York at Her Feet

C OBBLESTONES AND JOLTING CABS" were Melba's first impressions of New York City when she arrived there
after a stormy crossing from Le Havre late in 1893. It was
the year of the Chicago World's Fair, which featured the
world's most sensational attractions — naturally including
Nellie Melba, The Greatest Prima Donna on Earth, the Diva
with the Longest Trill.

New York must have been a wonderful place. Fifth
Avenue was "comparatively sleepy," Melba writes. William
K. Vanderbilt's town house at the northwest corner of Fifth
Avenue and Fifty-second Street (where the Tishman building stands now) was considered "quiet and secluded." When
Melba told Vanderbilt it would be too bad if the neighborhood were to become noisy, he laughed and said, "Oh this
will never get busy . . . We grow fast in New York but we
don't grow as fast as all that."

It was Melba's first encounter with American millionaires
and American democracy, "that debatable quality." (Perhaps
this wasn't her "democratic Australian" day.) She had "an

unusual experience" when she arrived one cold afternoon outside the door of the Metropolitan Opera House before a Sunday-evening concert in which she was starred. It was snowing heavily, and Melba tried to go in by the subscribers' covered entrance. She was promptly stopped by a uniformed man who asked for her ticket.

Melba, hardly looking at him, said "Please, let me pass," and when he told her that no one passed there without a ticket, she straightened herself out regally and said, "Surely you know who I am. I am Madame Melba."

For some reason the magic word didn't work. The man refused to let her pass without a ticket. A man behind Melba at once offered her his ticket. She shook her head.

"Thanks. If I can't get in here without a ticket, I won't get in at all."

A dire crisis was averted by the breathless appearance of one of the directors, summoned by someone who had recognized Melba. "Otherwise," Melba said later, "I would have turned around and the thousands of people who were waiting inside would have gone away disappointed."

The doorman was later sent to her dressing room to apologize. He gave a shrug. He was not subservient at all. "Sorry, Ma'm, but I've only done my duty."

Melba was impressed. She smiled and told him he was right. Democracy had prevailed after all.

If the celebrated prima donna of Brussels, Paris, London and Milan had hoped to take over New York's Metropolitan Opera House with a sustained high C and a long trill, she was soon disenchanted. American audiences were not overwhelmed and the critics were decidedly lukewarm. New York's fashionable world ignored the prima donna. There was no Lady de Grey to take her under her protection. In New York, Melba soon found out, an artist was just an artist. There was always, she noted with some acerbity, "a subtle difference" between a prima donna and the Four Hundred.

Melba's debut on December 4 had been under a bad cloud. She hadn't quite recovered from the bad crossing. She was used to the underheated rooms of England, and felt extremely uncomfortable at the Waldorf Hotel, where the steam heat came through the walls even after she had turned off all radiators. Also she had made the mistake of selecting for her debut *Lucia di Lammermoor*, which was known as "a Patti opera" in New York, where Madame Patti had a large and enthusiastic following. Madame Patti was at that time making one of her "farewell tours" through the United States (all in all, she made half a dozen of them) and her devoted fans considered Melba's choice a provocation.

There had been no grand opera at the Metropolitan during the previous fall season after the fire of August 27, 1892, which, according to Irving Kolodin, "consumed, along with the Metropolitan's wood and walls, the softer elements of the membership — so that only those who cared enough about opera not to count or those who had so much money that the cost didn't matter took up the burden of refinancing and reconstruction." Melba had to sing in a brand-new house (the house that is still known today as the Metropolitan Opera), and the very thought gave her the jitters. On the eve of the performance the baritone Eugene Dufriche, one of the principal singers, had to cancel because of laryngitis,

and she had to sing with an Enrico who had not properly rehearsed the part.

By Melba's standards, her debut was no success. A few
people in the boxes applauded — which didn't please the
audience-at-large, who "suspected the box-holders of foreign
sympathies." These were, it seems, the early predecessors of
the Congressional Subcommittee for un-American Activities.
After the Mad Scene there was applause around the
Diamond Horseshoe and elsewhere, and her fellow artists
complimented her, but the reviews the next day were just
"mildly favorable." Only the *New York Tribune* called her
vocalization "the finest example heard on the local stage
since Sembrich made her debut here ten years ago."

The Metropolitan had many great voices during that season, among them Emma Eames, Emma Calvé, Lillian Nordica, the de Reszkes, the tenor Ferrando de Lucia, the great
bass Pol Plançon. The season's most popular diva was Emma
Eames, an American girl born in Shanghai and brought up
in Bath, Maine, who had also been a pupil of Madame
Mathilde Marchesi in Paris at the time when Melba was
studying. Marchesi and Eames hadn't got along well; Madame Marchesi had been very hurt when Eames, after her
triumph at the Paris Opéra, gave her teacher no credit.
Eames had been Gounod's first choice for Juliette; but this
part was eventually given to the more powerful Patti, who
sang in the *première* with no success. Eames appeared as
Juliette in March 1888 at the Paris Opéra (a few weeks before Melba made her debut there) and won a triumph.
Gounod had been right.

Ever since then Melba and Eames had been competitors,

waging a persistent cold war. Officially, they pretended to love each other very much. The awful truth became known only later when the two divas published their respective now-it-can-be-told memoirs. Melba completely ignores Eames in her autobiography; Eames mentions Melba in *Some Memories and Reflections,* but not by name. She merely refers to "the soprano who prevented my debut in Brussels." Eames retired in 1912, after farewell performances as Tosca and Desdemona with the Boston Opera Company. Melba, six years older, sang for another fourteen years. When somebody mentioned Melba's durability Madame Eames, who had been an authentic American beauty in her younger years, said, "I would rather be a brilliant memory than a — curiosity."

Another rival of Melba, and a prominent member of the Metropolitan's galaxy, was Emma Calvé, also a former Marchesi pupil. It has been said that Calvé's beauty survived her voice while Melba's voice outlasted her looks. At London's Savoy, Madame Calvé once stared hard at Mary Garden who had arrived wearing a perfume especially created for her. (In those days, no real prima donna would touch a vulgar perfume also used by other women, even at nine dollars an ounce.) Madame Calvé knew her prima donna manners. She sniffed the air and loudly asked for another table.

At the Met, Calvé had a sensational success as Carmen. The opera was given twelve times during that season, earning the Met over one hundred thousand dollars. Melba and Calvé professed great enthusiasm for each other when they were sure to be overheard. *"Vous chantez comme une ange,"* Calvé once said to Melba in front of two critics. Melba answered in a similar sweet vein, but she drops Calvé's name only twice in her book, without any praise. Calvé is more generous in *My Life,* where she speaks of "Melba, whose pure voice soared like a skylark, intimate to heaven."

Melba pretended not to be discouraged by the lukewarm reception after her debut. "Let them talk about Madame Eames and Madame Calvé now," she said to a friend. "Before long they will talk about Madame Melba."

She was bothered by the acoustics of the Metropolitan, which seemed to her not as good as "the perfect conditions" at Covent Garden. (Later she often said it was "sheer joy" to sing at the Auditorium in Chicago, at Milan's La Scala or at Hammerstein's Manhattan Opera House.) But she loved American audiences, whom she called "among the most intelligent in the world."

"Americans know what is good and will never put up with a second best," she wrote. "They judge for themselves without waiting for the critics." She particularly loved to sing for the "matinee girls," "wearing huge posies of flowers at their waists," who would stream down the aisles at the end of the performance and throw flowers across the orchestra onto the stage.

And "gradually New York society . . . began to wonder who was this Madame Melba who was having so great a success, wondering if perhaps after all it might be interesting to make her acquaintance. I had not the faintest objection to allowing them to do so. I have always been perfectly happy whether my host is a millionaire or a bootmaker, provided that he possessed a sense of humor and sprinkling of brain."

Melba's arrogant optimism turned out to be right. She had such a success as Juliette that a great many Eames fans deserted their goddess and went over into the Melba camp. Within a few weeks Melba became the acknowledged star of the Sunday-night concerts at the Metropolitan. These concerts had been doing badly, but when Melba began to appear in them, they were always sold out. The season ended with a performance of *Faust* in which Melba appeared with Jean and Édouard de Reszke. *Faust* was always a favorite with New York audiences and given so often that the Metropolitan was called "the *Faustspielhaus.*" But rarely was it performed so well as with Melba and the de Reszkes. The *New York Herald* said that "since Christine Nilsson there has been no Marguérite the equal of Melba's."

At the end of the performance there was "a tempest of enthusiasm," and then the de Reszkes, gallant as ever, pushed a piano out on the stage, and Madame Melba sang "Home, Sweet Home," with "darling Jean" accompanying her on the piano. Some people said that was the best part of the evening. It just goes to show you: Melba had conquered New York.

During the World's Fair, she sang at the Chicago Auditorium — where the papers gave more attention to her dress than to her voice. It was reported that she had paid twenty-five hundred dollars for the dress she wore in the second act of *Tannhäuser,* "where the text demands an appearance of real magnificence." In the second act of *Rigoletto* she sang, as was her custom, the end of her aria *"Caro nome"* while walking up a high stairway — an effect which never fails to impress the audience, since only a coloratura with perfect breath-control can sing difficult staccato runs while she walks. Melba passed along a balcony, emitting her famous trill, entered a door — and suddenly the trill came to an abrupt end. People in the audience sensed that something must have happened, but they didn't know that Melba almost had an accident. Behind the door was a narrow platform. The stagehands had forgotten to put up a railing, and Melba almost fell down from the platform to the stage underneath. She managed to stop just in time by throwing herself backward against the scenery. "The trill was never finished," the papers reported the next day. Obviously Melba had grasped the essentials of American publicity.

She had bad luck one night when she was touring with the Chicago Opera Company. During a performance of *Faust*, with the tenor Lucien Muratore, Melba decided on the spur of the moment to appear in person in the tableau of Marguérite at her spinning wheel which is shown to Faust to lure him into perdition. The off-stage part had always been taken care of by an anonymous member of the company, but for some reason Melba wanted to be Marguérite both on and off stage that night.

Lady Susan Birch, Melba's great friend, who often went with her on tour, sat in the audience waiting for the tableau to appear. At the moment when the broad cloth veil was about to be lifted, there was a tremendous crash behind the scenes. The curtain came down. Lady Susan Birch rushed backstage. She found Melba lying in a faint in her dressing room. The doctor thought she might have broken her thigh.

Everybody was standing around in confusion. Then the manager ordered one of the singers to get dressed as Marguérite so the performance could continue. But Melba, who had come to, was not defeated. She rose to her feet and exclaimed in her marked Australian accent, *"Moi, je chante."* And she sang.

After Melba's first performance in Boston "it was generally concluded that no such singing had ever been heard here." Melba met "the world's finest body of musicians, a superb institution with a great soul" — proper talk that endeared her to all Bostonians, since she was referring to the celebrated Boston Symphony Orchestra. "I grew to love that orchestra almost as though it had been a human being," she later said. She immensely admired Major Higginson, the orchestra's great patron, "one of the very finest types of American, the type that says, 'I want the best and I don't care how much I pay for it.'" Outside the building she was delighted to see long queues of students who had waited from five o'clock in the morning in the rain and cold to obtain admission at twenty-five cents. "So much for those who say that America is not a music-loving country," Melba remarks. But it took a long time to overcome this prejudice. There were to be quite a few divas, long after Melba, who came to America with similar preconceptions and were greatly surprised.

In the annals of the Boston Symphony, Melba will be remembered as "the woman that dared stop the rehearsal." When she was rehearsing Handel's *Allegro ed il Penseroso,* with flute obbligato, one of the musicians played a C natural instead of a C sharp.

"C sharp! C sharp!" Melba shouted, pointing at the man who had made the mistake.

There was a dead silence. Then they all burst out laughing. Melba was later informed, perhaps not quite correctly, that "no one had dared criticize the orchestra like that since it had been founded."

"Yes," she adds in a typical Melba *non sequitur*, "Boston knew the best in music and always had it." The best included Madame Melba. She herself was so impressed by Charles A. Ellis, manager of the Boston Symphony — a man with a brilliant sense of organization and business acumen — that she made him her sole manager in America. And she remembers the good people of Boston who had "the same quiet appeal which one finds among one's friends in England."

One Bostonian whose appeal was perhaps not so quiet was Mrs. Jack Gardner, Melba's "ideal of what a rich woman should be." Mrs. Gardner, who "didn't know how many millions she had," impressed Melba because she spent her millions "in the service of beauty." In that service Mrs. Gardner brought over from Europe an entire Venetian palace, stone by stone, and had it set up in Boston, stone by stone. And Mrs. Gardner was more painstaking than Mr. William Randolph Hearst, another noted stone-by-stone importer. She insisted that real Italian plants be imported in their original pots and filled with Italian earth. In fact, Mrs. Gardner imported everything from Italy except the air and the sunshine. Melba heard strange rumors which swept

Boston. It was said that a noble Italian prince "languished in prison because he had allowed one of his old Italian paintings to be smuggled out" in return for a paltry two hundred thousand dollars.

Melba was among the first privileged few who were permitted to see Mrs. Gardner's palace. It was on a bitterly cold winter day, and a blizzard was raging; but when Melba arrived at the Boston *palazzo* two tall Italian servants opened the door and she found herself in an exquisite garden full of spring flowers. The courtyard had been glassed in, and there was "a very fair counterfeit of Southern warmth."

Mrs. Gardner was a stickler for detail. An immense, dark room called the Van Dyck was lit with hundreds of candles. The mail was brought in a basket each morning, just as in Venice. Before dinner a little ceremony would be held in the service of beauty. The guests would gather at one end of a long, dimly lit Italian gallery, with white statues on both sides, while the hostess would light a taper and slowly walk down the gallery to the other end, "a tiny figure in white draperies." She would then light two candles in front of an altar at the far end.

Mrs. Gardner's favorite guest list included John Singer Sargent, who painted her portrait. She loved to give presents and knew the art of giving. Once she came to see Melba at her hotel, chatted for a while and just before leaving gave her a little parcel wrapped in white tissue paper. "I brought you a little souvenir — I thought you might like it."

The "little souvenir" was a large yellow diamond. "One cannot help wondering," Melba muses, "how some other people of one's acquaintance, if they had so far forgotten themselves as to part with a yellow diamond at all, would have given it."

When Melba got back to New York she had become so thoroughly infected with "the American spirit of getting things done in the briefest possible time" that she got caught in an artistic disaster.

On a Saturday morning, during breakfast, she read in the *New York Herald* that she had been announced to sing Elisabeth in *Tannhäuser* — a part she had never studied — on the following Friday. Whether the surprise announcement was a mistake of the management or an intrigue of her competitors, Melba has never explained. Instead of doing the sensible thing and asking the Metropolitan to cancel her performance, Melba, infected by "the spirit of adventure in the air of New York," sent a special messenger down to the opera house for a *répétiteur*, and began to study the part of Elisabeth the same morning. She learned the part in three days. "Though I really did not know it, I sang it on Friday, and got good notices." She sang the part again "fairly well" on the following Tuesday, but the next performance in Philadelphia "found her out."

It was, by her own admission, "a horrible evening." She forgot some of her words in the Prayer, and several times the orchestra had to go on without her. It was an ordeal, and for several days afterwards she felt like a wreck. Back in New York she sent for the coach again and said, "Now I am *really* going to learn Elisabeth."

Exactly five months after her unsuccessful debut in New York in *Lucia* Melba appeared again in that opera at the Metropolitan. At the end of the performance there was so much cheering that the curtain had to be raised, a piano was wheeled upon the stage, and Melba sat down, playing and singing "Home, Sweet Home."

"The house was hushed and, as she left the stage, people in the audience said to each other, 'Melba is crying,' and they were right," wrote the impressionable *New York Herald*.

The following evening Melba made her farewell appearance at a Sunday-night concert in a mixed program with Nordica, Calvé, Scalchi, Eames and the de Reszkes. Everybody was there — on the stage as well as in the auditorium. After the Mad Scene from *Hamlet*, Messieurs Grau and Abbey, the managers of the Metropolitan, appeared with Madame Melba before the curtain. Again she was asked to sing "Home, Sweet Home." She did; though one would assume that everybody was a little tired of that song by now. She was followed to the Savoy Hotel by the orchestra of the Metropolitan and a large number of box-holders and subscribers. Melba fans were no longer "suspected of foreign sympathies." The orchestra serenaded Melba in the main lobby. The diva listened from the balcony overlooking the lobby. Afterwards she invited everybody to supper in the dining room. In one short season Melba, according to Henry C. Lahee, the American critic, "acquired popularity almost equal to Patti's in her best days."

"The Melba rage which has possessed New York," wrote the *New York Globe*, "will always be remembered as one of the most extraordinary manifestations of enthusiasm for the art. It is doubtful whether demonstrations of equal intensity have ever before been witnessed in the metropolis."

Yes, they were no longer talking about Mesdames Eames and Calvé. They were all talking about Madame Melba, just as she had predicted.

All her life Melba had a deep, unrequited love affair with the music of Richard Wagner. She could talk endlessly about the great composer. She often said she wished she had lived a little earlier and had known Wagner. At the Donizetti Centenary Exhibition in Bergamo, she was moved to tears when she saw copies of Donizetti compositions which Wagner had made in his younger years to earn a little money. She needn't have worried; the experience did no harm to Richard Wagner's strong personality. "As my musical instruction did me no good," he writes in *My Life*, "I continued in my willful process of self-education by copying out the scores of my beloved masters, and in so doing acquired a neat handwriting, which in later years has often been admired."

Melba always wanted to sing the great dramatic Wagnerian parts, for which her voice was totally unfit. She had sung in *Lohengrin* with modest success at Covent Garden, and in her first New York season she appeared in *Lohengrin* and *Tannhäuser*. Lyric sopranos often sing the parts of Elsa and Elisabeth, but Melba's white silvery voice lacked the heavier texture and darker lower register which are absolutely necessary for a good Wagnerian soprano. She never bothered to study German, singing the part of Elsa in

French and of Elisabeth in Italian. It is bad enough to hear Verdi sung in German, a guttural language not ideally suited to the melodious beauty of the Italian genius, but it is worse to hear Wagner's dramatic alliterations diluted in mellifluous Italian. Wagner's gods and heroes never were meant to sound like that. Melba once planned to sing the part of Senta in *The Flying Dutchman,* but luckily for her she gave up after a few weeks of trying.

In 1897, when she was the prima donna *assoluta* in New York, able to dictate her terms even at the Metropolitan, Melba reserved for herself "exclusive rights" to the dramatic part of Brünnhilde in *Siegfried.* This didn't ingratiate her to Madame Nordica, who was a superb Brünnhilde. But Nordica got her satisfaction.

Years earlier, Melba told Madame Marchesi in Paris that she wanted to sing Brünnhilde. Madame Marchesi's answer had been "a horrified expression and a great fluttering of the hands," as if Melba had threatened to cut her throat, which was exactly what she was about to do. Melba didn't pursue the matter further. Then she heard her favorite tenor, Jean de Reszke, in one of his favorite parts as Siegfried. "Darling Jean" told her, perhaps jokingly, that she would make a fine Brünnhilde.

For once Melba's common sense failed her. Despite all warnings she began to study the part with Herr Kniese in Paris, after Madame Marchesi refused to have anything to do with that. She sang it at the Metropolitan the evening of December 30, 1896. Jean de Reszke was Siegfried, brother

Édouard was the Wanderer, and the great Wagnerian conductor Anton Seidl conducted.

It had been noticed already, during previous rehearsals,
that Melba, usually so sure of herself, was scared to death.
Once or twice she wanted to quit, but Jean told her that
Richard Wagner must have had in mind exactly such a voice
as hers when he wrote the "exalted" music of Brünnhilde.
Didn't Nellie have perfect breathing power? Didn't she
know the music? Well, then, why did she worry? "Darling
Jean" was a charming colleague, but the world's worst judge
of voices. He later defended himself: he had indeed urged
Melba to sing in *Siegfried* — "the small part of the Waldvogel, not the terrific role of Brünnhilde." He must have
known that the great prima donna wouldn't have consented
to sing the invisible part of the Waldvogel, in which the
singer is only heard off stage. "If dear Nellie had been endowed not only with the voice of a lark but also with its
soul she would have made a triumph in the tiny part," he
is said to have explained.

But it was too late; she couldn't back out any more; people
might talk. She was terribly nervous the day before the
performance and didn't sleep all night long. Brünnhilde
appears only in the last scene of the last act. Even seasoned
hochdramatische Wagnerian sopranos find it strenuous to
have to hang around until eleven o'clock, and then to sing
some of the most formidable passages in the entire literature
of opera. It is truly wonderful, "exalted" music, one of the
greatest love duets in all music, and its scaring climaxes are
crowned by two ringing high C's.

Melba was beaten before she started. As soon as she

began to sing she knew that Madame Marchesi had been right and that she had been utterly wrong.

David Bispham, the noted American baritone, who sang the part of Alberich that night, gives us an eye witness account in his book *A Quaker Singer's Recollections:*

> I remember wishing her luck when, having finished my part in the second act, I found her upon the stage with Jean de Reszke. . . . I took my place in a box to witness the remainder of the performance. Melba was extremely nervous, because she was singing not only in a language to which she was unaccustomed, but in a part entirely unsuited to her and one which, though she knew it perfectly, she was ill-advised to have attempted at all. . . . She was apparently forgetful of the Wagnerian tradition, to remain well within the scene, and Jean, in the heavy fur coat of Siegfried, was kept busy patrolling the forward part of the stage to keep the white-clad Melba from rushing into the footlights, over which she had sung so many times to delighted audiences.

It was a minor tragedy. "Madame Melba's share in the performance cannot be discussed even in general terms," wrote Henry Krehbiel.

Melba admitted her defeat. "The music was too much for me. I felt as though I were struggling with something beyond my strength. I had a sensation almost of suffocation, of battling with some immense monster — a very different feeling from the usual exaltation which I had experienced in other roles."

She doesn't remember how she managed to get through the ordeal. When it was all over, she threw a dressing gown around her shoulders and sent for Mr. Grau.

"Tell the critics that I'm never going to do that again. It is beyond me. I have been a fool."

Few prima donnas ever made such an admission in public.

"The world can ill afford to lose a Melba even if it should gain a Brünnhilde," wrote the *New York Tribune* diplomatically. "But it will not gain a Brünnhilde."

W. J. Henderson, then the music critic of the *Sun*, told her a few days later, "You were quite right, Madame Melba. Your voice is like a piece of Dresden china. Please don't smash it." The same Henderson wrote, over thirty years later, after hearing Flagstad as Brünnhilde: "No other singer except Melba ever equalled her in liberation of voice, in the utter freedom from all constraint of production and articulation." Freudians will perhaps read some guilt in this subconscious comparison of one of the best Brünnhildes of all times to one of the worst.

The piece of Dresden china was not entirely smashed but the performance had done "very great harm" to Melba's voice. She sang twice afterwards, but the doctors told her that unless she took a long, complete rest at once, she might never be able to sing again.

Melba canceled all engagements in the middle of the season, went back to her home in Paris and for three months kept an enforced silence. "I implore young singers not to attempt to sing roles which are beyond their power," she writes. But opera singers learn from the mistakes of others as rarely as do other people. The world's great opera houses are populated with singers who ruined their voices prematurely by singing parts that are beyond their power.

Melba's infatuation with the music of Wagner continued despite her painful setback. In 1906, when she was in New York again, singing for Hammerstein's Manhattan Opera, which was then actively competing with the Met, the directors of the Met placed a box at her disposal for the first performance of *Parsifal*. She had sung the night before in *La Traviata* and was tired and feeling low when she got to the Met at the ghastly hour of eleven o'clock in the morning. She was in a "very nervous condition" and "ridiculously annoyed" by the bald head of the conductor. "I wanted to hit that bald head, to throw things at it, to cover it up." And then the lights dimmed and the cellos began to play the prelude. Melba forgot everything around her, as so many people have done during the prelude of *Parsifal*.

> I cannot explain what happened to me during the unforgettable act that followed [she wrote]. The bald head vanished, the theatre ceased to exist, I ceased to exist. But I do remember that at the end of the act, when the curtain fell, and the house remained wrapped in silence, I put my hand up to my head, and felt that I had a hat on. A hat. It seemed something unreal, grotesque. And then Ada Sassoli, that great little harpist, sitting by me, said something which made me realize I was on earth. She took my hand, and at the touch of the warm, human contact I leaned back in my chair and sobbed.

She was taken out by friends, and walked up and down the snow-covered pavements for some time. Slowly, gradually, she felt "returning to earth from the strange sphere" where the music had transported her. "Coming back was infinitely painful, and when I had to go out to lunch, the tinkling of the little orchestra in the restaurant was so torturing that I asked them to stop, otherwise I would have gone mad."

A great many people have gone through a similar emotional experience during the first act of *Parsifal*. I will remember the afternoon in Bayreuth when I stepped out of the Festspielhaus after the deeply moving first act and had a sense of revulsion when I saw the people in the nearby Festspiel restaurant drinking beer and eating *Wurstbrote* and mayonnaise eggs. It was quite an effort to go back to the auditorium and to become wrapped up in the music of the second act.

Melba remained absorbed in *Parsifal* for the rest of the day. She had frequent spells of weeping. She was depressed. "Here I am going to sing in *La Traviata* tomorrow," she would say "How can I do it? Heavens, how can I do it?"

The next day she sent for the score of *Tristan und Isolde*. She spent the day singing the part of Isolde and dreaming of the music. Many lyric sopranos have had that dream, and some try to sing the part, usually to the detriment of their vocal cords. Melba had learned her lesson in *Siegfried*. Much as she loved to be Isolde, she never attempted to sing the part.

≛ 13 ≛

The Bitter Taste of Fame and Fortune

IT WOULD BE superhuman for a prima donna to enjoy the success of her rivals. Melba was very human. When young Claire Dux created a sensation as Pamina at London's Drury Lane in the spring of 1914, and Melba, Destinn, Caruso, and Chaliapin came to listen, Sir Thomas Beecham reports in his autobiography, *A Mingled Chime*:

> . . . Naturally, it was the opinion of Melba, a soprano of world fame, that was most eagerly awaited, and I was almost as gratified as Claire herself when the formidable Nellie hailed her in my presence with the words: "You are my successor."

It must have been Melba's red-letter day. She was usually terribly jealous, and she admitted it.

"C'est plus fort que moi," she once said to Bemberg in the presence of Colson. "If any other artist gets as much applause as I do in any opera or concert at which I am singing, I simply can't bear it."

But she was generous when she listened to a rival as long

as the rival didn't appear on the same program. She never lowered herself to the technique of dumb applause when she was in the audience listening to a rival prima donna. Dumb applause — which is much used, not only by practicing prima donnas — can be defined as the skillful, silent clapping of one's hands for the benefit of the onlookers, without producing any sound. You would be surprised how often it is evident in the opera houses and concert halls of the so-called civilized world.

When Melba for the first time heard Adelina Patti, with the de Reszkes, in a performance of *Faust* conducted by Gounod at the Paris Opéra, she was overwhelmed. "When the moment for Patti's entrance came, and when I saw the light suddenly shine on the woman who had always been my goddess, I felt as though I should choke." Melba was young and impressionable. Many years later, when she wrote her autobiography, she neutralized her early exhilaration, adding: "Patti's best days are past. . . . In the Waltz-Song she made a tiny slip, and I could have kissed Gounod for the cleverness with which he managed to conceal it with a mere twist and a sudden gesture of his baton." This is prima donna writing at its best, with the stiletto hidden inside the pen. (*"Elle est la première dans son genre mais son genre n'est pas le premier,"* writes the great Catalini about her rival, the great Sontag. Ha!)

Melba was too big a woman to resort to petty tricks such as dumb applause. She was genuinely shocked when a famous pianist (whose name she doesn't reveal) once told her that he applauded his competitors only when he discovered false notes in their performance and never when they played faultlessly. But when Melba wanted to hit her target, she always scored a bull's-eye. She was the authentic prima donna who rises to her finest form in the presence of a rival.

When Madame Melba sang in Bergamo in 1897 for the festival honoring the centenary of Donizetti, one of the members of the company was Madame Alva, whose voice, according to Melba, "was not of the quality which would arouse superlative enthusiasm." Somehow or other, Alva's name was not mentioned in any of the reviews which praised Melba and Joseph Joachim, the celebrated violinist and Melba's great friend. Alva made the mistake of complaining, in a letter to the music critic of the *Daily Telegraph*, that she'd had, after all, "as much success, if not more, than Madame Melba"; why had her name not been mentioned?

The *Daily Telegraph* printed the letter. Alva and others accused Melba of having organized this exposure. There is no reason to disbelieve Melba's assertion that she had never seen the letter until she saw it in the paper. "I was exceedingly sorry for the unfortunate woman who had been so misguided as to run her head against the critics," Melba wrote later. She wouldn't have bothered to organize a psychological warfare campaign against Madame Alva, who simply was not in her class.

Melba's punctuality was the delight of her stage managers and the despair of her smart hostesses. She would always travel with several alarm clocks in her luggage; she was obsessed by the fear of being late for a rehearsal or an appointment. For Melba, eight o'clock meant eight o'clock sharp, not eight-fifteen. Once she appeared at a party at the appointed time, found the house dark and her hostess taking a bath. Madame Bemberg, the mother of the composer, always asked Melba to come half an hour later than she'd invited the rest of the people. "It meant," said Madame Bemberg, "that Nellie would show up at the same time they did."

Melba never let anyone wait for her at a rehearsal. She had no patience with sloppy artists. At the Metropolitan, during a rehearsal of *Tristan und Isolde* on the day of the performance, she heard a small-part singer say to Madame Nordica, the famous Isolde, "Nothing on earth would make me rehearse Isolde on the day I sang it." Melba turned to the speaker. "Don't worry — you will never be asked to do it."

Melba would never send an understudy to a rehearsal, as Patti had often done. Prima donnas don't often sing smaller parts, and when they do, they mention the fact in their memoirs because it is so unusual. Melba reports that when she decided to sing the small but beautiful part of Micaëla in *Carmen,* at the Opéra Comique in Paris, "out of courtesy to the management," her friends were astonished. "It is not a star's role," they said. "You will be eclipsed."

> Why on earth a prima donna should not sometimes sing small and secondary roles, I could not see [Melba writes]. I hate the artistic snobbery of it. The part of Micaëla has some exquisite music which I loved singing. I sang it at Covent Garden with Calvé, and later in America with Zelie de Lussan.

Not too often, however; and quite a few times she happened to be "indisposed" when she was to sing Micaëla.

Like all singers, Melba was plagued by imaginary colds

and nervous throat ills. A prima donna worries about her reputation and can't afford to sing when she isn't in top form. On her American concert or opera tours Melba would often call her manager, Charles A. Ellis, in the late morning to inform him that she couldn't sing, she couldn't sing a tone, she would probably be sick in that terrible weather.

Ellis knew how to treat a prima donna. He would listen to her patiently and sympathize with her. After a little while he'd get up saying, "See you tonight, curtain at eight" — and Melba would be there, singing in her best form.

"Everybody, who has known fame has also known the agonies which fame brought," Melba writes. She was referring to rumors that always followed her everywhere. The most persistent repeated her fondness for drinking, but there is no evidence that Melba ever hit the bottle. Elena Danieli, who often appeared with her in the prima donna's later years, always saw a thermos bottle with black coffee in Melba's dressing room, never a drop of alcohol.

"We've often wondered how these rumors were kept alive," Tom Hazelton-Cochrane says. "Melba liked a glass or two, like any sensible person, but she was much too careful about her voice and health to drink much. She didn't need liquor; she never had bad depressions. In her house there was always wonderful food and her wines were exquisite, but there was never enough champagne. She would serve half a bottle for four or six people. No one dared ask for more; they wouldn't dare ask her for anything. People were never quite relaxed in Melba's company. You are not relaxed in the presence of a queen. When she took us out for dinner she would discourage us right from the start by saying, 'I'm not having any champagne. Do you want any?' Naturally, no one spoke up. She was very upset about these silly rumors. I wonder why they never said she was smoking cigars. She didn't, but she liked the smell of a good cigar, and encouraged the men in her company to smoke a cigar after dinner."

Melba realized early in her career that all was well as long as people kept talking about her. The real trouble would come when they no longer so talked. Instead of denying the various rumors, she once set them down in her tidy, methodical way. According to her account of the talk that followed her rise to fame in London, the reasons that she could sing were,

1. That I had no roof to my mouth.
2. That I consume three raw eggs before each act of *La Bohème*.
3. That I show off in church by singing psalms an octave higher than the rest of the congregation.
4. That I am a German Jewess whose father was born in Stuttgart. [What's wrong with Stuttgart?]
5. That I am a Roman Catholic, a Nonconformist, a Christian Scientist, a Unitarian, a Theosophist, and a Spiritualist.

Usually supremely indifferent to what people were saying about her — in that respect she was Edwardian — Melba seems to have been badly stung by persistent rumors of her "autocratic ways" at Covent Garden and by stories of machinations of an alleged "Melba clique." Even now, rather late in the day, such insinuations raise the blood pressure of Melba's old friends.

I gather [I was supposed] to have instituted a sort of cabal at Covent Garden, [a system] by which those who endeavoured to obtain a hearing there were first referred to me and then, if they showed any promise, were summarily dismissed without a word of explanation [Melba writes at the very end of her autobiography]. Professional singers will realize how utterly fantastic such stories must be, but the general public . . . are more easily deluded. It is the general public I love, not the professional musicians, and it is for them, therefore, that I am including a copy of a letter from Mr. Harry Higgins who has been for so many years the directing spirit of all that concerns Covent Garden.

[Here follows Higgins's letter]:

Regarding suggestions that you were in the habit of using your position at Covent Garden to influence the management . . . I can honestly say that I have never known such to be the case. After all, no one had had from the very beginning of your career less cause to fear competition than you, apart from which you always appeared to me to wisely imitate the example of the gentleman who earned £10,000 a year by minding his own business.

You know as well as I that inefficient artists are always ready to put forward every sort of excuse for their failure, and never attribute it to the obvious cause, their own incompetence, and I think that accounts for the rumors you referred to.

The tactful Higgins (who happened to be the brother-in-law of Melba's great and powerful friend, Lady de Grey) then tells the story of a well-known and popular general who once asked a prima donna, "a mutual friend of ours," whether the intrigues among her colleagues were not of the most terrible sort. "They were nothing," she replied, "compared to those among the generals at the War Office."

"And I have no doubt she was right," concludes Harry Higgins.

The facts, alas, don't always support the chivalrous Higgins. In 1903, the young Italian baritone Titta Ruffo made his Covent Garden debut as Enrico in *Lucia*.

> He was so successful and created such an impression at the dress rehearsal of *Rigoletto*, which he was due to sing with Melba, that she protested that he was too young to play her father, and he was removed from the cast [reports Harold Rosenthal, in *Two Centuries of Opera at Covent Garden*]. He never sang again at Covent Garden. Several years later, when he had become an international celebrity, he had his revenge: he and Melba were billed to sing in the same work at another famous opera house, and this time Ruffo objected — on the grounds that Melba was too old to be his daughter.

"The absence of Geraldine Farrar, the early disappearance from the London scene of the American prima donna Emma Eames, and the infrequent appearances of the popular Austrian coloratura Selma Kurz have been attributed to the jealousy of Melba," writes Desmond Shawe-Taylor.

Melba didn't often use a claque. After her rapid rise to fame she had a large and enthusiastic following wherever she went and didn't need a body of hired applauders. Supremely confident of herself, she didn't have to have the encouragement of hand-clapping enthusiasts. But she rarely went to the opera without a large "house party" — members of her personal staff, admirers and friends. And she had skilled amateur *claqueurs* in "very high circles." "She had that magnetism which is the most valuable gift the gods can bestow on an artist," writes Colson.

Melba's great partner Caruso believed in using a claque. He would never make an entrance unless he was sure that at least sixty or eighty friends, admirers and "paid enthusiasts" were strategically scattered all over the house. He wanted to be sure that they would applaud and cry "Bravo!" at the right moment. He would spend two hundred dollars' worth of seats at every performance, and sometimes he would personally inspect the house before buying the seats in order to have his followers properly placed in strategic key positions. He was one of the greatest singers of all times, but he freely admitted that the right applause at the right time helped him to give his best.

Caruso knew that blasé people in the orchestra stalls and in the boxes often applauded too little and too late. He said there was nothing wrong in getting a little help from well-meaning friends and enthused *claqueurs*. There wasn't, and isn't. Genuine applause is contagious. It gives the artist more confidence, the audience more enjoyment, the performance a special gloss.

Melba was severely handicapped in this Department of Enthusiasm. She had no husband, and her lovers were much too discreet to run what Berlioz called a Success Bureau. Melba depended on rank amateurs for applause and approval. But she seems to have done quite well.

✄ 14 ✄

Home, Sweet Home

Y OU MUST UNDERSTAND first and foremost that I am an
Australian," Melba says at the beginning of her autobiography. In May, 1886, an obscure amateur singer, Mrs.
Helen Porter Armstrong, had left Australia. Sixteen years
later, in September, 1902, Madame Nellie Melba, the world's
most famous prima donna, returned to her native land.

For years rumors regularly swept Australia from time to
time that Melba was coming back, and were just as regularly
followed by Melba's official denials to the press. "These
rumors . . . have not been authorized by me, as the difficulties to such a venture have proved unsurmountable." The
regal style of these denials created bad feeling (and many
Melba jokes) in Australia. No one thought she would ever
come back to "an uncivilized country which doesn't even
have a single opera house."

No one except Melba's closest friends knew that she had
actually been homesick for Australia all these years. "The
very mention of the name made me long for the sight of the
tall white gum-trees, for the flash of the yellow wattle in the

bush, for the brilliant crystalline sunlight, for the great open spaces. And above all, for the sight of my Daddy."

In November, 1901, Madame Melba sent a cable to the Australian Press:

IT GIVES ME GREAT PLEASURE TO INFORM YOU THAT . . . I SHALL SAIL FROM ENGLAND IN AUGUST, AND GIVE A SERIES OF CONCERTS IN MELBOURNE, SYDNEY, BRISBANE, AND ADE-LAIDE, DURING THE MONTHS OF SEPTEMBER, OCTOBER, AND NOVEMBER. . . . I CANNOT TELL YOU HOW DELIGHTED I AM IN LOOKING FORWARD TO A VISIT SO FULL OF POTENTIAL PLEASURE TO MYSELF IN THE RENEWAL OF OLD FRIENDSHIPS WITH THE PEOPLE AMONG WHOM I WAS BORN AND BROUGHT UP.

It was the pronunciamento of a queen announcing a state visit, but Melba's homecoming was truly a royal progress. It was also one of the great ordeals of her life.

She sailed from Vancouver on August 22 on the *Miowera*. It was a terrible journey. The *Miowera*, soon known among the passengers as "The Weary Mary," had a habit of breaking down, sometimes for twenty-four hours, in the sweltering Pacific. This was before the days of radio, and Melba had no way of letting her father know that they would be delayed. He was over seventy and would worry, and that worried Melba. When the *Miowera* was three days overdue, wild rumors swept Australia. The ship was said to have been wrecked in Moreton Bay; everybody was dead. (A reassuring telegram was later received from Cape Moreton.) The uncertainty built up terrific advance publicity for the prima donna.

The *Miowera* arrived in Brisbane on the evening of September 17, three days late. Melba had said, with that charming modesty which is such an endearing trait of all great prima donnas, that she wished no special reception. But she would have been very annoyed if the Mayor and the Corporation of Brisbane hadn't come aboard to welcome her. There were red carpets, long speeches, and large bouquets of wattle blossom, Australia's national flower.

She was to meet her father the following morning in Albury, a town two hundred miles south of Melbourne. The train was scheduled to arrive in Albury at seven o'clock. Melba was up at five and dressing, taking "great pains to look my best in my prettiest frock and most becoming hat." She was no longer a great prima donna but a young girl going to her first date. "I almost reduced my maid to tears with my exacting demands. Sixteen years is a long time, and when one has somebody whom one loves very much to meet at the end of the journey, one wants to look one's best." After all the attractive men she had met in her life she still thought her father was the best of all.

"A quarter to seven, ten minutes to seven, five minutes to seven . . ." And then they were in Albury. She leaned out of the window; her large hat was almost blown off. In the distance she saw flags and heard the cheers of the crowd at the station.

The train stopped. Melba got out. A roar went up, people crowded around her. She looked around but there was no Daddy.

"Where is my father?"

There was an inarticulate murmur, and then silence.

"Where is he? What happened?"

She saw a gap in the crowd. A strange man dressed in black stood there, with a nurse at his side.

"Where is my father?" Melba asked him, with a sinking heart. The early morning sun beat hard in her face. The faceless crowd surged around her but she saw only the man in black, a doctor. He told her that her father was alive but very ill, lying in a house near the station. He had been so upset by the delay of the *Miowera* and the rumors that he had suffered a stroke. She must be brave. She would be allowed to see him but it was doubtful whether her father would recognize her.

Melba stared vacantly at the crowd, the flags, the flowers. "All the triumph, all the glory seemed to have vanished, and I remember thinking bitterly, 'What is the use of it all now?' "

She walked as in trance, following the doctor. The crowd seemed to have disappeared. There was something unreal about the whole scene. They walked across a field into a small house.

"You may go in," said the doctor. "But please don't speak to him."

A woman came out, Mrs. Griffith, the owner of the house.

"Go in. He seems better. He will recognize you."

The room was very dark after the strong sunlight outside. Melba stood still until her eyes were used to the dimness. She saw her father lying very still in bed. She tiptoed toward him, knelt down by the bed, kissed his hand.

And after a long time he opened his eyes, slowly and wearily. "As he saw me, the tired mouth switched itself into a little smile."

The nurse put a warning finger across her lips but Melba forgot all about the doctor's order. She had to speak to her father. She was going to stay here. She would cancel her whole program and nurse him until he was well again.

He managed to shake his head. Melba saw "that little gesture of unbreakable will which I remembered as a child." Then he said, almost inaudibly, "You must go on." Once more: *"You must go on."* His strict Scottish Presbyterian sense of honor wouldn't tolerate it if she let the people down.

"Do — not — disappoint," he said, wearily.

She understood. She had always understood her father, who said so little and meant so much.

> I went on [she writes]. How, I did not know. They had kept the express waiting for me for a whole hour. I went straight to my carriage and I began to cry. But I went on.

It was a harrowing experience. They had installed her in the state car which the Prince and the Princess of Wales had used when they toured the country a few months earlier, after the proclamation of the Commonwealth. All along the route thousands of people stood waiting to see Melba. The railway buildings were decorated. At every stop there were deputations, speeches, cheers. Melba had to make platform appearances, to smile, to thank the people.

Melbourne had proclaimed a public holiday. Thousands stood around Spencer Street Station. "The platform presented a scene of animation only equalled by the reception accorded to the first Governor General," reported a news-paper.

Melba's brother and sisters had boarded the express earlier at Seymour. (She never mentions any of them in her auto-biography.) Now other relatives and old friends greeted her. When she stepped out of the station, bedlam broke out. Melba rose to the challenge in perfect prima donna style. She began to tear up the heaps of flowers that filled the seats of the carriage and threw them to all sides. An inde-scribable mêlée ensued. "Men almost came to blows in dis-puting the right to a daffodil, women looked unutterable things at one another over a few damaged violets, while boys, with a keen eye to business, gathered all they could, and had a brisk market in the sale of Melba mementoes," wrote the conservative newspaper *Argus,* with a note of faint reproach.

The journey through the city whose name Melba had adopted was a fantastic triumph. Flags everywhere. Bands playing. The trams had stopped running. The streets were lined with people, all windows were occupied. In Collins Street the members of the Stock Exchange came out waving their hats in the air. Melba passed Allan's Piano Warehouse, where she had gone up the narrow stairs for her first sing-ing and piano lessons. A band was playing "Home, Sweet Home," and the house was covered with flags. A little farther away was a new office building where her grandmother had once lived in a quaint little rambling house. Nellie had often climbed the wall "to gather the ripening peaches which grew against it."

She kept smiling bravely, "but all the time I was thinking

of my father." When she was alone in her room, she broke down. She had to postpone her first concert. Not until two days later, when she had a telegram that her father was recovering nicely and might soon be able to return to Melbourne, did she begin to sing and get ready for her concerts.

The citizens of Melbourne, who still found it somewhat incredible that the legendary Melba had come home after all, gave her a tremendous welcome. There were receptions, parties, entertainments in her honor. The Presbyterian Ladies' College, whose teachers had been shocked by Nellie Mitchell's early accomplishments in the art of whistling and by "the funny noise" in her throat, received its most famous alumna with open arms. At a matinee performance of "Sweet Nell of Old Drury" in Melba's honor at the Princess's Theatre "thousands of people gathered in the vicinity, and the crowd cheered when Melba's carriage drew up at the door. As she entered the theatre, the orchestra played 'Auld Lang Syne,' and the vast audience stood up to greet the world's Queen of Song," reported the *Leader*.

No prima donna in history has ever been honored that way.

Melba's first concert in the city whose name she had adopted was one of the worst ordeals of her life. "No audience," she said, "is as trying as an audience of friends." There was little Nellie Mitchell, who had left Australia and returned as the world's undisputed prima donna *assoluta*. Was she really that good? Wouldn't her concert be an anticlimax after the terrific welcome?

People queued up all night long in the street to get a ticket. The better seats were fifteen dollars, four times the usual price; at later concerts they were even more expensive. Several hours before the concert, such crowds has assembled around the Town Hall that mounted police had to be called to cope with the traffic jam.

When Melba appeared on the platform, the entire audience got up and broke "into a wild tumult of cheers." Melba stood quietly in the center of the platform, "looking taller than her wont in that hour of exquisite triumph," reports her laudatory biographer, Agnes G. Murphy. She wore a simple (and very expensive) white gown, and a single (and very precious) string of pearls. She was pale and hardly smiled as the ovations continued. She bowed her head and people in the front rows thought she was hardly able to control her emotions.

Still the applause got stronger. "Melba now seemed quite overwhelmed by the greeting. There were many who felt that it would surely be impossible for her to sing." Another minute and she might have broken down. For once Melba had lost her proverbial *sang-froid.* So much had happened in the past few days that she thought she couldn't go on. Yet somehow she pulled herself together, "rose with a superb effort to the demands of the occasion, and sang as she had rarely sung before."

Encores and more encores . . . At long last Melba sat down at the piano and gave the people the song everybody was waiting for, "Home, Sweet Home."

"The applause that followed had in it something of a

great suppressed sob," writes Miss Murphy, almost breaking down herself.

Little Nellie Mitchell had come home.

Her father arrived a few days later in Melbourne and was able to attend Melba's second concert. She sang for him his favorite song, "Comin' thro' the Rye." It was Melba's tragedy that her father, whose acclaim was more important to her than that of any composer, critic or musician, had never heard her in any opera performance. His bad health had prevented him from making the long boat trip to Europe. Melba never got over it; she had wanted so much to prove to him that she'd made good after all.

Sitting there in Town Hall in the midst of all the excitement, old David Mitchell must have been wondering how he could have been so utterly wrong when he had opposed Nellie's early efforts to sing. Perhaps he was a little puzzled by all the uproar caused by his "lassie." But he was no longer puzzled when she told him how much she had earned with her concerts; his stout Scottish heart was always warmed by impressive cold figures.

The highest fee that had been paid to any prima donna anywhere any time on earth, until Melba came along, was ten thousand dollars which Jenny Lind had received for her first appearance in America under the management of Phineas T. Barnum — who had held a rather undignified auction for the sale of the tickets. Caruso had received fifteen thousand dollars when he sang in opera in Mexico City. But Melba established the prima donna's world's record when she received two thousand, three hundred and fifty pounds (eleven thousand seven hundred and fifty dollars) for her third concert in Melbourne, with no special advertising and no paid promotion, in a comparatively small community, and at a time when Australia was suffering from a bad drought.

"May I be forgiven for saying," Melba notes with pride, and for once the prima donna should be forgiven, "that from five concerts in Melbourne and four in Sidney I netted the sum of £21,000." One hundred and five thousand dollars — healthy, solid, uninflated gold dollars — for nine concerts, and hardly any income tax.

Wherever she went, it was the same story; tumultuous welcomes, endless ovations, crowded halls, record prices. She went back to the small township of Lilydale, twenty-four miles from Melbourne, where she'd spent her holidays as a kid. Her father now owned a beautiful wine-growing estate at nearby St. Hubert's, and proudly took her on a tour of his cellars. He was a remarkable man, starting new enterprises at an age when most people are glad to retire. The diva mounted her brother's dogcart and drove round the carriageway at a terriffic pace. For a few minutes she was Nellie Mitchell again, frightening all the bystanders with her wild temperament.

People from all over the countryside came to greet her. "Horses, carriages, bicycles, and people were all adorned with rosettes and ribbons in blue and gold, the family colors of the diva," writes Miss Murphy. The day ended with a monster picnic, which her father gave at Cave Hill Estate, another of his properties where Melba had often spent her

holidays. The *Lilydale Express*, the local newspaper, appeared in a "gala edition" with gold print on blue paper.

It was a time of triumph but there were moments of
trial. Sometimes Melba wished she could take the next boat
back to Europe. Melbourne wasn't Mayfair; the local standards of comfort were not what she had become used to.
Once she invited a few friends for dinner on a Sunday
evening, her only free day between concerts. On Saturday
morning her cook came to ask whether it was true that
Madame intended to give a dinner on the Sabbath day.

"Yes. Have you any objection?"

"I'm not going to cook for you on the Sabbath, and furthermore, I should like to give a week's notice."

"You needn't do that," Melba said angrily. "You can go
now."

She soon regretted that she'd lost her temper. She could
find no one in Melbourne who would cook a dinner on Sunday. Her father got her out of the predicament by lending
her his own cook. The cook consented to come only after
Melba had seen the director of the local tramway company
to have the cook's fiancé transferred to a line going nearer
her house. No diva is a prima donna to her cook.

Malicious gossip almost spoiled her homecoming. A
woman journalist whom Melba had offended in London in
one of her "painfully straight" moods had sent a collection
of juicy tidbits and inside dope to the Australian papers.
"The favorite rumors which attach to all politicians" as she
contemptuously wrote, now circulated: Melba was said to
"drink"; to be a morphia addict ("looking at my exceedingly

healthy face in the mirror I smiled at that one"); to have affairs with her tenors, baritones and conductors ("it did not seem to matter very much which"). Fame, Melba had found out long ago, has its bitterness, and success its agonies.

She had a particularly upsetting experience in the Tasmanian town of Launceston. She had arrived there after a bad crossing through rough seas in a small paddleboat. She had been terribly seasick, her throat was badly inflamed, and she was more dead than alive. The concert was to begin in a few hours. A local doctor examined her, told her it would be madness even to attempt to sing for several days, and gave her a certificate.

It was too late to notify the people who were already on their way from all over Tasmania to Launceston; and there was no way of letting her audience know that the concert had to be canceled. Many concertgoers arrived in Launceston after an arduous trip through the Bush only to be told that Madame Melba was unable to sing.

Immediately new rumors began to spread. Some said she couldn't sing because she'd had too much champagne. Somebody had heard from somebody who had seen a man who knew, from a woman, that a bottle of champagne had been taken up to Melba's room. Word got around that Melba would leave town by the first train to catch the next boat for New Zealand, and a few infuriated ticket-holders came to hoot her as her train steamed out of Launceston station.

This was the low point of Melba's homecoming. She never forgot the humiliation. When she returned to Australia five years later, she insisted that her itinerary must include a concert in Launceston. She wrote to her flutist and manager,

John Lemmone, to arrange the concert so it would coincide with the arrival of a big steamer; she had enough of paddle-boats.

"Please do this, for I would not disappoint the people of Launceston again," she wrote him.

When Lemmone arrived in town to make the arrangements he was told that Melba would be "hooted out of the hall" if she dared to come again. Lemmone had to go to the local club to prove that Melba had compensated her manager for the canceled concert; and then he went to the newspapers and showed them Melba's letter. (No one had gone after the facts of her sickness; the doctor who had attended her years ago had never bothered to explain the situation.) Melba came, sang and conquered. She was not hooted out of the hall. Instead, "all the flowers of Tasmania seemed to be heaped in front of me." There was such excitement that people took the horses from her carriage after the concert and dragged the carriage with the prima donna through the streets to her hotel.

Unharnessing the horses, once the classical tribute to a great diva, is no longer practiced these days for want of horses. The students of Göttingen University once unharnessed the horses from the coach of the great Henriette Sontag, pulled her home, and then threw the coach into the Leine River so no one else would ever "desecrate" the vehicle. Taking out the carburetor wouldn't be the same thing at all, and no one would push a nice Cadillac or Bentley into a river. Today's fans have no opportunities left. Their adored prima donna is already on the way to the airport to catch the next jet plane.

In September, 1909, when Melba was at the height of her fame and drawing power, she gave up a few months of large fees in Europe and America and made a sentimental journey through the remote back blocks of Australia, something she'd wanted to do ever since she became famous. This meant a trip off the beaten track, "far beyond the regions usually visited even by the smallest and most intrepid travelling circus." It was a challenge and an exciting experience. She had the acclaim of the greatest living composers, the praise of the sternest critics, the adoration of the most blasé audiences in New York, Milan, London, and Paris, the friendship of kings and queens — but she wanted more: to be accepted by her own people.

"I started that tour with an emotion which I had not felt during my greatest successes in Europe and America," she remembers. Would they really come to hear her? Would they understand her singing? Would she be able to get her music through to her own people?

They did come. They came from remote places in the wilderness of the bush, in carts and trucks and sometimes on foot. "Mark Twain would have enjoyed himself on that tour," she wrote. At every stopping place Melba was given a reception "of which even royalty could not have complained."

It was very moving. As the tiny train puffed into the station, Melba would be greeted by the shrill voices of school children standing lined up to greet her. The Mayor and his councilors would greet her officially. A "darling little lady" would drop her a curtsy and hand her a bouquet of glorious flowers. The children would sing "God Save the King," the

Mayor and everybody else would stand at attention, and Melba would be taken to the only hotel in town. The local establishment often made her think wistfully of London's Savoy or the Ritz in Paris. The Bush hotels didn't have quite the same comfort, although Melba, the passionate antique hunter, often noticed a genuine Sheraton book case brought out by some ancestor from the old country, pieces of authentic Chippendale used in the kitchen, or rare first editions on bedroom bookshelves.

At one of these dilapidated hostelries the proprietor had thoughtfully purchased a brand-new suite of furniture for Melba's sitting room. She thought it was a very touching gesture until, at the end of her stay, she noticed that the suite of furniture had been added to the bill. Manager Lemmone coped efficiently with the problem. He told the proprietor they would be delighted to pay for the furniture but would naturally take it along with them. The price of the suite came off the bill quickly.

In towns with a small newspaper the current issue would be devoted entirely to "highly colored accounts" of Melba's doings. If there was no newspaper, the town crier would spread the word. Once Melba and Lemmone went to listen to one.

"Oyez! Oyez!" he cried. "She's arrived. She's here. She's nothing to *me*, you know, I don't know anything about her. But when I tell you that she's sung before all the crowned heads of Sydney, she ought to be good enough for this one-horse town."

After that, Melba didn't bother to listen to another town crier.

Some people resented her. They tried to be rude to the former Nellie Mitchell who had become rich and famous. They objected to her "fancy attitudes" and were shocked by her manservant. They refused to serve her food after a concert. Melba took these minor irritations in stride. She really liked the people; she had mellowed; she enjoyed herself tremendously; she was having much more fun than when she'd been singing in London or New York.

> Nellie Melba was much more at home with her own people in Australia than with the great cosmopolitan society [says Hazelton-Cochrane]. They reminded her of her childhood. She knew that they didn't know better. They had lived all their life in the Bush. She was a different woman on these trips. She was no longer the imperious prima donna. She was herself.

Melba always tried to arrive in a place the evening before the concert. She wanted to have time to look around. In the morning on the day of the concert she would be roused out of sleep at dawn by the carts and trucks and bullock-wagons rolling in from the outlying districts. "Sometimes, in those early hours, a lump used to come into my throat as I thought of the gift which God had given to me to draw all these people from miles and miles to listen to me, Nellie Mitchell, the tomboy that used to fall into the mud rather than go to church."

The local halls were never large enough to hold all the people who wanted to hear "that Nellie Mitchell from Melbourne." Managers adjusted the inexorable law of supply and demand by selling a great many more tickets than there were seats in the hall. Some places were so crowded that

Melba "had to refresh herself behind the scene with a bag of oxygen," which she always carried around. In one town Melba was bothered during her first numbers by a strange noise underneath the platform where she was standing. She was told that the hall was built on wooden pillars because of the dangerous white ants. A number of connoisseurs of *bel canto* were lying between the pillars, sometimes bumping their heads against the floor of the platform.

Another time Melba noticed a large silent crowd outside the hall — people who had been unable to get in. They stood in silence and listened, and after each number joined in the applause from inside. Melba was so moved by their devotion that she told Lemmone to open the doors. There was bedlam. People rushed in, chairs were overturned, women screamed and fainted, and the police had to restore order. Afterwards Melba was more careful about having doors opened.

In another town some *aficionados* decided that they would like to hear Melba without paying for it. They milled around the hall with the paying concertgoers before the beginning of the concert, and then surreptitiously disappeared toward the rear where the community gardener was known to leave his high ladder standing against the flat roof. The hall had a large skylight which was left open in the damp heat. These thrifty music lovers got up on the ladder and enjoyed the free concert and the cool air on the roof.

Then, during the concert, the community gardener remembered his ladder. With so many strangers around he thought he had better put it away in the tool shed for the night. The connoisseurs on the roof didn't notice him, being thrilled with Melba's (free) trills. When the concert was over and the paying audience had left, the *cognoscenti* wanted to get down from the roof and discovered they were unable to do so. They spent a very long and uncomfortable night up there until they were rescued at five in the morning by a policeman who brought them a ladder.

"I can well believe that that policeman lived comfortably on blackmail for the rest of his life," Melba said when she heard of this bit of Maupassant.

No day went by without another adventure. In one town they hurriedly built a makeshift hall for Melba's concert. When she went to take a look at the place a few hours before the concert and stepped on the platform, there was a tremendous crash. Melba rushed out afraid the roof had fallen, but it was only the floor that had caved in, not strong enough to support both the piano and the prima donna. Fortunately the village carpenter had "an ear for music" and managed to patch up the piano in time for the concert.

Melba never allowed an intermission during these bush concerts. "We used to create an atmosphere and kept it," she wrote. "Intervals would be fatally disturbing."

After a concert a man came to her and said happily, "Madame Melba, I just want to tell you I loved your singing."

She thanked him with a smile.

"I've heard the best singer in the world, Madame Galli-Curci, and you are the next-best." Melba's smile became a little strained.

Another time a very old man waited for her and said, "You were worth the money. You were all prizes and no blanks, and I know something about singing. I was in a circus myself once."

The greatest compliment on this tour was paid to her by two small boys who were crouching by the stage door on a rainy night. She told them to come in. They listened breathlessly. After the concert Melba said, jokingly, "There, you owe me a guinea each."

"Madame Melba," said the smaller boy earnestly. "We owe you much more than that." She gave him a kiss. He deserved it.

When she returned to Melbourne, Lord Kitchener, who was then a guest at the Government House, asked her for dinner there. Melba had met him in London and admired him greatly. To her impressionable soul he seemed a romantic figure, very lonely, very quiet, with "the voice of a poet rather than of a soldier."

After dinner at Government House Lord Kitchener, followed by the Governor General and the Governor of Victoria, came in from the dining room, approached Melba and pretended to fall on their knees.

"I know what you want but I won't," she said, and laughed.

Kitchener looked her straight in the eyes. "Madame, I have been an exile for eight years. Won't you — won't you sing me just one verse of 'Home, Sweet Home'?"

She went to the piano and sang. Afterwards Kitchener came over with tears in his eyes and kissed her hands. "And when I've heard people say that Kitchener had no heart, I think of that moment," Melba remembers with her incurable romanticism.

ᨒ 15 ᨒ

Pêche Melba and Melba Parties

"MY NAME HAS BEEN printed fairly often and I suppose it will figure on menus long after I'm gone," Melba wrote in a prophetic moment. To most people today "Melba" means a dessert. Many celebrated chefs have claimed to be the creators of the world's most famous peach. The honor belongs exclusively to Auguste Escoffier, one of the greatest practitioners of all times of *la haute cuisine*.

Melba herself has put the fact on record. She was often irritated by famous chefs in hotels and restaurants all over the world who claimed to be the creators of Pêche Melba.

"They think my memory is particularly short or imagine I am a fool," she once said to her friend Tom Hazelton-Cochrane. One day she was walking with him in the gardens on Monte Carlo when they met a slim old goateed gentleman in black who turned out to be the celebrated M. Escoffier, living there in retirement. He kissed Melba's hand with old-fashioned gallantry, and began to talk rapidly in French.

"M. Escoffier was very upset," remembers Hazelton-Cochrane. "A story had just been published in an American magazine in which another chef was said to have invented Pêche Melba."

Poor M. Escoffier was almost in tears. "Ah, *Madame Melba, mais vous savez que ce n'est pas la verité,*" Escoffier said, wringing his hands. Melba was quite upset. She had a strong sense of fairness — except perhaps when another prima donna was concerned — and she had great loyalty to her friends.

"Right then and there," says Hazelton-Cochrane, "she promised to write up the truth in her autobiography, and she did. She was fond of M. Escoffier. She invited him to come for lunch with us. Afterwards she said to me, 'You already have my autograph, and now be sure to get M. Escoffier's, Tommy. He is the greatest chef of our time.' I understood. Monsieur Escoffier was to the art of the *haute cuisine* what Madame Melba was to the art of *bel canto.*"

The famous dessert was created one glorious morning in spring, probably toward the end of the past century, when Melba lived at London's Savoy, which was then under the personal management of César Ritz. The *chef de cuisine* was the formidable Auguste Escoffier.

Melba was having her lunch in her room. She was very hungry — she was always blessed with a healthy appetite — and was given "the most excellent luncheon." This I find easy to believe. The world's most famous chef was an ardent admirer of the world's most celebrated prima donna. He always made "special little things" for her. Melba liked light food, and M. Escoffier came up with wonderful creations of fish, poulard, or sweetbreads, and with glorious *grande cuisine* masterpieces of pheasant and partridge.

Toward the end of that excellent lunch a small silver dish arrived and was uncovered before the diva with a message that M. Escoffier had it prepared especially for her. And, "much as Eve tasted the first apple," Melba now tasted the first Pêche Melba in the world.

"It's delicious," she said. "Ask M. Escoffier what it is called."

Word came back from the kitchens that the dessert had no name, but that M. Escoffier would be honored if he might call it Pêche Melba. Melba said he might, with the greatest of pleasure, and thought no more about it. Soon afterwards, Pêche Melba was the rage of London.

Melba's memory may have failed her, for Escoffier himself has written that he created the famous dessert as early as 1894, after Melba had sent him two orchestra seats to a Covent Garden performance of *Lohengrin* in which she appeared with Jean de Reszke. The next day she gave a supper party for the Duc d'Orleans and a few friends. Escoffier had enjoyed *Lohengrin* and wanted Melba to enjoy his new dessert, which he served in a large silver cup placed between the wings of a swan — the *Lohengrin* swan — made of ice. "Pêche Melba became, however, popular only after the opening of the Carlton in London in 1899," he concludes. At any rate, Melba soon realized that Monsieur Escoffier had given her a touch of immortality.

The authentic recipe of Pêche Melba is in Escoffier's own cookbook, his world-famous *Guide Culinaire:*

After peeling the peaches, poach them in vanilla-flavored syrup. Put them in a *timbale* upon a layer of vanilla ice-cream, and coat them with a raspberry purée.

Melba calls Escoffier "an artist if there ever was one." She adds, with her customary flair for hot business deals and her occasional disregard for cold figures, "I once tried to calculate exactly how much he would have made had he charged a royalty of one penny on every dozen Pêche Melbas that were consumed but gave up when I realized that it would total many millions of pounds."

After the world-wide success of Pêche Melba Escoffier created Poires Melba, Fraises Melba and other variations, but the celebrated peaches remained the smash hit while Poires Mary Garden (syrup-cooked pears with raspberry sauce, sour cherries and whipped cream) and Coupe Emma Calvé (vanilla ice cream, kirsch-flavored stewed cherries and raspberry purée) are long forgotten. Gastronomically, Nellie Melba has clearly defeated all other prima donnas.

Melba never mentions "Melba toast" in her memoirs, since it was neither inspired by her nor made by the great chef, but her friends remember that she liked Melba toast and often had it made for them. She never accepted a penny for the commercial exploitation of her name from makers of soaps, ribbons and ruffles, and once became very indignant in New York when she discovered that it had been pirated for a perfume. (She became resigned to "Melba cigarettes," and always kept a supply in her home for her guests. She herself didn't smoke.)

She discovered the "Melba" perfume in the window of a large drugstore on Forty-second Street, where they had an enormous display with glaring advertisements and large pictures of the prima donna. Melba thought she "deserved a bottle of this," went into the store and asked to try the perfume. The clerk sprayed some on her wrist.

One sniff was enough. "I hated the stuff."

She asked politely who had given them permission to call their creation "Melba."

"Oh, that's all right. We found out that her real name is Armstrong. We've got as much right to call this stuff 'Melba' as she has."

"I am Madame Melba," said the Queen of Song, in her most regal manner. "Don't you think you might have asked my permission?"

The clerk shrugged.

Melba expressed her opinion of these methods "fairly freely," leaving them in no doubt about what she thought of them. She made sure that the incident was not repeated, and had her name patented throughout the United States.

As long as Ritz and Escoffier were around, Melba remained faithful to them. She once said Ritz should have a monument in London with the inscription HE MADE US COMFORTABLE. London hotels were terrible before the arrival of Ritz. "The cooking was execrable, the carpets were dirty, the linen was mediaeval, the service was an insult."

César Ritz, "the slim, silent Swiss with dark, close-cropped hair" changed all that. When Melba took up residence at the Savoy, she felt as if she had "landed in Paradise." Ritz next opened the Carlton in London, which he launched with the help of Lady de Grey, and then the Ritz in Paris. Melba

was one of his first clients there. She was distressed to see
that "success turned Ritz' head." He became less thin and
elegant, and got bloated and flabby. His hotels were still
excellent, but he had lost his fastidious sense of responsibil-
ity and old-timers discovered some subtle difference.

Melba heard all kinds of stories about Ritz. Somebody told
her, for instance, that he had walked into the shop of a
famous goldsmith on Regent Street, announced grandly
that the Prince of Wales was dining with him next week, and
ordered a very fine set of gold plate.

"And of course," he said, "everything in the room must
be solid gold too. I must have gold carpets, gold furniture,
gold curtains. Nothing but gold."

Melba saw the great *hôtelier* for the last time in the dining
room of the Ritz Hotel in Paris. The headwaiter brought him
over to Melba's table, but Ritz didn't recognize her and
talked to her vaguely. As he walked away, he said to the
headwaiter, "Madame Melba? I haven't been talking to her.
I don't even know whether she is staying at the hotel."

A few months later Melba read of his death.

The Ritz-Escoffier performances of their better days at
London's Savoy belonged as much to the glories of the Ed-
wardian era as the Melba-Caruso performances at Covent
Garden. Melba loved singing with Caruso.

"The higher he sings, the easier it seems to him," she once
said to a friend. "In the third act of *La Bohème* I always
feel as if our two voices had merged into one." She called
Caruso "the most wonderful tenor I ever heard" though he
was perhaps a notch below her "god," Jean de Reszke. She

loved "the truly golden richness of Caruso's voice which rolled out like an organ." In those days Caruso's voice was pure metal and had magnificent strength, though his artistic approach was not as subtle as later on when his voice was no longer in its prime.

The Melba-Caruso nights must have been wonderful, perhaps among the greatest events in the history of *bel canto*. They sang together for the first time at the inauguration of the Monte Carlo opera season in 1902 in *La Bohème*. They had their greatest success together in Puccini's masterpiece, and later made operatic history in *La Bohème* at Covent Garden and the Metropolitan.

"Madame Melba, even in her access of fervor, didn't exactly balance the passionate heat of Caruso, but they were on the same level," wrote the *Daily Telegraph*. "She even had the rare and precious quality of pathos when she sang with Caruso and was carried away by him."

Melba thought Caruso was "a simple, lovable creature." She loved his generous heart and was touched by his complete lack of snobbishness. She even put up with his fondness for spaghetti, heavy Tuscan wines and strong cigars. Once she backed a hundred-to-one outsider at Sandown only because the name of the horse was "Caruso." After the start "Caruso" began to kick and bolted off in the wrong direction.

Sometimes Melba got a little tired of Enrico Caruso's sense of fun. His specialty was brightening up the lachrymose scenes in grand opera, of which there are so many. He was particularly eager to dispel the gloom in the last act of *La Bohème*, when poor Mimi is dying in a simple iron bed in the middle of the stage, surrounded by beautiful melodies. Rarely a performance went by without Caruso's coming up with something to cheer up the despondent Bohemians and the tearful listeners. His taste in high jinks was not as impeccable as his high C's. Once Melba staggered onstage as the dying Mimi. Rodolfo's friends quickly pushed the bed from the wall to the center of the stage, when a collective gasp went through the dignified auditorium of Covent Garden. Caruso had secretly placed a chamber pot under the bed, which stood revealed there in splendid isolation.

During another *La Bohème* performance, in Monte Carlo, before "a fashionable audience thick with Grand Dukes and Princesses" — all of them carried away by Melba and Caruso, many with tears in their eyes — Melba was just dying in perfect legato melody when suddenly she thought she heard a strange squeaking noise. She went on singing. For a moment she was afraid Caruso might have become ill. His face was solemn and his eyes were sad, as befits the broken-hearted lover of the dying Mimi.

Then Melba saw that Caruso was holding in his hand a tiny rubber toy which he pressed against her ear during the most doleful melodious passages. Melba almost stopped singing in mid-breath.

"It is difficult to stop laughing when you are supposed to be solemn but when you are supposed to be dying the temptation is almost too much to be borne," she wrote. She often complained to her closest friends about Caruso's jokes, but she herself once literally stopped a performance of *La Bo-*

hème at Covent Garden with her own idea of good, clean fun.

She was singing Mimi and Madame Fritzi Scheff sang the part of Musetta. Madame Scheff possessed "a pretty voice and a dainty figure." Henderson thought she was "chic to her fingertips." To say that the two divas were not on the friendliest terms would be an understatement.

Toward the end of Musetta's waltz, just as Madame Scheff was embarking — with some difficulty, it was noted — on her B natural, a clear, angelic voice elsewhere on the stage was heard to take up the tone with perfect ease, and to sing the rest of the phrase *unisono* with Madame Scheff. Experts in the audience smiled knowingly and there were whispers, "Melba." No one was very much surprised. At that time Melba practically owned Covent Garden, and the cold war between the two divas was no secret. Some of Melba's high-class admirers even thought it was a capital joke.

After the fall of the second-act curtain there was an unusually long intermission. Then Neil Forsyth, the manager, came out to announce that "owing to a sudden indisposition of Madame Scheff" the third and fourth acts of *La Bohème* could unfortunately not be given. Madame Melba had kindly consented to conclude the performance with the Mad Scene from *Lucia*.

Some incorrigible Melba fans even applauded. Other people in the audience thought Mr. Forsyth looked a trifle shaken. And well he might: there had been some hand-to-hand fighting backstage, where the cold war had become very hot. Madame Scheff had tried to scratch Madame Melba's face and had to be taken away "in a fit of hysterics."

It was not unusual in those days to have great fun on the stage at the expense of the music and the audience. During a performance of *Les Huguénots* at Covent Garden Melba in the part of the Queen got so engrossed in private conversation with her ladies-in-waiting that she forgot her cue. Even the phenomenal Mademoiselle Bauermeister, who was said to know everybody's cue, was unable to help her.

> In this predicament [writes Agnes Murphy, quite pleased] the Australian prima donna substituted for the Meyerbeer passage some impromptu phrases of her own, ending with a brilliant cadenza. Monsieur Plançon as St. Bris was due to continue after her with the phrase, "Madame, I will go and bring my daughter," but noticing Melba's lapse he sang instead, "Madame, I will go and tell Meyerbeer." Mancinelli, the conductor, had to bury his face in the score in order to hide his amusement at Plançon's sally.

It must have been quite a night at the opera, even without the Marx Brothers.

Once, at a concert, when her accompanist Ronald Landon played the accompaniment of an encore by heart, four notes too low, Melba turned toward him and said loudly, "My dear sir, you are in the wrong key. I am not a contralto." This friendly correction "greatly entertained the audience." A prima donna could, and did, get away with murder.

Mimi in *La Bohème* was Melba's greatest part. "My friends like it better than anything else I sing," she once wrote. "I have very great faith in Puccini's gifts. I delight in singing his music and I believe him to be the coming Italian composer." She said this in 1899 when there were still many people who considered Puccini "an imitation Mascagni." Melba, who was often accused of not being very musical, showed sounder musical judgment than some of the highbrow critics. One of them, H. G. Krehbiel, objected to "Puccini's shrieking cantilena until there is no relief except exhaustion."

Melba studied the part of Mimi with Puccini in 1898. She went down to Lucca, the small town in Tuscany where Puccini was born. He would come every day to her studio, and they would go through her part bar by bar. Her score was full of Puccini's pencil marks and annotations. Puccini called her the Mimi of his dreams.

In the United States an unauthorized version of *La Bohème* had been given by the Bagetto and the Royal Italian Opera companies, without much success. Melba changed all that. With her as Mimi, *La Bohème* became one of the biggest box-office draws in the Metropolitan history. At Covent Garden, *La Bohème* had been given without particular success until Melba came along. She had so much faith in the opera that the management consented to put up a new production of *La Bohème* with Melba, the tenor de Lucia as Rodolfo, and Madame de Lussan as Musetta, on July 1, 1899.

Melba's success was enormous. No other soprano on earth could touch her as Mimi. Hazelton-Cochrane tells me that the moment when Mimi's voice was heard offstage, before her first entrance, remains one of his most vivid memories of Nellie Melba.

"In *La Bohème*," he says, "there was nothing wrong with

her acting. Her voice alone expressed clearly all emotions. Her phrasing was perfect, and her heavenly *legato* would move you deeply. You didn't think of Melba. You were happy with Mimi, you loved and suffered with her, and when she died in the last act, you always died a little with her. Melba knew it. Once she said to me, 'If I don't make them cry in the last act, I know I have given a bad performance.'"

The most remarkable tribute comes from Melba's erstwhile competitor, Mary Garden. In *Mary Garden's Story* the great prima donna writes:

> . . . I once went to Covent Garden to hear Melba as Mimi. You know, the last note of the first act of *La Bohème* is the last note that comes out of Mimi's throat. It is a high C, and Mimi sings it when she walks out the door with Rodolfo. She closes the door and then she takes the note. The way Melba sang that high C was the strangest and weirdest thing I have ever experienced in my life. The note came floating over the auditorium of Covent Garden: it left Melba's throat, it left Melba's body, it left everything and came like a star and passed us in our box, and went out into the infinite. I have never heard anything like it in my life, not from any other singer, ever. That note of Melba's was like a ball of light. It wasn't attached to anything. It was out of everything . . . My God, how beautiful it was!

Melba claimed that Puccini had written *Madama Butterfly* for her. This is a doubtful claim. In April, 1897, Puccini was in London, "a better and more interesting place to stay than Paris." He didn't understand English. "I know the numerals, first ten," he wrote home, "and I have some addresses to which I can go in a cab." Melba took Puccini

to the Duke of York's Theatre, where they saw David Belasco's dramatization of John Luther Long's short story,
Madama Butterfly. Although Puccini didn't understand a
word of the play (which contains few numerals) he was
so moved by the love and death of little Cho-Cho-San, the
lovely Japanese girl, that he went back to Italy, and told
his publishers to get the rights to Belasco's play. He made
one of his finest operas out of it.

Puccini hoped that the Mimi of his dreams would become
the Madama Butterfly of his visions, but unfortunately
Nellie Melba and Cho-Cho-San couldn't get together. Melba
made a special trip to Venice to work on the part with
Puccini, but found it too dramatic. Her friend, Lady Stracey,
who had rented a small *palazzo* with Melba, once stepped
into the library just as Melba hurled the score across the
room shouting, "Damn the thing, I shall never learn it!"

Puccini sat at the piano unhappily. "*Patienza, cara sig-
nora,*" he said. "*Patienza.*" But the dear lady had no patience
and never learned the damn thing.

La Bohème would be the opera on a typical "Melba night"
during the Edwardian era — a synthesis of great singing and
social splendor, of lavish elegance and beautiful music, of
gala cast and gala audience.

A gala audience is not usually distinguished for its musicality. After all, a certain number of white ties and gorgeous
evening gowns will give any audience a gala look. "It is,"
writes Irving Kolodin, "the audience for the opening of the
opera, late to arrive, early to leave, ill-mannered and very

clean, the despair of the ushers and the desire of every press-agent." The best audience — the audience of dedicated opera lovers — has no gala look.

I believe there has never been anything like the Melba nights of the late Victorian and the Edwardian eras. The openings of the Metropolitan, to which Mr. Kolodin refers, are pseudo-social rather than genuine musical events. Big nights at the Vienna Court and later State Opera, and at Milan's La Scala, were distinguished musically and vocally; but only at Covent Garden towards the end of the rule of Queen Victoria and during the short and happy reign of King Edward VII was there that inimitable mixture of music and glamour, of art and splendor, when what happens in the audience is as important as what goes on onstage. There were prima donnas on both sides of the orchestra pit. For Western civilization it was the last epoch frankly devoted to the pursuit of exorbitance. The Roman Empire was like that shortly before its decline — but they had no Melbas then, no Carusos, in fact, no grand opera.

The Edwardian era outdid the late Victorian period. These Edwardians did everything on a lavish, luxurious scale. Opera programs were printed on silk for state performances, with photographs of Melba and other great stars in suitable frames. Nellie Melba was the epitome of that happy epoch, which began with Prince Albert Edward's influence in the nineties and lasted until 1910, when Good King Edward VII died.

The season was considered really to have begun only with the arrival of Melba late in May.

The Opera presented a brilliant spectacle [says a London newspaper about a typical Melba night]. The house was crowded with well-dressed women, and jewels galore were to be seen in the stalls and boxes. Madame Melba received quite an ovation after each act, and sang superbly the title part in *La Traviata*, wearing a succession of lovely Paris gowns designed by Maison Worth. On such a night it is almost difficult to say who was *not* present — all London seemed in evidence. Baron and Baroness Cederström [Mme. Patti and her third husband] watched the performance with the greatest interest, the one diva applauding the other vigorously. It was a typical Melba night [ends this typical Melba report].

A typical big Melba night — *La Traviata* or *Lucia di Lammermoor* or *La Bohème* — with her and Caruso, "by Desire of Their Majesties," would be the climax of the London season, on one of those magical evenings in May or June when the stately buildings of the noble city receded behind a slight haze and the lights seemed to float over the Thames. No one was in a hurry. People would go to Covent Garden in a comfortable hansom cab at a civilized speed which gave them a chance to enjoy their ride. There was so much to see: the flowers, the trees in the parks, the lights; above all, the people.

Arriving in Long Acre you would join a long queue — an Englishman wouldn't be happy unless he had a chance to join a queue — and then there would come a sharp thrill of pleasure as you stepped into the red-gold splendor of the Royal Opera House. It was always an exciting experience, no matter how many times you had seen it before. Prices had been substantially increased; a Melba night was

predominantly a social event. Covent Garden is a dignified
house, with its shades of red plush, its sloping floors, the arrangement of boxes and galleries, the liveried footmen, the
fine staircase, its excellent acoustics. It was the perfect
setting for the beautiful stones displayed in it, the magnificent tiaras and jewels of the women. The men would wear
court dress, parade uniform or full evening dress, with decorations. There was the sight of beautiful women, the scent
of expensive perfumes, the beauty of many flowers. During
the Gala Performance on June 26, 1911, celebrating the
coronation of King George V and Queen Mary, the auditorium was decorated with 100,000 rose blooms, "the scent
of which caused many ladies to faint during the course of
the evening." As much as five thousand dollars was offered
for a box and five hundred dollars for a single seat. Madame
Melba was on hand then too, singing in the second act of
Roméo et Juliette. Doubtless the audience did not follow
the opera with the rapt attention and the deep enjoyment
which we young "opera fools" displayed during *Tristan
und Isolde*, when we were in the fourth gallery of the Vienna
State Opera. Five ecstatic hours were filled with intense
excitement. Some people kept their eyes closed most of the
time, not because they were as sleepy as some of the box
holders but because they gave themselves completely to the
magic of the music.

During a Melba night, people in the audience kept their
eyes wide open so they wouldn't miss a single detail. They
cared more about the auditorium than the stage. This
doesn't really matter, once in a while. I have learned, since
my idealistic claque days, that grand opera needs the sup-

port of both the dedicated gallery standees and the blasé box-holders. One group contributes enthusiasm and the other money. Grand opera needs both to survive.

A Victorian statesman once startled the House by asking in the course of a financial debate the eminently sensible question, "What *is* a pound?" His son happened to be a young man about town, and *Punch* supplied the son's reply:

> A pound, dear father, is the sum
> That clears the opera wicket;
> Two lemon gloves, one lemon ice,
> Libretto, and your ticket.

Obviously a night at the opera was perfect entertainment for a fashionable young man, and he would not go there without a libretto. People considered operagoing a serious business, and many prepared themselves for the performance. Victorian and Edwardian librettos have the original text on one side and the translation on the other. Sometimes the music of the principal airs is included. It was customary to jot down one's impressions on white pages, thoughtfully provided for this purpose by the publisher. Not all the listeners were ignorant, as is often claimed today. To be sure, there were snobs among them, but also many who knew the music well. They had heard so many great voices that they had developed a limited but genuine understanding of good singing.

Audiences should be given credit for a great many other things. Yet Hector Berlioz writes, "The public is of absolutely no use in the theater. It is not only of no use, but it spoils everything. As long as the public is allowed at the opera, the opera will not get along." There is certainly a great truth in this, because a bad audience is worse than no audience at all; but opera's public has one important function. It has become the last element distinguishing the leading opera houses of the world.

Don't look surprised. Airplane travel and the star system have created a deplorable *Gleichschaltung* (uniformity) of repertory, casts and performances. Today's great singing stars enjoy a monopoly. No one dares start anti-trust action against them. They know their indispensability and take advantage of it. The very same artists produce, conduct, and perform opera from Barcelona to London, from Vienna to New York, from Milan to Munich. People talk about Knappertsbusch's not Wagner's *Ring,* about Karajan's not Verdi's *Falstaff,* about Hotter's Wotan and London's Dutchman. Each new Isolde is measured up against Nilsson's, and any new Norma will be compared to Callas. Highly polished productions by radio, television and on long-playing records have established definite impeccable standards in the ears of many listeners. As always, when too much polishing is done, the human element loses out. The world's opera stages have become set for the same vast seasons during certain months of the year: September in Berlin, winter in Milan and New York, spring in London and Vienna, summer in Bayreuth, Salzburg, Munich and the festival circuit — but the same works, the same productions, the same singers, the same conductors. Only the audiences are different.

No wonder audiences are often more interesting than the performers on stage! Local ones have their municipal prejudices, their loyalties to local favorites, as well as national idiosyncrasies.

In different places people come to the opera for different reasons, expecting different things. Italians love opera; Austrians and Germans were brought up on it; the British are fond of it in their own way; Americans go to it for a variety of reasons, but they could live without it — which Europeans would find very very hard. New Yorkers want entertainment at the Met; Italians go for excitement to La Scala; and the Viennese go for inspiration to their Staats-oper.

Some people come late to the Metropolitan, others leave early; quite a few stay at the bar during the second act. People keep their topcoats and hats on their laps (in opera houses on the Continent, one can always spot Americans, because they are reluctant to check their coats and sit with their London Fogs and Burberrys in their arms — as the Europeans do only at the cinema). In New York ushers play around with flashlights during the lovely pianissimi in the fourth act of *Otello* while Desdemona sings *"Salce."* Dedicated artists who have to sing important arias at the beginning or toward the end of the opera, are just out of luck at the Metropolitan — although lately word has got around that the *"Liebestod"* comes at the end of *Tristan und Isolde,* and most people will keep their seats until the end.

American audiences are learning fast. They have now a new, genuine crush on opera, and are extremely appreciative. Once they find out that Wagner, Verdi and Strauss often saved their finest inspirations for the final scenes of their works, they will all stay to the end. They will even

learn to appreciate their performers less for good looks
and forceful voices and more for feeling, style and musicality.

London's opera audiences are well-informed and well-
mannered. They don't exude Italian enthusiasm, or Viennese
flair for criticism, but they are grateful for a good performance and loyal to their favorite performers. No one munches
candy during the overture, and no one tries to explain to
you the libretto of *Trovatore* — an impossible task anyway.
Covent Garden's audiences politely overlook shortcomings
that would cause grave head-shaking in Vienna and noisy
invective in Milan or Rome. English opera lovers reserve
their temperamental outbursts for festival performances outside of England. In Salzburg and Bayreuth they drop their
national reserve and cheer with the rest of the crowd, and
in Italy I've heard them boo with the gallery.

At Barcelona's Liceo, the claque is unpredictable. No applause after Cherubino's *"Non sò più"* in *Le Nozze di Figaro*,
but terrific tumult after the "Letter Duet" (*"Che soave zef-
firetto"*), which is often repeated though the ink was not
spilled. People come very late, although the performance
rarely starts before ten P.M. and ends before two A.M.; but
here the stars are smarter than in New York: important arias
are switched from the beginning toward the middle of the
opera, when everybody is present. No liberties must be taken
with Wagnerian scores, however; and a few years ago I
witnessed a terrific scandal during the second act of *Siegfried:* parts of the boring Alberich-Mime duet had been cut.

Milan's audiences are not as impeccable as the strict standards which they demand from their singers. La Scala's *afi-*

cionados know a great deal about the art of *bel canto* but are lenient against offenders who show a deplorable lack in musical taste. They have a sense of drama and flair for singing, though they haven't discovered yet the divine beauty of Mozart. Theater scandals are quickly arranged and quickly forgotten; performers are often booed and cheered during the same performance. For the *prime* (first nights) at La Scala the audiences are the world's most elegant today.

From the performer's point of view the "good" audiences in Vienna and Germany (you have to be lucky to catch a "good" one) are perhaps the most rewarding. They are appreciative and critical, nostalgic-minded and frankly prejudiced. They take operagoing seriously. It's easier for a singer to establish contact with the audience in Vienna, Bayreuth or Stuttgart than in New York, London, or Paris. The younger people already share the American predilection for cold, brilliant perfection — the sort of singing that is standard on the expensive records — but the older ones still prefer warmth and emotion. The audiences are critical and uncompromising, but generous with their praise. Many among them have grown up with opera as American children grow up with jazz: in the small provincial town where they went to school there was usually a small "provincial" opera house that played ten months a year, a fine school for young singers and young listeners.

The atmosphere at the Vienna opera house is hushed; it is a little like going to church. No one is permitted to enter the auditorium while the performance is going on. Candy munchers are immediately spotted as hopeless barbarians from abroad. *Aficionados* judge their favorites not by how they sing tonight but how they used to sing at their very best. A personal relationship exists between the singer and his public, although most people have never met him or her. Score reading is so popular that the Vienna Opera provides certain seats in the gallery with reading lights. The listeners know the importance of a good orchestra (the Vienna Staatsopes has the best opera orchestra in the world, the Vienna Philharmonic) and they know that it is the conductor, not the prima donna, who makes or breaks a performance.

The most lavish spectacles of the lavish age were the state performances. No nation, not even the imaginative French, surpasses the English for the splendor of colorful pageantry. Artistically, however, these evenings were mixed blessings. The state performance in 1897, commemorating Queen Victoria's Diamond Jubilee, featured the third act of *Roméo et Juliette* (with Melba), the second act of *Tannhäuser,* and the fourth act of *Les Huguénots.* It must have been a nightmare for discriminating music lovers, but perhaps not many were present.

How the singers managed to get through these evenings is hard to understand. When Melba was invited by her great admirer, King Oscar of Sweden, "the smiling giant" with the sweet tenor voice, to sing in a gala performance at the Stockholm Opera, the King selected personally the following program for her:

1. The Balcony Scene from *Roméo et Juliette,*
2. The Second Act of *Lohengrin,*
3. The Third Act of *Lucia,*
4. The Fourth Act of *Faust.*

"I smiled when I read the program for it was as arduous a selection as any singer could undertake," remembers Melba. "However, in those days four of the most strenuous acts in four different operas deterred me not at all, and I was inclined to congratulate the King on his good taste."

Good taste!

Melba was the Queen of Covent Garden, and a "Melba party" (not to be confused with a "Melba night") was the smartest form of private entertaining — provided you could afford it. Melba's fee was five hundred guineas (twenty-five hundred dollars) but quite a few people in London thought her name printed very large on the invitation cards was worth a great deal more. She asked twice as much in America, where she often got five thousand dollars for singing for her supper. Her hosts naturally thought nothing of spending twenty or thirty thousand dollars for an evening. Melba reports that sometimes half that amount was spent on flower decorations alone.

A "Melba party" was not strictly a musical event. The program might consist of some songs of the "salon" type, a couple of operatic arias, "nothing-too-difficult-my-dear," a few short piano or violin pieces played by a famous virtuoso, possibly a recitation by a famous actor. Some highbrows took a dim view of such popular entertainment, but if they were invited to the party they were sure to go. "It wasn't every night that you could hear Melba, Kreisler or Paderewski in one evening, for free, and get an excellent supper in addition," writes the irreverent Colson. Hostesses who couldn't get Melba would feature Calvé or Nordica, but the "Calvé party" or "Nordica party" was never quite the same thing.

Madame Melba, naturally, would have to be consulted in advance about the other artists who would have the honor of appearing on the same program. She was very fond of Paderewski. "I would have married him at once," she once said, "but alas, he never asked me." She was very much amused when she overheard one woman saying to another at a Paderewski concert, "If he married Melba, what a lot of money they would make between them!"

Melba had a weakness for great violinists. Joachim, Ysaÿe, Kreisler and Kubelik were all her friends. She always tried to have one of them invited to a "Melba party." She would ask for her friend Herman Bemberg as accompanist and she would sing a couple of his charming songs. (Bemberg, the millionaire-composer-about-town, was naturally more desirable to the hostess than a "professional piano player.") Another Melba protégé was Theodore Byard, a gifted singer with a lyric baritone voice who made the mistake of studying, against Melba's urgent advice, with Jean de Reszke, who persuaded him that he was really a tenor. After a year's study with Jean poor Byard was no longer a baritone and not yet a tenor. "Darling Jean" knew little about any voice except his own.

The audience at a "Melba party" was socially impeccable and musically impotent. Colson once asked a certain peer, "If you come here to listen to Melba, why don't you subscribe to the opera? Your brother does, and he is quite deaf!"

To which his lordship answered, "My dear fellow, if I were as deaf as my brother, I too would subscribe."

♭ 16 ♭

Manhattan's Wonderful War

OSCAR HAMMERSTEIN I, dynamic, high-spirited, formidable, aggressive — a former cigar maker, a playwright, composer, theatrical entrepreneur and opera enthusiast — was, in Melba's words, "the most American of Americans, and the only man who ever made me change my mind."

Hammerstein was what the Viennese call an *Opernnarr* — a man who dreams, sleeps, breathes, talks, thinks and lives opera. Unlike the sweet fools who talk constantly about opera and do nothing about it, Hammerstein had the energy, determination and money to do something about his folly, "that insane desire to produce opera." The greatest managers have always been a combination of idealist and businessman; they could read a balance sheet as well as a score; they had great love for opera, but knew its financial drawbacks. Managers who consider producing opera either just a business or an avocation alone have always failed.

Hammerstein was no man to do things in a small way. He challenged the supremacy of two of the world's great opera houses, Covent Garden and the Metropolitan. In London he failed badly after one season. He couldn't break the monopoly which Covent Garden had on operas and singers. His enthusiasm cost him two hundred and fifty thousand dollars. The London Opera House which he built became a variety hall and cinema. Earlier, in New York City, where he conceived, designed, built, owned, managed and operated the Manhattan Opera House, he gave the Metropolitan Opera House the only serious competition it ever had. During four exciting seasons, from 1906 to 1910, Hammerstein all by himself fought the most sensational war in the history of grand opera.

Against the powerful, entrenched Astor-Morgan-Vanderbilt directorate and Wall Street's financial forces that stood behind the Metropolitan, Hammerstein was underdog, upstart and challenger. The American public and the press, traditionally champions of the underdog, were enthusiastically on his side. Oscar had sound flair, gambling instinct, and great showmanship. The newspapers loved him. It was a relief to have an opera war in Manhattan on the front pages, instead of a revolution in South America. The music critics of the big papers became (unaccredited) war correspondents. They reported the battles as they saw them without worrying about the judgment of history. They were frankly partisan: war correspondents rarely take the enemy's side.

Some of these correspondents — W. J. Henderson, Richard Aldrich and Carl Van Vechten of the *New York Times;* Henry Krehbiel of the *New York Tribune;* James G. Huneker of the *New York World* — knew a great deal more about opera than Hammerstein and had a good idea of what he was up against. They watched him with fascination and with regret, for they had no doubt that their shining knight of opera would lose his fight. "It was not strange that many observers refused to believe that Hammerstein was of the stuff out of which opera managers are made," wrote Krehbiel. "He did not seem illogical enough."

But time went on and it became apparent that Hammerstein was not going to lose. He might even come out the winner. The critics' reluctant fascination turned into ardent admiration.

Hammerstein's Manhattan Opera House was going up on Eighth Avenue and Thirty-fourth Street: an imposing structure with a Louis Quatorze auditorium in red and gold, which the papers described as "modern French," with thirty-one hundred seats. (The Metropolitan has thirty-eight hundred seats.) Hammerstein signed up a first-rate orchestra and recruited a chorus from students of local voice studios; he imported some seasoned choristers from Italy. He also signed up conductors and singers. He let it be known that the conductors would have all the rehearsal time they needed. Hammerstein made it clear that he was quite serious and intended to produce first-rate opera.

It was a hazardous undertaking, to say the least. The Metropolitan was backed by many of the richest people in America. It had subscriptions for four hundred thousand dollars. Hammerstein had no outside backing whatsoever. He financed the Manhattan Opera House with the profits from his own vaudeville house, the Victoria Theater. Most Americans cared little about grand opera, but they watched

Hammerstein with breathless excitement. He had dared take on the long-time champ and the odds were heavily against him. The David versus Goliath comparison was inevitable. It was a sporting contest rather than an operatic one.

Almost every day throughout 1906 the New York newspapers carried special stories of Hammerstein's progress. Hammerstein "hoped" to get Jean de Reszke out of retirement. The skeptics smiled. They knew that even a fee of thirty-five hundred dollars a performance (which Hammerstein was willing to pay) wouldn't lure Jean from pleasant retirement in sunny Nice. But when Hammerstein claimed he was still "negotiating" with Jean and with Édouard de Reszke, the skeptics became curious. What about Caruso? Hammerstein admitted he could not get Caruso, who had a sure-fire, absolute, ironclad Metropolitan Opera House contract; but he had "managed to sign up" Alessandro Bonci, "the most famous tenor after Caruso." Hammerstein's able press agent, William J. Guard, even got front-page space with a (phony) story that Caruso had challenged Bonci to a duel. Later the battle of the tenors became a veritable duel but it was fought with high C's on the stage in front of thousands of people instead of with pistols at dawn before a couple of seconds.

Hammerstein jubilantly announced that he had engaged Maurice Renaud, the great French baritone whom Melba calls "a consummate musician, a superb artist with perfect phrasing and acting." Hammerstein also secured the young, handsome dramatic tenor Charles Dalmorès, the basso Victor Vittorio Arimondi, the buffo Charles Gilibert. It was an-

nounced that Hammerstein was "negotiating" with Arturo
Toscanini, but the maestro preferred to stay at La Scala in
Milan. Hammerstein got the next best man, Maestro Cleofonte Campanini, older than Toscanini, "a remarkable in-
spirer of great operatic performances." In his younger years
Campanini had conducted during several seasons at the Met,
but he disliked the interference of financiers and society
ladies and had not returned to the States for many years. He
was revered by his artists as an indefatigable worker; he
had that electrifying effect on orchestra and singers that
works like magic and makes all the difference between a
mediocre opera performance and a great one. He was a terrific success. After his first season at the Manhattan, Campanini was offered twice his salary by Heinrich Conried,
general manager of the Met. Campanini, a loyal artist,
didn't even bother to inform Hammerstein of Conried's offer.

More Hammerstein stories broke. Hammerstein had
signed up the great contralto Eleonora de Cisneros. Hammerstein would "soon" sign up Mary Garden and Emma
Calvé.

As the Manhattan Opera House neared completion Hammerstein himself broke the biggest story of all. He was going
to sign up Nellie Melba, "the most famous singer in the
world." Even his friends refused to believe this. Melba was
a pillar of the Met. She had sung at the Met every season
between 1893 and 1904. She was in demand by every major
opera house in the world. Her contract demanded that she
must be paid in cash before the rise of the curtain. Hammerstein predicted loudly that Madame Melba was going to sing
for him, only for him. And he added that she would sing

better for him than she had ever sung for anybody else.

There was only one catch in Hammerstein's noble scheme. He didn't really have Madame Melba. She had no intention whatsoever of coming to America.

The summit meeting between Melba and Hammerstein, those giants of the opera world, is one of the great legends of musical history. Unfortunately, Hammerstein never got around to writing his version; but Melba wrote hers, and the only way to recapture the mood of the *entretien* is to quote her:

> One day, when I was in my flat in Paris, thinking what fun I was going to have in my coming season, Mr. Hammerstein called. I had an idea of what he wanted, and I wouldn't see him.
>
> Hammerstein went straight off to Maurice Grau [the former manager of Covent Garden and the Metropolitan Opera House] who was very ill at the time, and persuaded him to give him a letter to me. I felt obliged to give him an appointment. But I kept saying to myself: "I'm not going to America. I'm not going to America."
>
> When Hammerstein arrived, my first impression was of a determined man of Jewish persuasion, shortish, thin and dark, dark, with piercing black eyes. He carried a top hat with a very wide brim in his hand, and he addressed me in a strong American accent.
>
> HAMMERSTEIN: "I'm out to do the big thing in opera. I am building the biggest and finest opera house in the world. And I can't do without you."
>
> MYSELF: "In what way do you want me to help you?"
>
> HAMMERSTEIN: "I want you to come and sing."
>
> MYSELF: "I'm very sorry, but I have no intention of going to New York next year."

HAMMERSTEIN: "I can't do without you."

MYSELF: "That's a great pity, because I'm not going."

HAMMERSTEIN: "I shall give you fifteen hundred dollars a night."

MYSELF: "Please don't discuss terms, Monsieur Hammerstein. I assure you it is useless."

HAMMERSTEIN: "Oh, you'll come all right." (Pause.) "What do you say to two thousand?"

MYSELF: "If you offer me twenty thousand, I shall still say the same thing."

HAMMERSTEIN: "It'll be the biggest thing you have done yet. Oscar Hammerstein says so."

MYSELF: "And Nellie Melba says 'No.' I have no intention of going. Good morning, Mr. Hammerstein."

Had anybody else been so importunate, I should probably have been very angry. But there was a naïve determination about Mr. Hammerstein which appealed to my own character. He knew what he wanted, and did not hesitate to say so. We therefore parted good friends, and I regarded the matter as closed.

Not so Mr. Hammerstein. At intervals of six days during the next month he either called, wrote notes or telephoned, always prefacing his remarks by "Now that you have decided to come to America . . ." I merely sat tight and set my lips. On one occasion, I remember, he obtained an entry into my rooms while I was in my bath. Not in the least deterred, he came and battered at the door.

HAMMERSTEIN: "Are you coming to America?"

MYSELF (*between splashes*): "No!"

HAMMERSTEIN: "I'll give you two thousand five hundred a night."

MYSELF: "Not for ten times the money."

HAMMERSTEIN: "And you can sing as many nights as you like."

MYSELF: "Go away."

Shortly after that, Mr. Hammerstein decided on his Napoleonic coup. I had just breakfasted and was sitting down, reading *Le Figaro,* when he burst into my rooms in a great hurry.

HAMMERSTEIN: "It's all settled. You're to have three thousand dollars a night."

MYSELF: "But I've told you a hundred times —"

HAMMERSTEIN (*interrupting*): "Never mind about that. Three thousand dollars a night, and you open in *Traviata.*"

Here, to my astonishment, he drew from his pocket a bundle of thousand-franc notes and began scattering them over the floor like cards, until the carpet was littered with them. I was so surprised that I could say or do nothing, and before I could call him back, he had swept out of the room like a whirlwind, crying that he had to catch his train and had no time to wait.

I picked up the notes, smiling quietly, and found that in all he had strewn my carpet with one hundred thousand francs. Today it may not sound such a very vast sum, but then it meant four thousand pounds. And even nowadays one does not go strewing thousands of pounds on people's carpets.

I took the notes at the earliest possible opportunity to the Rothschild Bank, telling them they were not mine, and that they must be kept there safely until Mr. Hammerstein called for them.

However, he did not call for them. Instead, he called once again for me, in the early morning.

HAMMERSTEIN: "Well, and so you've made up your mind at last. Didn't Oscar Hammerstein say you would?"

MYSELF: "He did, and Oscar Hammerstein was wrong. As I've told you before, I am not going to America."

HAMMERSTEIN: "Oh yes, you are. You've got all my money."

MYSELF: "The money is in the bank. It has nothing to do with me."

HAMMERSTEIN: "Was there ever such a woman? Still, you'll come. Mark my words."

Hammerstein was right. Melba had already made up her mind. She signed a contract with him the next morning, for ten performances at three thousand dollars a night.

"I never regretted doing so," she writes. "I was to experience one of the most brilliant epochs in my career, and I was to know the exhilaration of battles, rivalry, difficulties galore. And I love a good fight."

She also loved the fee of three thousand dollars, because it was the highest ever paid to an opera star in America. Financially she had established herself as the prima donna *assoluta* of all times. Caruso was then getting a measly one thousand, four hundred and forty dollars at the Met, and he never got more than two thousand, five hundred. Madame Calvé and later Madame Nordica got one thousand, five hundred a performance from Hammerstein.

Still, Melba was already rich and independent. Money meant little to her unless it was a little more money than her rivals'. People began to speculate why she had signed the contract with Hammerstein. Some said she was dissatisfied with the Metropolitan, where she had sung only once in *La Bohème*, in 1904, and never since. She had not been in her best form, was ill, and had canceled all other performances. There was the usual rumor mill. Some said she was afraid to come to America because people were "talking" about her and the Duc d'Orléans. Others said, on the contrary, that she wanted to get away from Europe to forget the Duc, with whom she was still desperately in love.

Old legends never die. There were so many rumors about Melba that something in each of them was probably true. Melba's own version of why she defected from the Met and decided to sing for Hammerstein was quite different:

> At the Metropolitan I should have had to sing when and where they wanted. My roles would have been dictated for me. No artist gives her best under those conditions. I said to myself, "I am Melba. I shall sing when and where I like, and I shall sing in my own way." It may sound arrogant but arrogance of that sort is not a bad way to get things done.

There was another reason, as we shall soon see. Melba had admitted, "I love a good fight." She was forty-eight now, and there was, in the words of her friend Bemberg, "not a hole in Nellie's voice." She knew that this time she was not just singing against another prima donna but against one of the world's great opera houses. It was an exciting challenge, the ideal challenge for the greatest living prima donna.

"Battle was in the air," Melba remembers with her usual sense of gusto as she set foot on American soil, on December 29, 1906. The erstwhile tomboy from Australia was rolling up her sleeves and spitting in her hands. During her trip on the *Caronia* she had received marconigrams almost every day. Hammerstein sent exciting reports from the front lines. Melba's friends implored her to give up the whole thing before it was too late. "Don't associate yourself with an obvious failure!" they warned her. She knew that after the sensational opening on December 3 the receipts of the Manhattan

Opera House had steadily fallen. Around December 12 they had reached a lamentable low of less than a thousand dollars a night. Hammerstein seemed to have lost his fight before it really started. Several singers whom he had previously signed up in Europe had lost heart and canceled their contracts.

Hammerstein had never learned the meaning of compromise; he always considered attack the best form of defense. He had originally planned to open his Manhattan Opera House on the same night as the Metropolitan opened, November 26, but had had to postpone his opening for a week because his house was not ready. As a matter of fact, the Manhattan Opera House was ready five minutes before the beginning of the opening performance. *The New York American* of December 3 headlined: *LAST WORKMEN TO LEAVE NEW MANHATTAN AS ARRIVAL OF AUDIENCE BEGINS.*

Reading the reports of the big event I can't help wishing I had been there. It must have been great fun. Long before the opening hour, "automobiles and wagonettes" were moving in a slow procession through Thirty-fourth Street, a strange no man's land for seasoned operagoers in New York. Traffic police were unable to prevent chaos: violent mob scenes occurred at the single entrance of the Manhattan Opera House. (The Metropolitan has several entrances. The following morning the newspapers admonished Hammerstein to take better precautions.) Many ticket-holders had to literally fight their way through dense crowds around the entrance until they were able to get in.

Inside the auditorium, there was confusion confounded.

The ushers were unfamiliar with the new house. No one could find his seat. A dense mass of standees filled up the space around the periphery of the auditorium. By the time many people had at last reached their seats, they were completely exhausted.

The performance had been announced for eight o'clock, but Hammerstein held the curtain for half an hour because so many were still outside struggling to get in. Official society — the older elements of New York's elite, known as "Knickerbocker gentry" — paid little attention to the "upstart venture," but the social set was sufficiently represented by H. H. Flagler, Rawlins Cottenet, Miss May Callender, E. Berry Wall, James de Wolf Cutting, Mrs. Charles Childs. The more conservative members of the Four Hundred had demonstratively gone to the Metropolitan to hear Caruso and Sembrich in *Marta*.

Hammerstein, a romantic figure in black cape, white tie, silk hat, with an unlit cigar in his mouth, was a great sight. He showed himself everywhere to the crowds — at the box office, in the auditorium, in front of the house. He was the star attraction of the evening and enjoyed himself tremendously. He savored the excitement as a gourmet savors the aroma of fine food that drifts out of the kitchen before the beginning of a great meal.

The house lights dimmed. Maestro Campanini appeared on the conductor's platform. There was an ovation, the first of many ovations that night. Campanini raised his baton, and the orchestra began to play. Connoisseurs closed their eyes blissfully. No doubt, the acoustics of the new house were wonderful, much much better than the Met's.

Hammerstein had chosen Bellini's *I Puritani* as the opening work. Hardly anyone in New York knew the opera. Hammerstein's sole reason for selecting it was the tenor part,
which was made to order for his star, Alessandro Bonci,
"the only tenor of the century who could sing the terrific
range without transposing the music." The century was only
six years old, but the claim was not exaggerated. Caruso had
sung in *I Puritani*, but later dropped the part because his
voice didn't have the colossal range that was needed. Hammerstein was gambling on "the duel of the tenors," which
had already consumed more newsprint than the average
Balkan war.

After a rough start owing to bad stage fright, Bonci displayed his "extraordinary vocalism." There was frenetic applause. There were other ovations for Madame Regina Pinkert, a Polish soprano (later dropped by Hammerstein
because of her "fits of hysteria") and the "opulent" baritone
Mario Ancona (later fired because he was "too fat"). Campanini had the greatest success of all the artists that night.

At the end of the final curtain, Hammerstein joined his
artists before the curtain and made a memorable curtain
speech. "Ladies and gentlemen, I'm very much gratified,"
he said, after a burst of wild applause. "I can only say that
this is an effort toward the furtherance of industry and
music. I am compelled to add that I am the only one who
has created this institution. I have had no assistance, financially or morally. I have no board of directors, nobody to tell
me what I should or should not do."

There was laughter, and some people in the audience
stared rather provocatively at Messieurs Otto Kahn and

Eliot Gregory, members of the Metropolitan's board of directors, who sat stony-faced in Proscenium Box 13. Several other directors and singers of the Met were scattered among the audience and feeling not very well.

"I have never expected to make a dollar out of this enterprise," Hammerstein went on. "Many people endow libraries ("One on Carnegie!" shouted a voice from the gallery) and hospitals, but I have yet to see one who has endowed opera. When the curtain falls tonight it is the beginning of a series of trials — nothing else.

"The ensemble which surrounds this institution is so large and is composed of so many celebrities of music that every opera for the next three or four weeks is experimental, and depends for success or failure on this audience and this city."

There was much applause and people cheered.

Even without Mr. Hammerstein's bellicose speech, the Metropolitan's forces realized that he was in this fight to the bitter end. The very design of his new opera house was provocative proof of his operatic Blitzkrieg tactics. At the Met, the box-holders could view each other — which to some of them was certainly far more interesting than to look at the stage. The Manhattan's forty boxes were so arranged that the box-holders could see the stage perfectly well but were not seen by all the people in the other boxes, and not at all by the people in the orchestra stalls.

The auditorium is designed for seeing and hearing but not for the display of jewel and gowns [the *New York Times* society reporter wrote with deadpan style]. On matters sartorial the first-night audience followed a go-as-you-please style of dressing. Not only were the standees clad, as

are many of the same class of genuine music-lovers at the
Metropolitan, in white cotton blouses and plaid walking-
skirts topped by serviceable but nonornamental headgear,
but they wore these in many of the orchestra as well as gallery seats, removing, of course, the view-obstructing cha-
peaux, while next to them sat women in the most gorgeous
of highly colored or white dinner and evening gowns, wearing lofty aigrettes of pearls, diamonds and other precious
gems. . . . [The society reporter's style becomes no longer
deadpan.]

The occupants of the first tier of boxes (which at the Metropolitan was called "Diamond Horseshoe") could be seen
only from the front of the orchestra and they were not interested in the admiration, if there was such, of oboe players
and second fiddlers. It was a real provocation. People in the
stalls had, however, a "splendid view of the stage." And the
all-important intermissions were much shorter than at the
Met. Hammerstein made it quite clear that he intended to
produce good opera without the support of the Four Hundred. At one time he had even planned to give performances
at popular prices, but gave up this idea when he began to
realize how much he would lose.

He lost a lot of money, even so, during the first four weeks,
before Melba arrived. And he almost lost his gamble. After
the initial sensation had worn off, half the orchestra seats
and many of the boxes remained empty. The gallery was always crowded, but you can't run opera for the gallery. Hammerstein didn't want the support of the Diamond Horseshoe
set — and he didn't get it. The Met subscribers avoided the
Manhattan like the plague.

Considering attack the best defense, Hammerstein had an-

nounced that his Manhattan Opera House would perform
on the same nights as the Metropolitan — on Mondays,
Wednesdays, Fridays, and twice on Saturday. He could
easily have put on opera on Tuesday and Thursdays when
the Met was closed, and he might have lured away some
Met patrons; but he wanted a fight.

He did other incredible things. He knew as well as everybody that *Aïda* had always been one of the Met's box-office
hits, that it was well-produced and beautifully sung at the
older house. During the sixteen years when Caruso appeared
as Radames in America, *Aïda* was given one hundred and
one times at the Met; Caruso sang in sixty-four performances. Yet the amazing Mr. Hammerstein had the nerve to
produce his own *Aïda*. Campanini conducted, "with very
great success," wrote the critics. Two days later the Met's
Aïda was said to be "merely boisterous." Thus encouraged,
Hammerstein scheduled *Aïda* the same night it was given at
the Met!

Something akin to the spirit of the World Series had infected everybody at the Manhattan. They were all trying to
outsing, outplay, and outdo their opposite numbers at the
Met. During the first intermission of that simultaneous performance of *Aïda* news reached the Manhattan — which was
completely sold out that night — that the Metropolitan was
half empty. The curtain was down at that moment and there
was pandemonium backstage. Singers, stagehands, musicians, the conductor and Hammerstein formed a circle and
danced a triumphal war dance.

But that came later. For the moment Hammerstein had
tough going. Looking over his half-empty house during the

first weeks, he must have wondered whether Melba would save him. Thank God, she was on her way, aboard the *Caronia*. If she couldn't do it, no one could.

Melba arrived on the morning of December 29, sniffing with delight "the clean sparkling air which seems peculiar to New York." (If Melba is to be trusted, that air must have been better in 1906 than it is today.) A large crowd was waiting for her at the Cunard pier: friends and admirers, curiosity seekers and celebrity hunters, photographers and reporters, policemen, and plainclothesmen. Hammerstein had thoughtfully informed the press that in her first performance in *La Traviata* Madame Melba would wear "a large portion of her famous jewels" and that he would provide two detectives to guard her day and night.

Hammerstein was guided by precedent for this bit of operatic protocol. At one of her farewell performances in *La Traviata* at Covent Garden, Adelina Patti wore a magnificent white dress studded with thirty-seven hundred small diamonds worth a million dollars. "It was necessary to include amongst Flora's guests a couple of detectives from Bow Street Police Station," writes Harold Rosenthal. "All in all it must have been an unforgettable evening."

A crowded, animated press conference was held in the *Caronia's* main lounge. The newspapermen, a shocked Mr. Colson notes, displayed "all the usual impertinences peculiar to American reporters." Did Madame Melba realize that she was about to ruin her career in America? Did she have any surprises up her sleeve? How much was she being paid to sing for Hammerstein? Was she singing for him because he paid her more than the Metropolitan? Did she know that the directors of the Metropolitan were furious at her impudence? How many times a week was she to sing? All very "impertinent" questions, as can be seen.

The Queen of Song glared imperiously at the brash reporters. An Edwardian prima donna might "confide her views," but she was not in the habit of being asked direct questions. Melba acted with the aplomb of an Elder Stateswoman. She knew nothing. She was going to sing for Mr. Hammerstein. It made no difference to her whether she sang "at the Metropolitan, at the Manhattan or at a barn." If people wanted to hear her, they would come, and if not, they would stay away. And, as she had already said, she knew nothing more.

At the Hotel St. Regis the excitement continued. One of Melba's first visitors was Mrs. Jack Gardner, who had left the warmth of her original Venetian palace in Boston to venture into Manhattan's cold, windy Siberia because she just had to wish Melba luck — darling Nellie would need it; the Metropolitan people were "beside themselves with rage"; they were "massing all forces to sing for the old firm." Mrs. Gardner was thrilled, and promised to attend Melba's performance, possibly "in the service of beauty" in which she excelled. She was followed by another friend, Mrs. LeRoy Edgar.

"My dear Nellie, how exciting! New York society is talking of nothing but the war."

"The war?"

"Well, the war between the Metropolitan and the Manhattan. How terribly fascinating. I predict that your first appearance will be one of the most remarkable events in the whole history of the American stage."

The Manhattan was a madhouse. The demand for tickets for the first "Melba night" — on January 2: *La Traviata,* with the tenor Bassi, the baritone Ancona, and Campanini as conductor — was so heavy that Hammerstein had decided to put in a great many extra chairs. On New Year's Day, when Melba came to the opera house for a rehearsal, the chairs were arriving in vans while the rehearsal was in progress. She had to sing to the accompaniment of fortissimo hammering.

"I left the theater with a sinking heart," she writes of a rare moment of self-doubt. "Should we ever pull through?"

Melba was extremely nervous on the morning of Wednesday, January 2, 1907. She now realized that she was playing for high stakes. If she failed, it might be a severe shock to her position. And it might be the end of Hammerstein's courageous experiment. Everybody was going to be there tonight, her friends and her enemies. Tomorrow New York, America, the whole world would know that Melba was still the greatest prima donna of all — or that she was on her way out. In this ruthless business you never knew when the beginning of the end might come. So many were waiting in the wings. . . .

Visitors, letters, telegrams, packages, fruit, flowers, last-minute wishes arrived constantly at her suite at the St. Regis. The members of her staff were on the verge of collapse. There were half a dozen of them, maids, secretaries, her doctor, her manager; unlike some of her celebrated tenor partners who traveled with a retinue of ten or twelve people, including lawyer, cook, barber and *chef de claque,* Melba had only a modest-sized staff. (Today she would probably have her accountant, press agent and private psychiatrist going everywhere with her.)

She had forgotten to ask Hammerstein for seats for her staff. Now he told her he couldn't get any; even he was unable to buy them back from ticket-holders or speculators. They would have to stand up, but under the circumstances they didn't mind.

The hotel was "dreadfully overheated." Melba and the staff had turned off all radiators but so much heat came through the walls of the adjoining rooms that she was very uncomfortable. She made arrangements to get out of the hotel the next day when an apartment in West Fifty-eighth Street was offered to her by Mr. Navarro, and cabled to London "for linen, silver and servants." During the next three months she would keep house there for her friends. Quite a few planned to come over from London to see how the opera war was going.

The telephone rang incessantly. Melba told her maid to take it off the receiver, and to cover the bell of the front door with wadding. The members of her staff noticed that Madame was alternately irritated and in high spirits, a sure sign that she was very nervous. During the morning she went through her warming-up exercises and scales. She reached the top D with no effort, and knew she was in good form.

She went for a quiet walk in Central Park, had a light lunch at the Savoy, came back to the St. Regis, and played bridge. She loved bridge, which she played in a straight, un-subtle way; some people said she was too eager to win. Around four in the afternoon she tried to catch some sleep, but was too nervous and got up again. The people, the heat, the noise were too much for her. She slipped out of the hotel for a long drive "down the Hudson Road." When she came back, she felt better, "ready for the worst, or rather, the best."

There was time for a game of dominoes — anything to take her mind off the approaching ordeal. Then she got ready to go to the theater, taking along her jewels. She was escorted by the two detectives whom Mr. Hammerstein had so thoughtfully provided. He didn't want Melba to be held up now (much as he would have liked the publicity). Ten years ago the "Melba Suite" at the Auditorium Hotel in Chicago, where the prima donna usually stayed when she was in town, had been invaded by "two well-dressed men of gen-tlemanly appearance." They had knocked at the door of "the Melba suite" and when the lady who then occupied the rooms opened, they had pointed their guns at her and asked her for her jewels.

> The astonished lady explained that she had none [writes Miss Murphy]. They swore she had, gagged and bound her and made a complete search, but failed to find Melba's jewels. They locked the doors and disappeared. The poor lady was found hours later in a state of exhaustion. She wasn't Melba, who during that trip to Chicago had taken a different suite. . . . When the diva heard of the terrifying experience which the lady had been subjected to because she'd been mistaken for Melba, she paid her a visit of sym-pathy.

Hammerstein was waiting for her at the stage door.

"I shall never forget his look of agitation and fatigue," Melba remembers. She had been told that a few weeks ago he had fallen out of a box into the stalls during rehearsal and had suffered a severe concussion from which he had not fully recovered. "In fact, he was never quite the same again."

He was trembling with emotion. "Every seat is sold," he said. "By Jove, I'm going to win out."

Melba was so moved she could only shake his hand.

He looked at her anxiously. "For God's sake, keep well, won't you?"

Melba laughed. "I'll do my darnedest. Angels can't do more."

"Come on the stage and listen to the audience," Hammerstein said.

They walked across the dim stage. From the auditorium behind the curtain came the dull roar of many voices which tells of a packed house, and always shoots an extra supply of adrenalin through an artist's veins. Melba noted with some astonishment that her hands were shaking. She tried to tell herself that it was "from exhilaration, not from fright." Or, was she — afraid?

She was getting ready, wearing her "amazing collection of diamonds." The call boy came to say, "Five minutes, Madame Melba." She walked out of her dressing room towards the stage. She heard the end of the overture. The curtain rose. From where she stood in the wings Melba could see "many familiar faces that were pillars at the Metropolitan." The defection had already begun. The Met management had countered Melba's initial appearance with a de luxe *Tosca*, with Madame Eames, Caruso and Scotti; but so many "pillars" had deserted their operatic bastion on that night that the Metropolitan Opera House must have been trembling in its foundations.

And now Melba's fear was gone, and her Australian pluck was evident again. "Very well, I vowed to myself, I should sing as I had never sung before."

She stepped out on the stage. A storm of applause broke down on her. For a moment she stood motionless as if blinded. And then . . .

. . . Silence again, and I heard my voice ring out [Melba writes]. In thirty seconds — I must say it though it may sound boastful — I knew I had won.

It does sound boastful, but she was right. The rest of her performance was "one long triumph." And after the first act there were ten curtain calls for Melba.

"I am delighted," she said. "I am as happy as a king."

At the end of the performance she came out ten times, first alone, then with the cast, and finally with Campanini and Oscar Hammerstein. "As the singer appeared with the intrepid impresario," writes Melba's adoring Agnes G. Murphy, "the enthusiasm of the audience passed all bounds, and for some minutes there was a deafening uproar, during which hundreds of people waved their handkerchiefs, and the younger members of the audience threw their floral buttonholes at her feet."

She was still the prima donna *assoluta*.

When it was all over, and Melba walked through the corridors "full of massed bouquets" . . .

. . . I felt the emotion which Cecil Rhodes had described
to me as the supreme sensation of life — power!

So now at last we know why she decided to sing for Mr.
Hammerstein.

The next morning Richard Aldrich wrote in the *Times:*

> Melba's voice has its old-time lusciousness and purity, it's
> exquisite smoothness and fullness; it poured out with all
> spontaneity and freedom. Her singing was a delight from
> beginning to end.

The critics also liked Hammerstein's production, with its
1848 sets and costumes. It was remembered that less erudite
producers of *La Dame aux Camélias* had dressed up the
story in seventeenth-century décor. The critics admired
Campanini, the conductor, but didn't like Amedeo Bassi, the
tenor. Hammerstein wasn't surprised; he hadn't wanted
Melba to share the spotlight that night with a first-rate tenor.
This was her night exclusively.

There are still a few people in New York who have heard
about that performance from their parents or older friends.
It must have been the sort of opera evening that no one
who was there will ever forget.

"The success of Melba in this season surpassed anything
she had ever done in America before," writes Vincent Sheean
in his *Oscar Hammerstein I.* Melba enjoyed herself enormously in the fiercely competitive air. She had won her
private battle against the entire Metropolitan.

At the Met they had at first watched Hammerstein with
the indulgent attitude displayed towards innocuous upstarts

and precocious children. Heinrich Conried, the general manager of the Metropolitan, was known to refer to the Manhattan merely as "that house on Thirty-fourth Street."

But this attitude of unconcerned arrogance soon changed
as Melba continued to draw growing support from the Metropolitan audience. On "Melba nights" the Manhattan began
to look more and more like the Metropolitan, as the elegant
members of the Diamond Horseshoe set made the hazardous journey to "that house" on Eighth Avenue while the
Metropolitan was half-empty. It was reported that the de-
fectors even *liked* the performances at the Manhattan Opera
House! The Manhattan's receipts, which had been as low
as one thousand dollars a night only a few weeks ago, were
said to be reaching an average of ten thousand a night.

At the Met's offices there was now a bleak mood of despair. In vain did Conried try to match the "Melba nights"
with his strongest attractions. His luck ran very low that season, while Hammerstein's luck reached high tide.

Heinrich Conried knew much less about opera than Hammerstein. He was a Silesian-born, Vienna-trained former
actor and stage manager, who had run several German-
language theaters in New York. (As a profitable sideline, he
provided the Hamburg-America Line with the steamer
chairs that were rented to passengers. It is doubtful whether
today's board of directors at the Met would permit Mr. Bing
to indulge in such outside activities.)

Conried was a self-made man, shrewd and tough and
"lacking in those small courtesies which people like." He
knew little about voices, and less about music. He made the
mistake of turning down all new French works that were

offered to him by the Parisian agent Gabriel Astruc, including Debussy's *Pelléas et Mélisande* and Charpentier's *Louise*. Hammerstein snapped them up and later produced them with great success.

Conried once astonished the press by walking into the press room on the grand-tier floor, during the second act of *Tosca*, where some of the critics worked on their reviews, and threatening to banish them from the house unless they came back to listen to Caruso sing *"E lucevan le stelle"* in the third act. The critics were amused.

One week after her triumphal initial performance Melba appeared with Bonci and Renaud in *Rigoletto*. This was a first-rate cast: the greatest prima donna, the "tenor of the century," one of the greatest living baritones, and Campanini conducting. The house was sold out days in advance. The newspapers printed irate letters from readers who had been unable to get tickets. The activities of the ticket speculators were scandalous. Hammerstein was blamed by the press for his inability to stop the black market in Melba tickets. It must have been worse than during the early run of *My Fair Lady* exactly half a century later. Melba autographs were sold like hot cakes at a dollar apiece, with the proceeds going to the Long Island Home for Blind Children.

On the evening of that unforgettable *Rigoletto* performance, standing-room tickets fetched from five to ten dollars, and the brass barrier of the box office was broken away by an angry crowd. The police must have been lenient in those days, for the Manhattan sold so many standing-room tickets that "all aisles and corridors were dangerously crowded."

Rigoletto belongs to those operas (like *Carmen, Lohengrin, Cavalleria Rusticana, La Gioconda, Mefistofele, Andrea Chénier*) that are great musical theater when they're superlatively sung, played and produced, but can be easily ruined by mediocrity, and then become insufferably dull. On the evening of January 11, 1907, everything was perfect: great singing, great staging, great playing, great conducting. The critics reached for their rarest superlatives. Melba was "magnificent," Bonci's luscious tenor "surprised even his warmest admirers." Melba and Bonci were no great friends but Hammerstein had made them bury the hatchet "for the duration." It was Bonci's bad luck to be considerably shorter than Melba, and their love scenes sometimes had an involuntary comic effect. Melba, that great practical joker, didn't like to be laughed at, and poor Bonci was in disgrace. That night in *Rigoletto* everything went beautifully; perhaps Bonci wore elevator shoes and Melba low heels. The *Times* called it "The best production of *Rigoletto* seen in New York for many years."

And on the same evening, the Metropolitan put on a revival of Meyerbeer's *L'Africaine* with Fremstad and Caruso. It got such bad notices that it had to be dropped. There was now unconcealed panic at the Met. Conried began to send cables to Toscanini, imploring him to come to New York and save the Metropolitan.

It must have been very pleasant for Melba to compare the Metropolitan's bad notices with the Manhattan's rave reviews. Even a saint would have rejoiced, and prima donnas have scant hopes of ever attaining sainthood. The reference books' standard phrase is that "Melba saved Hammerstein

from disaster"—but she did more than that. She brought
real glamour to the Manhattan, and made it a full-fledged
competitor of the Metropolitan. She improved the morale
of everybody connected with the Manhattan. As a result,
everybody worked just a little harder—with the imperceptible extra effort that makes all the difference between
a good opera night and a great one.

Not only were the "Melba nights" spectacular events.
Even when she wasn't singing, the Manhattan's performances were getting better all the time. The public and the
critics showed mounting enthusiasm. On January 18, Hammerstein produced Meyerbeer's *Les Huguénots* with a cast
which included no stellar names, but the Manhattan Opera
House was packed to the rafters and the critics were raving.
On the same evening the Metropolitan gave the American
première of Puccini's *Manon Lescaut,* in the presence of
the composer, with Caruso and Lina Cavalieri, a former
dancer and perhaps "the most beautiful woman ever to appear on the operatic stage," who created havoc among the
male element in the audience. Opera was now as popular as
baseball in New York, thanks to Madame Melba and her
"intrepid" impresario.

How serious the situation had become around the Met
was evident from the "gaps among its audiences" when
Melba was singing at "the other place."

"It seemed as though the directors would be forced to do
something desperate," Melba writes. The "desperate" action
occurred a few days later, when some of the directors—
"and very charming, gallant, American gentlemen they
were"—called at her flat. There was some diplomatic

shadow-boxing on both sides, but it is not hard to guess why they had bothered to come up.

One of them, acting as spokesman, said, "Why don't you come and direct the Metropolitan for us, Madame?"

Melba admits it might have been said in a laughing way, "but there perhaps was more than mere jest in it." You bet there was. The charming, gallant gentlemen promptly denied having made any overtures to Madame Melba, but they didn't go up to her place just to congratulate her on her successful efforts on behalf of Mr. Hammerstein.

Melba laughed and thanked them for the proffered honor. "Had I accepted it, I am quite certain that I should not have been alive today," she wrote in her autobiography.

She knew the risks. It was better to remain a prima donna than to become a manager.

The Metropolitan's dignity did not permit an all-out, open attack against "that house on Thirty-fourth Street." Instead, subtle psychological underground warfare was now waged against Hammerstein. Melba alludes to this with her customary reticence (when she prefers to be reticent).

"Victory didn't come at all easily to us," she records, and brushes over the matter, saying she cannot attempt "to describe all difficulties." She was referring to the *cause célèbre* of *La Bohème*.

That affair was then a puzzle to most people, and still is something of a musical mystery hidden in a legal enigma. The skill of the legal experts and the inevitable passage of time have beautifully camouflaged the issue, but there is no doubt that the Metropolitan was trying everything short of murder to prevent Hammerstein from producing *La Bohème*. Hammerstein shouted from the rooftops that he could see the fine Italian hand of Heinrich Conried. Conried claimed piously that he had nothing to do with the matter — it was all between Hammerstein and the Italian publishing house of G. Ricordi in Milan, which owned the rights to all works of Puccini.

Hammerstein wanted to produce *La Bohème* at his house because his prima donna *assoluta* wanted to sing in it. When Melba had appeared in *La Bohème* in 1904 at the Met she had been ill and neither she nor the production had been a success. After one performance she had canceled all engagements for the rest of the season and returned to Europe. Now she had the opportunity to sing the part of Mimi, her best part, under different circumstances. No real prima donna would pass up such a chance.

A year earlier, in March, 1906, Hammerstein had made an oral agreement with George Maxwell, the New York representative of the firm of G. Ricordi, Milan. According to this agreement Hammerstein claimed "to have the right to produce *La Bohème* and all other Puccini works."

This was emphatically denied by G. Ricordi in Milan. They brought suit in the United States Circuit Court seeking an injunction to keep Hammerstein from producing *La Bohème*, on the ground that "the Metropolitan Opera owned exclusive rights to *La Bohème* and all other Puccini operas in New York."

Hammerstein answered that "his oral contract with Maxwell was valid and would be proved in court."

Public opinion and the entire press were on Hammerstein's side. It was well known that G. Ricordi had given other opera companies permission to produce *La Bohème* in the United States and even in New York. The traveling San Carlo Opera Company and the Henry Savage Opera Company had both produced it. In point of fact anybody could produce it as long as he paid Ricordi the sum of one hundred and fifty dollars a performance for royalties. The cautious consensus was that the Metropolitan's claim to "exclusive rights in New York" might be legally valid but that it was certainly rather surprising — quite possibly a legal maneuver to keep Mr. Hammerstein from getting *La Bohème* and Madame Melba from singing in it. It was a wonderful time for opera lovers and "opera fools," lawyers and musicians, gossipmongers and prima donna partisans.

Possession is nine tenths of the law. Ricordi had possession of the orchestra score of *La Bohème;* Puccini's score had never been printed. There existed about a dozen written copies of the original score, which Ricordi treated like the blueprint of a top-secret mobilization plan. These copies were carefully numbered and kept in vaults in various parts of the world.

The Metropolitan tried to promote its case and to improve its public relations by inviting Giacomo Puccini to come to America as guest of the Metropolitan. They had a perfectly valid reason: on February 11, 1907, his new opera *Madama Butterfly* would have its American *première* at the Met, with a splendid cast — Geraldine Farrar, Louise Homer, Enrico Caruso and Antonio Scotti.

Puccini arrived on January 18, just in time to catch a performance of his *Manon Lescaut* (which didn't make him too happy), and at once took part in the preparations of *Madama Butterfly*, his favorite opera — perhaps because it had caused him his greatest heartbreak a while ago when its *première* at Milan's La Scala was an utter failure and turned into an ugly theater scandal. At his arrival in New York Puccini was asked what he thought of "the *La Bohème* affair." He was asked the question almost every day during his six-week stay in America.

Puccini said, in a statesmanlike manner, that he knew nothing about the matter. He would neither confirm nor deny. The whole matter didn't concern him. It was strictly between the firm of Ricordi and Mr. Hammerstein. Puccini was an honest man with common sense. He certainly had not been "bribed" by the Met, as some people insinuated. But he was no fool. He did not want to get involved in a fight with his publishers, or in a fight with the Metropolitan, or in a fight with the Manhattan (which might come out on top, you never know), and certainly not in a fight with Madame Melba, the Mimi of his dreams in *La Bohème*. "Nobody was eager to offend Madame Melba, whose powers in several opera houses of the world were at that time very great, possibly as great as those of Ricordi," writes Vincent Sheean. "Her popularity in America was such that it may have influenced even the courts. Certainly it influenced the press."

The Metropolitan did its best to identify itself, as they

would nowadays say, with the image of Puccini. During the composer's six weeks in America, it presented not less than twenty-one performances of four Puccini operas — among them *La Bohème*, to be sure. The Met wanted to make it clear even to musical morons that Puccini belonged exclusively to the Met, that they owned not only the exclusive rights to all works of the composer in New York City but to the composer himself. Hammerstein, displaying a Mephistophelian grin, said this was all a carefully arranged, diabolical plan, and the press supported him happily. Melba's uncharacteristically cautious version is, "We could not get the music of *La Bohème* because it was possessed by the Metropolitan, and in some roundabout way they also possessed, I believe, certain rights of production."

But Hammerstein was a fighter who never acknowledged defeat.

He came round to see Melba.

"How about doing *La Bohème?*" he said.

Melba said she was "longing" to do it. "It's one of my favorite roles. But how can we get around the Metropolitan? How can we get the music?"

"Leave it to me," said Hammerstein. "I may have to go to Italy for it. I may have to fly to the moon for it. But I'll get it."

"And he did get it, by what mysterious influences I never discovered," writes Melba. It's a safe bet that Melba was one of the few people on earth who knew how Hammerstein got the music: he had made a world-wide search, hired musical operatives and operatic private eyes, and after "a diligent search" succeeded in getting the music of *La Bohème,* but not the whole music; he got hold of an incomplete, badly mutilated score that had been used in America years ago by the Del Conti Opera Company, a touring outfit from England.

Melba was "in transports of joy." Then there arose another difficulty. Maestro Campanini was willing to prepare and rehearse the performance but he would not conduct it.

> He had scruples, had Campanini [writes Melba in her inimitable style]. He was also afraid of Ricordi, the music publisher, who was running around New York, in company with others, threatening lawsuits if we gave *Bohème.* In addition to which, quantities of anonymous letters were constantly arriving for myself, threatening the direst perils if I appeared as Mimi.

In her vivid imagination Melba saw herself as the heroine in a sinister plot. She was on the verge of death, just as Mimi is in the last act of *La Bohème.* Melba enjoyed the excitement. She read, with a pleasant shiver, the statements that were circulated among critics, musicians and interested opera lovers, in which terrible threats were voiced against Hammerstein and Melba. It was predicted they would be "committed to contempt of court."

Campanini (who was probably afraid of being boycotted by some opera houses in Italy, where the power of Ricordi was very great) officially had nothing to do with *La Bohème.* Actually he completely prepared and rehearsed the performance. He had conducted the opera so often that he knew the score by heart and was able to supply the missing parts.

Here and there he would supply a minor orchestral phrase. Rehearsals were held in strictest secrecy. Everybody worked overtime. Even Melba showed greater enthusiasm than for anything she had ever done.

La Bohème was announced for March 1, 1907, with Melba, her protégée Emma Trentini as Musetta, Alessandro Bonci, and Mario Sammarco. The house was packed. It was reported that "half an hour before the curtain went up representatives of the opposition *côterie* assembled in the vestibule of the Manhattan and loudly voiced their opinions so that all who passed might hear." Maestro Campanini watched from a box while his deputy Fernando Tanara raised the baton.

It was a spectacular success. "We gave one of the best performances of *La Bohème* in which it has ever been my privilege to sing," remembers Melba, and the critics agreed. "Melba sang the music more beautifully than she has done anything else in this season in New York," wrote the *Times*. Perhaps not all the notes in Puccini's score were played, but those played certainly sounded better than ever.

Melba was the heroine of the evening. She was at her best, "and even if she had been at her worst, she would still have received an ovation on that particular occasion." At the end of the third act, she brought Hammerstein with her before the curtain, and there was "another wild scene of popular approval, to which the people of New York had now accustomed her," writes the panegyrical Miss Murphy.

Melba appeared three times in *La Bohème*. After the third performance Hammerstein voluntarily withdrew his opposition to the case in court, and the court granted the injunction to Ricordi. But Hammerstein no longer cared: he had put on *La Bohème,* and won another battle.

He must have been a proud and happy man in those days. The Manhattan was doing better than he'd ever dared hope. And he had obtained a loan of four hundred thousand dollars from Frank Woolworth, the founder of the Woolworth stores, with the Manhattan Opera House as security. Woolworth was an opera lover who didn't like the Diamond Horseshoe people over at the Met. He subscribed to a box for every performance of the Manhattan.

Melba had contracted to sing ten times at the Manhattan when she signed up for Hammerstein in Paris, but she sang fifteen times. She was really devoted to him, and refused the most tempting offers of concerts in New York. She might have sung even more often at the Manhattan if she hadn't previously contracted several concerts in other American cities. Hammerstein tried to buy off the managers in these places, to enable Melba to sing for him; but no amount of money plus the substitution of another famous singer would compensate for her nonappearance, and where she had been definitely announced she had to sing.

It is often said now that today's great singers have shorter careers than those of the past because they travel too fast and sing too much. Well, here is Melba's traveling schedule for the week commencing Monday, March 18, 1907. That day she went from Chicago to Philadelphia; on Tuesday she sang in Philadelphia; on Wednesday she returned to New York and sang at the Manhattan Opera House; on Thursday she made the ten-hour train trip to Pittsburgh, where she sang on Friday and Saturday. Saturday night was spent on the train, and she arrived in New York on Sunday, March 24, where she began to make gramophone recordings; on Monday she made her farewell appearances at the Manhattan.

In Pittsburgh she drew "the largest audience since the establishment of the orchestra." In Boston, her final concert attracted "the record audience since the building of the Symphony Hall." In Buffalo the rows of carriages jammed all traffic for five blocks around Convention Hall. When Hammerstein was shown a clever cartoon by the well-known cartoonist Henry Mayer, the great manager laughed.

"Not bad," he said. "But you should see Melba draw."

Melba came through the ordeal gloriously. Her voice retained its fresh and pure quality through these arduous weeks, proof of her impeccable technique. Had she not sung so correctly she would have certainly shown signs of fatigue. She may have been stimulated by the general enthusiasm around her, and perhaps by her fees. Miss Murphy reports that "His Master's Voice" paid her a bonus of fifty thousand dollars for a week of recording, with more to follow in the way of royalties.

Melba's farewell New York performance, on March 25, as Mimi in *La Bohème*, was described by the city's most seasoned critics and oldest opera hands as "unique in the musical history of New York." The speculators did a brisk business; stalls were bought for thirty dollars each and some writers reported twice that price. At the end of *La Bohème*,

Melba sang the Mad Scene from Lucia, "by popular requests forwarded to the box office." Afterwards, so many floral devices were arranged around her on the stage that the prima donna was almost lost behind them. The audience left their places and rushed toward the footlights, and men and women threw little bunches of roses, violets and lilies-of-the-valley at her, "which they clamored for her to return to them as souvenirs and while she threw them back across the orchestra at her admirers the enthusiasm increased." The *New York Herald* remarked the next day that the Mad Scene from Lucia had been followed by a mad scene. Melba began to cry, thanking the people "in eloquent gestures," and the house lights were lowered; but the audience refused to leave. Melba called "Won't you go home?" People shouted "No!"

Then Melba told the stage hands to push a piano on the stage. The prima donna sat down and sang Tosti's "Mattinata" to her own accompaniment. Some who had been leaving rushed back to hear her, and there was pandemonium again. "A young fellow in the balcony, in an excess of ardor, having no other offering, threw a round empty cardboard box, which had contained flowers or candy, at her feet." By this time Melba had got into the spirit of the scene, caught the box, and put it on her head. "The brightest stage joke ever perpetrated could never have evoked such appreciation as this," reports Miss Murphy, completely beside herself. "Everybody joined in the roar of laughter and there were shouts 'Ain't she a crackerjack!' and 'She's all the candy!', with other vernacular compliments." Melba had to come out twenty-three times before she was permitted to retire, "utterly exhausted."

But the evening wasn't over yet. Hammerstein had arranged a banquet in her honor on the cleared stage. Tables were put up and the artists, with their wives or husbands, the staff of the opera house, the leading critics, and a number of New York's prominent citizens, sat down to supper — Suprême de Volaille Hammerstein, followed, naturally, by Pêche Melba. Gifts were given and received; Melba presented Hammerstein with a dress watch, and to Maestro Campanini and other heads of departments she gave scarf pins.

It must have been a wonderful party. Hammerstein had Melba, the guest of honor, on his right side, and Calvé on his left. Once upon a time, when Calvé was not yet a great prima donna, Hammerstein had tried to hire her for his vaudeville show at the Olympia Theater and had failed. Now she was to sing her memorable Carmen for him, after Melba's departure.

The orchestra played a potpourri, "Memories of the Manhattan Opera Season," which the Magnificent Oscar had composed especially for the occasion. (It is hard to see how he had found the time to do this too.) The guests at that wonderful supper party must have been particularly reticent people, or the two divas must have been on their best behavior; at any rate, no piquant anecdotes are remembered — which is a pity, since both Madame Melba and Madame Calvé were famous for the stiletto style of their repartee.

That night Hammerstein learned what so many great managers have learned before and after him: nothing on earth is as interesting as a great prima donna, except two great *prime donne.*

As he was going back to his modest rooms on top of his Victoria Theater, the great Hammerstein must have pondered the vicissitudes of operatic life. At the start of this season he had been given up and buried by the critics, lamented by his friends, ridiculed by the Met management. At the end of his first season his certified public accountants announced that the Manhattan Opera House had made a profit of 11,000 dollars. Hammerstein himself estimated his profits as closer to 100,000 dollars. Perhaps no accountant could penetrate the jungle of Hammerstein's triple bookkeeping, since he often took money out of his Victoria Theater to put it into his Manhattan Opera House. But there was no doubt that the box office of the Manhattan had taken in "over 750,000 dollars."

The Metropolitan Opera House had finished its season with a loss of 84,039 dollars — the first such loss in many years. The following year the loss was 95,806 dollars.

Hammerstein gave the Metropolitan three more seasons of unrelenting warfare, and New York's opera lovers the best three years of their lives. Hammerstein managed to fill his Manhattan even when the Met had both Gustav Mahler and Toscanini as conductors. The Met also had Caruso and his competitor Bonci, "the tenor of the century," whom Conried had bribed away from the Manhattan by paying him one thousand five hundred dollars for each performance instead of the one thousand which he would have got from Hammerstein during his second season. (Bonci said he had.

not known about these details, the sordid subject of money didn't concern him, only his agents.)

During one season Caruso sang fifty-one times at the Met, and Bonci twenty-five, and it also had Chaliapin; yet despite that formidable competition Hammerstein's Manhattan was more crowded than the Met. He made a profit of 229,000 dollars during the 1908–1909 season, while at the same time the Metropolitan had a loss of 205,201 dollars.

The following season New York City had three opera houses — the Metropolitan, the Manhattan and the recently completed New Theater. Certain operas — *La Bohème, Cavalleria Rusticana, Tosca* — were given by all three houses, and all of them were sold out. It seemed as if New Yorkers had gone opera-mad. A more sober explanation is the growth of the foreign-born element of New York's population by 700,000 people between 1900 and 1910. Many of the new immigrants were Italian-born opera enthusiasts.

At the end of the 1909–1910 season, the directors of the Metropolitan threw in the towel. On April 28, 1910, the *Sun* headlined *METROPOLITAN A MONOPOLY BY PAYING HAMMERSTEIN $2,000,000.* The fact was true although the figure was exaggerated. Hammerstein received a cash settlement of 1,200,000 dollars in return for which he agreed not to produce opera in New York and America for the next ten years and to give up his new Philadelphia Opera House. The Metropolitan also inherited the rights to several operas and contracts with several of Hammerstein's artists, as well as scenery, costumes and orchestral scores.

The astounding Mr. Hammerstein had won his four-year opera war. The Metropolitan had conceded defeat. Hammerstein had over a million dollars in cash, he still owned his Manhattan Opera House, and he had gained a world-wide reputation as a genius among opera managers. He had made New York opera-conscious for the first time in history and had advanced the cause of opera in Manhattan by at least fifty years.

Melba, as usual, had the last word. Before she sailed back to Europe — the day after the historic banquet on the stage of the Manhattan Opera House — she issued a royal farewell address:

> I have never enjoyed any season in America as much as the one now closing. All through I have been in splendid health and spirits, and I shall never forget the kindness with which I have been received. I am proud to have been associated with Mr. Hammerstein in his launching of New York's new opera house. What courage Mr. Hammerstein has shown, and what wonders he has done! I think there must be something in the conditions of American life to encourage him, for I know of no opera manager in any other city of the world who, single-handed and under circumstances of such difficulty and competition, would have risked his fortune in opera.
>
> His pluck appealed to me from the first, and I leave as I came, his loyal supporter.

⚞ 17 ⚟

Farewell Is Such a Very Beautiful Word

THE HARDEST THING for a prima donna is to realize that she is no longer one. She will never admit it, although she knows the danger signals — the first moments of terror that indicate the inexorable beginning of the end.

As long as she is fairly young and fairly healthy nothing ever goes very wrong. Of course, she has her off days, but so has every other artist. She may even suffer from a protracted vocal crisis, but she will always come back.

The fear, however, is forever there, in the back of her mind. The fear that someday it will be all over. As the great evenings and glorious opera seasons go by, the fear gets stronger. Then, one night, the prima donna has a little trouble in a difficult upward arpeggio. A sudden indisposition, nothing to worry about. Or . . . But no, that's impossible! Thank God, no one noticed it.

Then it happens again. She has some difficulty with her breath control in the long, sustained lower notes. And this time a few people who know about singing notice it. Two or three of her competitors were in the house, and immediately the tongues start wagging. Still, the audience doesn't know. The audience-at-large is with her as always.

Gradually the prima donna's brilliant high tones take on a certain sharpness around the edges. Her middle tones become somewhat colorless. Her florid technique is still impeccable, but her legato is punctured by invisible holes. One day X, the critic ("he never liked me") writes about it. The prima donna's friends rally to her defense. She is tired. She traveled too much, lost weight, slept too little, worked too hard. A minor fatigue, everybody suffers from it once in a while. But the fatigue develops into an acute crisis, and the crisis turns into a chronic *malaise.*

One night the prima donna's voice cracks as she tries to reach the high C, the all-important high C, the great climax of the evening.

Now everybody knows it. She is through.

Why don't they step back gracefully before the catastrophe occurs? The great nineteenth-century tenor Mario, husband of the celebrated prima donna Giulia Grisi, who had begun his career in England six years before the first Verdi opera was heard there and ended five years before the first production of *Aïda,* stepped down at the height of his fame (though not of his voice) — after several farewell performances, and perhaps after some prompting from his wife. (The aging prima donna had forbidden him to sing with the beautiful young diva, Pauline Viardot.) Jean de Reszke was still a matinee idol when he retired.

Few artists have shown such good sense. Lord Mount-

Edgcumbe writes of one Madame Galli, famous for her performances in Handel's oratorios, who was past seventy and impoverished, and had to sing again. "Her voice was cracked and trembling, but her school was good, and it was pleasing to observe the kindness with which she was received, and to mark the delight with which she seemed to hear again the music in which she had formerly been a distinguished performer."

Giulia Grisi gave nine farewell performances in 1861. That year a new prima donna, Adelina Patti, appeared on the stage. Thirty-four years later, Patti gave six farewell performances at Covent Garden, following up with several farewell tours. Patti specialized in farewell performances. Her first was in New York in 1887, and she gave dozens of them in the next ten years. "I can never forget the spectacle of Patti in her old age . . . ogling, dreadful, standing on the platform of Albert Hall, struggling painfully with 'Voi che sapete,'" remembers Colson.

Opera audiences are among the kindest people on earth. "When Mario came to take his farewell on the stage, there remained only a trace of that once matchless voice of his, and yet there seemed to linger on his perfect phrasing and ineffable charm," writes Patti's friend Wilhelm Kube. And when Patti, fiftyish, sang the part of the young peasant girl Zerlina in Don Giovanni, the critic Herman Klein wrote, "Such singing afforded a new experience for the younger generation of opera lovers." So much for the alleged callousness and cynicism of the cold-blooded critics.

The truth is that the critics suffer with their aging prima donnas. Opera is a romantic art, and opera lovers are romantic-minded people. In their younger years they were impressed by the giants of the past. When opera lovers reach middle age, they talk wistfully about the great voices of their youth, because such talk brings back nostalgic memories. No one likes getting old and it is painful to see one's heroes and heroines getting old on the stage, because it reminds you that you are getting old too, though perhaps not so publicly. And thus we listen to the prima donnas of our happier, younger days, and foolishly hope against hope that they will live and sing happily ever after. No other art has so much kindness, warmth and understanding left for its has-beens.

The critic who compares contemporary singers to the "golden" voices of the past gets himself into a trap from which no one can extricate him. He can't win. He is often disliked, sometimes misunderstood, frequently ignored, always quoted out of context. His readers are either prejudiced and dislike anything he writes or they try in vain to understand what he is after and give up in confusion. Even his few friends in the business don't always want to understand that no one is exempt from the critic's professional criticism.

People expect the critic to have knowledge and wisdom, taste and experience, style and tact; but do they ever expect a prima donna to be humble and broadminded, tolerant and altruistic, patient and generous? Perfection, friends, is rare on both sides of the orchestra pit. Sometimes a singer is out of pitch — and a critic out of tact. The artists claim that the critic cannot sing or play a simple scale, that they never learned the first thing about voice; how can he write about the mysteries of tonal production or the enigma of breath control?

A critic, friends, isn't supposed to perform but to criticize, which means to differentiate between a good and a bad performance. Ignorance is inexcusable but public ridicule will take care of ignorant critics if somebody else doesn't. They don't last. The great critics of the past whose judgments seem hilariously wrong in retrospect were not ignorant, though they were often prejudiced. Prejudice works both ways; sometimes it is just as hard to dislike an attractive mezzo as it is to like a score written in the twelve-tone scale.

I have no respect for artists who proclaim that they "never look at the reviews." The critic is the voice of the public. The artist who willfully ignores his public shows a deplorable lack of humility without which there can be no real art. I've never heard a singer say that the critic has the right to state his opinion even if he should be wrong. Singers, it seems, are not made that way.

Well, I will come out and fight for the performer's right to say in print what he thinks of his critics and public. It might not be a bad idea. Suppose a celebrated singer should write, "Last night's performance of *Don Giovanni* was attended by a restless, ignorant audience that gave no support to us, and coughed through the pianissimos. A couple of jerks came in during '*Deh, vieni alla finestra*' and ruined my legato. The applause after my '*Finch' han dal vino*' was sloppy and unco-ordinated. Mr. X, the critic, left during my scene with the Commendatore, which he later described as 'truly Gothic.' How the hell does M. X know whether it was true Gothic or phony baroque, since he wasn't there?"

In this era of flagrant corruption no hint of "payola" has yet touched music criticism. We know, of course, that Giacomo Meyerbeer used to visit the important critics in Vienna before one of his *premières* to pay them his respects and possibly something else, but you know what happened to Meyerbeer. All I can say is that no composer ever offered me anything. Modern composers are poor devils; they expect us critics to pay for the drinks.

Years ago when I was a novice in this hazardous business I was invited to dinner by the husband of a prima donna whom I had praised enthusiastically. Fool that I was, I accepted the invitation, which turned out to be a gastronomic experience. The diva knew her way around her range, and her chicken breasts with mushrooms in white sauce were as good as her *sotto voce* singing. Unfortunately, she gave a bad performance a few weeks later, which I was bound to record. She has never called me since, and when her husband sees me in the street he crosses over to the other side.

I should have known that the chicken breasts in white sauce were intended to create a stronger bond between us. It was my bad luck that I had to write for *Opera*, a magazine devoted to opera, on the prima donna's singing performance when I should have been writing for *Cuisine et Vins de France* on her Suprême de Volaille aux Champignons à Blanc.

I know better today and buy my own chicken breasts.

Much as I like the pleasures of dining and wining, the color of a man's claret will under no circumstances color my judgment of the color of his wife's voice.

A prima donna's healthy feeling for music is not always matched by a sound sense of proportion. She doesn't want to learn that the critic reports on an artist's performance, not on her character. I admire certain artists enormously between 7 and 10 P.M. in Europe (8 and 11 P.M. in America) on certain nights. But I wouldn't want to spend the rest of the night with them. I've had to praise highly artists whom I don't respect greatly as people; and I've had to criticize performers whom I'm proud to call my friends. Such are the pitfalls of the profession, the critic's eternal dilemma.

After the First World War, which Nellie Melba had spent in Australia and America, she sang in New York and went back to London in January, 1919. She didn't have to go on singing. She was very rich; she was sixty years old and she knew much too much about the art of singing to have any illusions about her voice. But Melba did not want to retire, or maybe she could not retire. Caruso once said, "When you hear that an artist is going to retire, don't believe it. As long as he keeps his voice, he will sing." Melba needed what no money on earth could buy: the exciting sight of the footlights, the intoxicating scent of backstage dust, the exhilarating sound of applause.

"I couldn't bear it if I couldn't sing any more," she said. "I just couldn't bear it."

She never forgot the night when she had "the honor of opening Covent Garden after the War."

"To drive to the old stage door, to walk upstairs and down the long corridor to a dressing room at the end of the passage; to sit down before the same mirror; to make up again; to put on once more the simple dress of Mimi, as though nothing had happened . . ." But Melba was a sensitive woman and she knew there were ghosts around her, "in every shadow cast by the lights, in the very air I breathed."

She tried not to think of the ghosts as she stood in the wings and heard Rodolfo sing his phrase, *"Non sono in vena";* was thrilled, as so many times before in her life, by the sweeping change of key in the orchestra, and heard herself sing, *"Scusi."* She sensed the ripple of excitement out there in the unseen audience. And then she opened the door and stepped once more on that stage "which was for me the scene of so much that is wonderful in life."

It was wonderful for a short while, as the candle dropped from her hands and the familiar phrases came from her lips "from long habit." She was still the youthful Mimi, the immortal *grisette,* not Nellie Melba, the middle-aged prima donna. But then she could no longer avoid looking into the auditorium, and she knew that she was singing to an audience of ghosts.

> Lady de Grey had gone, Alfred de Rothschild had gone, and so many others, all gone; and yet I felt them there . . . and it was for them rather than for this great audience that I sang.
>
> It was that night at Covent Garden which made me real-

ize the full extent to which London had changed. There was little of the old brilliance. Can you imagine in the old days men walking into Covent Garden on a "Melba night," sitting in the stalls in shabby tweed coats? I could not help feeling a sensation almost of resentment that men who could afford to pay for their stalls could not also afford to wear the proper clothes.

There has been a change. Opera was no longer a preserve of the rich, of "the real aristocracy," as during Melba's great days. She didn't understand, or didn't want to understand, that opera was getting really popular, that people all over the world were discovering the excitement of this old form of art, that this was the best thing that could happen to grand opera — and to its prima donnas.

During the First World War, Covent Garden had been a furniture repository. Gone were the members of the smart set for whom a night at the opera was just another chance to meet one's friends, who might have heard *Aïda* a dozen times without ever finding out what happened to the poor girl and her lover Radames, because they would always leave before the last scene. "People who sighed with audible pleasure over yet another *Roméo* with darling Jean, or another Melba-Caruso *La Bohème*." And gone were many of the great singers of Melba's epoch. Many people got bored by repetitious programs, always the same twenty-five standard repertory works, and became interested in orchestra concerts and the ballet. Others wanted to hear contemporary operas and "experiments." But the managers had not yet learned to adjust their repertoire to the new situation.

It was all very bewildering to old-timers like Melba. To

console themselves, they would endlessly repeat that grand opera was finished because there were no great voices left; that the art of *bel canto* was dead.

The art of *bel canto* has been declared dead and buried for a long, long time. Exactly a hundred years ago Manuel Garcia wrote, "Singing is becoming as much a lost art as the manufacture of china or the varnish used by the old masters."

Melba was bewildered by the postwar changes. She was shocked to see that London had become "gray and strange and very dirty." She was taken to lunch at a restaurant by the Duchess of Bedford, who brought along two little gold pots with butter and sugar. Melba couldn't get used to it all. Half of the men she had known were dead. She was depressed; she hated the very thought of old age and death. Once she drove with Beverly Nichols through Paris, talking about the new apartment that she had just bought.

"After all, I am still a young woman," she said.

"I shall never forget that moment," said Nichols later. "There she sat with diamonds glittering round her throat, and a lovely chinchilla fur round her shoulders, staring proudly ahead." When she was closer to seventy than to sixty she was "still a young woman." After a bad operation in 1922 that had lasted over two hours, her first question after regaining consciousness was, "Shall I be able to sing in three weeks?" She did sing, six weeks later, and she sang well. She gave special performances with the newly formed British National Opera Company in London, and later organized her own company for a season in Australia.

Melba loved life. She wished it would never end. "Getting

old is rather a fuss," she once said to Hazelton-Cochrane. When she became very ill with bronchitis and the doctors worried about her voice, Melba cried out, "God can't do this to me! He can't! I've always helped people all my life. . . . Can't He help me now?"

In 1923 Melba went home. She built herself a charming house in the Australian bush near the places of her youth that she had always loved.

She called her house Coombe Cottage, in memory of Coombe Cottage, Kingston Hill, London — seven thousand miles and a whole civilization away, the lovely house where Melba had at one time lived and where the Empress Eugénie had once been. Melba had often walked across the lawn to a nearby point from which Henry VIII had watched impatiently for the flag to be hoisted that would tell him Anne Boleyn had been beheaded. . . . Nearby also was Lady de Grey's Coombe Court, where Melba had spent some of her happiest hours.

Melba loved her Australian Coombe Cottage. It stood near the great bush region, almost at the fringe of civilization, "within sight and sound of the same trees and vineyards in which I played as a child." She loved the flowers and the hum of the crickets, the scarlet wings of the parrots, the tall gum trees and "the great blue mountains on the horizon." From her bedroom she could see the wide lawn. She had a fine vegetable garden and a swimming pool. She decided the pool should have a marbled effect, so she had it drained, went down herself, and painted the floor with a marble design.

She was not alone in Coombe Cottage. Her son and his wife lived nearby with their little girl, Pamela, whom Melba adored. And she had work. She was bringing over from Europe her own opera company, in spite of protests of local labor unions. Some singers and musicians, the stage director and the ballet mistress came from Italy. Melba was the star of her own company, as well as manager, press agent, artistic adviser, financial backer and general troubleshooter. "If you desire the season to run without any murders or assaults, you must be mother, father and sister to them all rolled in one."

The former prima donna *assoluta* was learning something about the other side of the coin. It was a hard struggle, but eventually Nellie Melba gave her native land its first taste of grand opera.

MELBA'S FAREWELL, said the program of the Royal Opera, Covent Garden, for Tuesday, June 8, 1926, at 8:15 P.M. The program consisted of Melba's greatest triumphs — the second act (with the Balcony Scene) of *Roméo et Juliette,* conducted by Percy Pitt; the "Willow Song" and "Ave Marie" from the last act of *Otello;* and the last two acts of *La Bohème,* conducted by Vincenzo Bellezza.

Several artists who had sung with Melba's company in Australia appeared with her on that historic night — among them Browning Mummery, who was Rodolfo in *La Bohème,* and Melba's protégé John Brownlee, who was making his debut. It was Melba's last Mimi and his first Marcello.

Brownlee had met Melba one night in 1922 when he sang in a performance of Handel's "Messiah" with the Melbourne

Philharmonic. There was great excitement backstage afterwards and then Madame Melba, surrounded by members of her court, made a regal entrance into the artists' room.

She stared at Brownlee, a young singer in his early twenties.

"Young man," she said. "You've got a fine voice. Go to Europe and study hard. Be sure to come and see me in London."

"I did," John Brownlee says now. "She gave me the best advice I ever had. 'Go off to the Continent and learn languages. Don't sit on my doorstep. I won't make a career for you.' She sounded painfully direct but later I found out that her straight approach screened a generous heart. Quite a few young singers were literally sitting on her doorstep hoping she would build their careers. Melba was really a warm, graceful, kind woman, but she had no time for humbug."

In the winter of 1925–1926 Brownlee was singing at the Trianon-Lyrique, a second-rate musical theater in the Montmartre district of Paris. One night, during a performance of Gounod's *Mireille*, there was again that sudden terrific excitement backstage as word got around that Madame Melba had come to see Monsieur Brownlee. This time she was very, very pleased.

"You sing very well," she said to Brownlee. "Why didn't you let me know that you were doing so well? If friends of mine hadn't found out you were singing here, I should never have heard you."

"You told me not to sit on your doorstep, remember?" Brownlee said.

Melba laughed. "Come to see me tomorrow afternoon."

She was then living in Bemberg's large apartment in Rue Victor Hugo. When Brownlee arrived, Melba greeted him perfunctorily and sat down at the piano.

"Let's have some music," she said, without wasting any time on social amenities.

"We did the duets from *La Traviata* and *Rigoletto*," Brownlee remembers. "She was then sixty-seven and she sang beautifully. Later she took me along to some parties, where we performed duets together. Fantastic parties! Looking back now, I almost feel they never happened. I remember the *soirées* in the house of Boni de Castellane, when the large place was lit by hundreds of candles. Women wearing exquisite gowns and wonderful jewels and men in full evening dress walked between rows of liveried footmen. The powerful and the rich and the famous of the whole of Europe were there, but Melba was always the center of attraction, the undisputed queen of these parties. There was something electrifying about her mere presence. She was more than the greatest prima donna of her time. She was a dynamic personality that attracted people magically wherever she went."

Melba usually called Brownlee at seven in the morning to invite him to another party. Brownlee didn't mind; getting up early, he says, is an old Australian habit. One morning Melba sounded different, and asked him to come over right away, it was important.

When he got there, she said with her usual directness,

"John, how would you like to sing in my farewell performance at Covent Garden?"

Brownlee was too overwhelmed to speak. He could only
nod.

"Do you know the part of Marcello in *La Bohème*?"

He had never heard *La Bohème*, but he managed to say
that he knew the part quite well.

"All right. Come back at the end of the week and we'll
go through the third and fourth act."

"I went home, my head swimming," Brownlee remembers. "Here was I, an unknown, inexperienced Australian
singer, and I was going to sing before the King and the
Queen in my debut at Covent Garden. I'd always learned
the music fast and I knew the part of Marcello at the end
of the week. We rehearsed in Melba's place with Maurice
Renaud, the great baritone, who helped me a lot and gave
me some of his costumes. It was an experience. Even rehearsing was exciting when Melba was around."

Brownlee remembers the night of June 8, 1926, as if it
were yesterday.

"Quite a night to make one's debut," he said wistfully
the other day, as we sat in his New York apartment looking
out on Central Park. In a corner of the large music room
there stands a lovely Empire commode which was once
used to store jewels. Melba brought it from Russia and gave
it to Brownlee as a wedding present. Her picture, with an
affectionate dedication written in her strong, characteristic
handwriting, stands on the piano.

"The King and the Queen were there, the Prince of Wales

(now Duke of Windsor), and other members of the Royal Family. Practically the whole of England had come to Covent Garden that night to pay homage to Melba. The auditorium was a sea of gowns and tiaras and uniforms and decorations and white shirtfronts. The atmosphere was charged almost beyond endurance. A lot of people had come with dire forebodings. They were afraid it would be a pathetic spectacle and wished it were over. Some were openly sorry for the old girl of over sixty-seven and for what they thought would be Melba's ordeal.

"It didn't turn out that way. Melba's ordeal became Melba's triumph. She confounded her stanchest admirers. She sang so beautifully that the years seemed to recede as in a fairy tale, and there stood again the great prima donna of a quarter of a century ago. The voice had almost a youthful charm and freshness. The heavenly legato was still there, and the wonderful technique. It was a miracle. The people who had come out of a sense of duty were as in a trance. Then they went wild with excitement. After the last act of *La Bohème,* the curtain came down and the stagehands quickly arranged onstage all the flowers that Melba had received. When the curtain went up, she stood in front of a six-feet-high sea of flowers. In all my life at the opera I've never heard another ovation that had such overtones of love, affection and adoration. Only the supposedly cold English can bestow such a tribute upon an artist whom they worship."

Electrical recording had just been invented. "His Master's Voice" placed several microphones in Covent Garden as an

experiment, and — unknown to Melba and the other performers — recorded the second part of the farewell performance. The result is a historical document and astonishing
proof that a great singer at over sixty-seven is able to command purity of tone and steadiness of voice if her technique
and vocal method have been perfect.

Melba had sung at Covent Garden for thirty-eight years.
She had outlived most of her colleagues. But she still had
her voice left.

> If a little of its old mellowness is gone [wrote the *Daily
> Telegraph*], no singer, not even the youngest of the day, is
> steadier in tone or hits the notes more precisely or accu-
> rately. . . . The art is still there, as shown in the extraordi-
> narily touching singing of "*Salce*" and the "Ave Maria" from
> *Otello*. A colossal night of music, and a glorious exhibition
> of the noble art of singing. . . . The enthusiasm of the au-
> dience knew no bounds.

A great and wonderful era in the history of grand opera
had come to an end.

At the end of the long ovation Melba broke down, after
a speech by Lord Stanley, the head of the London Opera
Syndicate. She stepped up to the footlights and began to
speak. Her voice, clear despite the emotion, comes out of
the recording:

LORD STANLEY:
    I thank you for all the beautiful things you've said of me.
I don't feel at all worthy, but I thank you all the same. I
have so many people to thank tonight. It is such a great and
glorious evening; but you can imagine what a terrible feeling it is for me to think that I shall never again perhaps sing

within these beloved walls. Covent Garden has always been my artistic home and I love it — I love it more than any place in the world perhaps. But all things must end. And now I have to thank the Management for their ready courtesy and kindness to me. I have to thank my dear, dear big public for their great faithfulness to me. I have to thank the orchestra for their patience at many tiresome rehearsals and who played so beautifully in the evenings. I have to thank the dear stagehands, always willing to help in any way they can, and even tonight they have presented me with a little souvenir, which will always be so precious. And I have to thank my dear old friend, Austin, who has been at the stage door for forty years, and out of those forty years, for thirty-six years he has put me in my carriage and always bid me good-night. . . . You can imagine — what I feel . . .

At this point Melba's voice becomes blurred and loses its steadiness. She broke down and wept and so did many people in the audience. And then a shout from thousands of voices went up and a cascade of applause broke down over her before she was able to finish her farewell speech.

Melba's concert farewell took place at the Royal Albert Hall in London on June 25, 1926 — an unforgettable night for those who were there. The concert program carried a line MELBA'S FAREWELL *is* FAREWELL, but this didn't turn out to be literally true. She sang again, at a charity performance in aid of the Sadler's Wells Theater Fund at the Old Vic, on December 7, 1926, appearing in the last act of *Otello* and the last two acts of *La Bohème*. After her Australian tour, Melba came back to England and sang again for charity — The Sussex Eye Hospital — at the Brighton Hippodrome on October 5, 1929. This was her last public appearance. She made another semipublic appearance, at a charity concert given at the Hyde Park Hotel in May, 1930. A few weeks later she left for Australia. John Brownlee and his wife saw Melba off.

"Melba had always been casual about departures," Brownlee remembers. "She was going away so much. It was bye-bye, see-you-soon, the smile and wave of the hand. But that day she broke down and cried as the boat train pulled out. She knew in her heart that she would never come back."

Melba had often said she wanted to die as "darling Jean" de Reszke had died, "surrounded by melodies." But her end was slow and painful, and there was no music in it.

For a long time she had suffered from an unknown virus. Her condition was aggravated by lingering diabetes. Even among her close friends, few knew how sick she was. Melba, the proud Edwardian prima donna to the very last moment, kept her troubles to herself.

She was undergoing treatment in Sydney, but her condition grew worse and finally she was stricken by an acute form of blood poisoning which partly disfigured her. It was the last, cruel, illogical blow to Nellie Melba, who had loved beauty and given beauty all her life. Her son and a few trusted friends were near her when she died on February 23, 1931.

Melba must have known for a long time that she was a very sick woman. In the archives of Covent Garden is a letter which she wrote in London five years before her death:

DEAR MR. FLADGATE,

In case of my death I am writing you a few final wishes which I know you will faithfully carry out. If I die in London I wish my body to be embalmed & sent to Australia where I am to be buried in the Lilydale Cemetery near my Father. I also wish to have a memorial service at either St. Paul's or the Westminster Cathedral with the most beautiful music that England can produce. If Landon Ronald is alive he will conduct. If Bertram MacKennal is alive I wish him to make my tombstone. I would like a tiny chapel with a tomb & Juliette (me) lying on it. A pretty effect could be made with windows of either blue or yellow glass. However I shall leave this to his taste which is perfect.

It is my wish that my son George Armstrong will keep up Coombe Cottage as though I were there & I hope he will never sell it; because I have put my heart's blood in this beloved little spot. *I would like my very faithful Covent Garden & Albert Hall public to be invited to the Memorial service.*

With many thanks for all your kindness,

Yrs sincerely

Nellie Melba

P.S. My last will is with Mr. Jo Redding, Crocher Building, San Francisco.

Melba was buried near her father in Lilydale. Her estate was over a million dollars. It is estimated that once her fortune had been at least twice that much, but the aftermath of the First World War and the depression reduced her holdings. Her generous will contained a large number of legacies. Friends, poor relations, impoverished colleagues, struggling protégés, old servants — all were remembered. Some people had disappeared long ago and had to be traced.

A large legacy went to Albert Street Conservatory in Melbourne, of which she was founder and president, to institute a Melba Scholarship, "in the hope that another Melba will arise." There have been great singers since, coloraturas and soprano leggiero divas, but there has never been another Melba.

The remainder of Melba's estate went to her son, George Armstrong, and to his wife. Melba left her jewels that she had loved so much to her adored little granddaughter Pamela. Some of these beautiful jewels were gifts that had been given to the greatest prima donna of all times by emperors, kings, queens and millionaires, and by people everywhere who were her friends. A small brooch of pearls and rubies is the rather modest gift of Queen Victoria after Melba's first command performance in Windsor Castle.

And now [Melba concludes her farewell speech at Covent Garden] there is only one more word to say, and that is "Farewell." I won't say "Good-bye," because "Farewell" is such a very beautiful word. I am sure you all know that it is part of a prayer and means "Fare thee well," which I wish you all — and I feel sure that you wish me the same.